POWER AND JUST TRANSITIONS

POWER AND JUST TRANSITIONS

Struggles for a Post-Coal Future in an Appalachian Valley

JOHN GAVENTA and
GABE SCHWARTZMAN

UNIVERSITY OF ILLINOIS PRESS
Urbana, Chicago, and Springfield

Manufactured in the United States of America
1 2 3 4 5 C P 5 4 3 2 1
∞ This book is printed on acid-free paper.

All royalties from this book are donated to the Power and Powerlessness Fund at the Appalachian Community Foundation to support grassroots organizing and empowerment work in the region.

Cataloging data available from the Library of Congress

ISBN 978-0-252-04693-3 (hardcover)
ISBN 978-0-252-08906-0 (paperback)
ISBN 978-0-252-04855-5 (ebook)

Contents

Preface vii

Acknowledgments xi

List of Abbreviations xv

Introduction: The Challenge of Just Transitions 1

1 Intersecting Inequalities and the Failed Promises of Development 19

2 Setting the Context: Power, Resistance, and the Rise and Decline of King Coal 39

3 Power and Transitions 53

4 Old Powerholders Cling On: How the Coal Industry Fights to Maintain Its Dominance 69

5 Protecting the Hegemony of Coal: The Rise of the Conservative Right 86

6 Financialization and the Rise of Corporate Conservation 104

7 Building Collective Power from Below 123

8 Bottom Up Meets Top Down: A New Policy Moment? 141

Conclusion: An Interregnum between Past and Future? 157

Notes 177

Index 223

Preface

Cutting across parts of four rural counties in Kentucky and Tennessee, in the heart of the Appalachian Mountains in the United States, lies an area known as the Clearfork Valley. Driving into the Valley on a small, winding mountain road one is met by a beautiful vista of rolling hills, rising mists, and in the spring, lush green forests. But alongside this beauty, there is another story. Once home to over a dozen small mining towns, today the mines are all closed, leaving behind intersecting legacies of ongoing poverty and inequality, environmental and climate injustice, and social and health crises brought on by opioid addiction.

Continuing farther down the mountain into the heart of the Valley, the signs of economic abandonment become more visible. What was once the largest coal-loading structure, the Marion Tipple in Rock Creek, from which trains and trucks carried hundreds of tons of coal a day, at the time of our research sat empty (see cover illustration). The tipple and the mines that supplied it were most recently run by the Kopper Glo Company, which, like many companies across the region, has now gone bankrupt, abandoning its mining infrastructure and leaving behind environmental destruction as a result of decades of strip-mining practices. The steel gates, once guarded with twenty-four-hour security, had been cut and flung open. Metal wires hung down, mining belts were strewn across the grounds, large portions of fencing were missing, and pieces of sheet metal were conspicuously gone, having been stripped for sale as scrap metal and recycled materials as part of an informal economy of survival. At the end of 2024 the entire site was demolished.

By contrast, alongside the loss of the coal industry are other stories of community resilience and action. In what once was a coal-company-run school in the former coal community of Eagan, a local organization runs a community center, which serves as a gathering place for events, workshops, and visiting volunteers. Up a nearby "hollow," a Community Land Trust offers a symbolic alternative to the otherwise absentee-owned land, while up the road in another direction, a water utility, health clinic, and post office have all been developed by local efforts. In small but multiple ways, community groups are organizing to demand that the legacies of the past mining be cleaned up, and that the residents have a say in a new economic future.

They do so in a rapidly changing economic landscape. For almost a century, the land on which the tipple sits in Valley Creek and much of the broader Clearfork Valley was wholly owned by the American Association, a British company, and later by various forestry and mining conglomerates. Today the ownership structure is very different. The land is owned by a private equity fund, known as the Cumberland Forest Limited Partnership, founded by NatureVest, the finance and investing arm of The Nature Conservancy (TNC), the largest environmental nonprofit organization in the world. Rather than making money through the extraction of coal, this project generates a return on investment through a new economy of conservation, selling credits on the California carbon markets, as well as through revenues gained from recreational leasing and logging. Yet to many community members, this is yet another form of extraction of wealth from which they see few benefits.

This book is about what happens to mining communities when their mines have closed, and new economic actors emerge. Writ large, it is about how the transition away from fossil fuels in the face of climate change will affect communities like those in the Clearfork Valley, whose history, politics, social relations, and identities have been built for over a century around the extraction of coal. Picking up on global debates on the need for a "just transition" toward a post–fossil fuel world, it explores the questions of who benefits in this transition, whose voices are heard, whose values and knowledge are recognized, and how communities at the front line of this change struggle to ensure that the transition is equitable, fair, and inclusive.

Through the lens of power relations, we ask how historically powerful actors cling on, whether new actors wield power differently, and how these changes have an impact on the possibilities of transformative and empowering citizen action. Although the literatures on the politics of climate change and the struggles for a just transition are rapidly growing, this volume is unique as a case study of the implications of coal's decline on power and mobilization in a single community, especially one that traces change over time and that takes a bottom-up perspective to understand critical national and global issues.

The book represents an intergenerational collaboration between two scholars who have studied and worked in the Valley over a fifty-year time span. In the early 1970s, John Gaventa began his research, which led to the publication of *Power and Powerlessness: Quiescence and Rebellion in an Appalachian Valley*. This early book focused on the power relations that derived from the absentee-owned coal industry, documenting how the coal companies and landowners kept close control of workers not only through political power, but also through the instillation of fear and a sense of powerlessness among local residents.

Today, seeing the wide-open gates and looting of company property, a long-time community organizer remarked to Gabe Schwartzman, the second coauthor, "People aren't afraid of the coal company anymore." Instead, the community faces new challenges of repairing the destructive legacies left by over one hundred years of coal mining and contending with new economic activities based on carbon offsets and recreation, both of which have little need for local labor—themes developed by Schwartzman in his 2022 PhD dissertation "Power, Development, and Post-Coal Politics in Appalachia," as well as other writings.

Gaventa first entered the Valley in 1971, as a student volunteer through a Vanderbilt University program called the Student Health Coalition. Told by residents that their Valley was owned by a British company, he subsequently used time as a PhD student in Oxford, England, to trace the Valley's ownership while simultaneously working with community residents to document their story. This led to his 1975 dissertation and the subsequent book published by Oxford University Press in 1980 and the University of Illinois University Press in 1982.

Schwartzman, who came to the area as coal was already declining, had known of community organizing work in Clearfork as early as 2010, when he was involved in the anti–mountaintop removal movement in West Virginia. In that process, he met a community leader from the Valley, Carol Judy, and heard about her organizing there. Coming to the Valley in late 2020, Schwartzman had already studied coal politics in Appalachia for a decade. Early on in that journey, Nancy Peluso, a professor at UC Berkeley, suggested that he replicate Gaventa's study in the Clearfork Valley. When The Nature Conservancy came to control the land in the Valley in 2019, he decided to do his dissertation research there, using Gaventa's former study as a historical comparison.

Meanwhile in 2022, Gaventa set out to revisit the subject of his previous book with the intent of publishing an updated version that added a chapter or two about the changes in the Valley since his work fifty years earlier. Schwartzman had just finished his dissertation on the Valley and wanted to continue his work there. Realizing that the story of change was much bigger and more complex than an update could tell, the two authors decided to join forces.

Over the period 2022–2024, Gaventa was able to revisit the Valley several times, interviewing residents and activists, some of whom he had interviewed and worked with fifty years earlier. Schwartzman had conducted dozens of interviews for his PhD work and was able to conduct further interviews, witnessing and following rapidly changing developments in the region even as we were writing the book. Meeting weekly online during the process of writing, we were able to co-draft this volume, brainstorming together on each chapter, with each of us taking the lead on certain parts of the project. The collaboration has been stimulating and enjoyable, and one which we hope has benefited the overall result through combining our perspectives.

As we were putting the finishing touches on this manuscript in November 2024, Donald Trump was reelected president of the United States, with a promise to unfetter the exploration and exploitation of fossil fuels. Just weeks before, massive storms had left communities across southern Appalachia flooded, and similar serious weather events were increasing across the globe. Hundreds of government representatives, industry lobbyists, and climate change advocates were gathering in Azerbaijan for the Twenty-ninth Conference of the Parties (COP) to the United Nations Framework Convention on Climate Change, the same body that had passed the Paris Agreement on climate change in 2015, and which in its twenty-eighth meeting in Egypt had called for a transition away from fossil fuels. Yet, fossil fuel emissions have continued to rise, and in 2024 are globally higher than ever before in history. All these factors remind us that the need to understand and transform power relations in order to create a just and inclusive transition remains urgent and critical—a project to which we hope this book will in a small way contribute.

John Gaventa and Gabe Schwartzman
November 2024

Acknowledgments

In working on this book, we were aided by many others to whom we are grateful. We offer our enormous thanks to the dozens of community members, activists, local government and corporate officials, and others who gave their time and insights for this process, a number of whom chose to remain confidential. However, we do thank you all for your hours either in person or online sharing your experiences with us.

We want to say particular thanks to members of Tennessee Appalachian Community Economics (TNACE), an informal organization that brings together several grassroots groups and individuals who work in the Valley. TNACE members not only participated in workshops around the themes of the book but also offered important insights throughout the process. Schwartzman spent countless hours in TNACE meetings, working on projects with members, writing grant proposals, and breaking bread together. These relationships and experiences deeply inform the insights shared here. Thanks especially to Tonia Brookman, April Jarocki, Bonnie Swinford, Adam Hughes, Jackie Waldrop, Marie Webster, Morgan Pennington, and the late D. Steele, members of this group.

Many others in the Valley were vital to our understanding of situations on the ground. Randall Hatfield, in particular, spent scores of hours with Schwartzman discussing and debating concepts posed in this book. Over the years, Gaventa has kept in touch with and learned from many local leaders and activists, including, to name a few, Marie Cirillo, now deceased, Maureen O'Connell, Charles "Boomer" Winfrey (also deceased), Dal Macon, Derek Douglas, and others, some of whom asked not to be named.

We were fortunate also to benefit from the help of several research assistants. Special thanks to Michelle Mockbee, who had worked previously as a volunteer in the Valley, for assistance in tracking down documents and statistics, fact and citation checking as well as for cleaning up and coding hundreds of pages of interviews. Additional thanks to Ricki Draper, an organizer who also had spent time in the Valley, and to Caleb Gore, a PhD student at the University of Tennessee, for their research assistance, aided by their personal knowledge of the coalfields.

We also benefitted enormously from the wealth of scholarship that has grown in the region. Fifty years ago, when Gaventa started his first book, there was little academic scholarship on the Appalachian coalfields to draw from. Today Appalachian Studies has emerged as a vibrant field, and we have learned a great deal from other scholars who have grappled with questions of power and hegemony in the coalfields, including, to name a few, Shannon Elizabeth Bell, Dwight Billings, Steve Fisher, William Isom, Phillip Lewin, Sylvia Ryerson, Judah Schept, Shauna Scott, Becky Scott, Barbara Ellen Smith, Bill Turner, and of course Helen Lewis, now deceased.

At the Institute of Development Studies, many thanks to the institute's small sabbatical fund for supporting some of Gaventa's time to work on this project, to Gary Edwards for assistance with tables and figures, as well as to a number of colleagues who encouraged the project and participated in an internal seminar with the authors in September 2023 to comment on a presentation of the early arguments in the book.

At the University of Minnesota, where Schwartzman conducted some of the research that contributed to this work during his doctoral dissertation, thanks to Kate Derickson for help crafting the project that led to parts of this book, to Vinay Gidwani, for helpful feedback and encouragement along the way, and to Adam Bledsoe, for support in developing research about Black communities in Appalachia. Thanks to colleagues in the Department of Geography, Environment, and Society Ned Wilbur, Merle Davis, Anya Kaplan-Seem, Elizabeth Calhoun, Keavy McFadden, and Julie Santella for reading early drafts of chapters that became parts of this book.

We also thank other colleagues who have read drafts of the work and offered useful comments. These include anonymous reviewers who reviewed the early proposal as well as the submitted manuscript, as well as Juliet Merrifield, who read and commented on all the chapters, and other colleagues, including Rosie McGee, Peter Newell, Rosalind Eyben, and Julia Haggerty, who read and commented on selected chapters. Thanks also to the participants in the Land Deal Politics Initiative's Global Land Grabbing Conference, in Bogota, Colombia, in 2024, and participants in the Global Coal Transitions conference in Columbus, Ohio, in 2024, for their feedback on a draft of chapter 6. Finally, our thanks to Leigh Ann Cowan and Alison Syring at University of Illinois Press, who encouraged and supported this project from the beginning, as well as to Megan Donnan, Marilyn Campbell, and Amaranth Tupelo for their assistance in copy editing and indexing.

We are pleased that all the royalties from the sale of this book will be contributed to the Power and Powerlessness Fund at the Appalachian Community Foundation (ACF). Thanks to ACF for managing this fund, as it has done with the royalties from Gaventa's previous book on the Valley. These proceeds will continue to provide small grants to support grassroots groups working to challenge and change unjust power relations in the Valley and surrounding Central Appalachian communities.

List of Abbreviations

ABCD	asset-based community development
ACF	Appalachian Community Foundation
AFL-CIO	American Federation of Labor and Congress of Industrial Organizations
AML	abandoned mine land
ARB	California Air Resources Board
ARC	Appalachian Regional Commission
ARISE	Appalachian Regional Initiative for Stronger Economies
BIL	Bipartisan Infrastructure Law
CCD	Census County Division
CCI	Clearfork Community Institute
CFP	Cumberland Forest Project
CJA	Climate Justice Alliance
CLT	community land trust
COP	Conference of the Parties
COPD	chronic obstructive pulmonary disease
DOE	Department of Energy
EPA	Environmental Protection Agency
ESG	environmental, social, and governance
IFM	Improved Forestry Management
ILO	International Labor Organization
IRA	Inflation Reduction Act
KFTC	Kentuckians for the Commonwealth, originally Kentuckians for Fair Taxation
LLC	Limited Liability Company
MACED	now Mountain Association

MAGA	Make America Great Again
MLP	Multilevel Perspective
MTR	mountaintop removal
NGO	non-governmental organization
NLRB	National Labor Relations Board
NRP	Natural Resource Partners
OCED	Office of Clean Energy Demonstration
OEO	Office of Economic Opportunity
OHV	off-highway vehicle
OSMRE	Office of Surface Mining Reclamation and Enforcement
PAC	political action committee
POWER	Partnerships for Opportunity and Workforce and Economic Revitalization Initiative
RECLAIM	Revitalizing the Economy of Coal Communities by Leveraging Local Activities and Investing More Act
SMCRA	Surface Mining Control and Reclamation Act of 1977
SOAR	Shaping Our Appalachian Region
SOCM	Save Our Cumberland Mountains, now Statewide Organizing for Community eMpowerment
SOCM	Statewide Organizing for Community eMpowerment
TDEC	Tennessee Department of Environment and Conservation
TIMO	timber investment management organization
TNACE	Tennessee Appalachian Community Economics
TNC	The Nature Conservancy
TWRA	Tennessee Wildlife Resources Agency
UMWA	United Mine Workers of America
UNFCCC	United Nations Framework Convention on Climate Change
UPS	United Parcel Service
USDA	United States Department of Agriculture
WMMT	Kentucky community radio station, associated with Appalshop

INTRODUCTION

The Challenge of Just Transitions

> I'm not sure who has the power now. . . . Is there anyone who's in power anymore? I mean I can think of a few people who have, like, more sway than others here or there, but nothing like [the coal company].
>
> —Community development leader, Clearfork Valley, 18 October 2022

Sitting around a table in a community center in Eagan, Tennessee, a small former coal-mining town in the remote eastern Kentucky-Tennessee border region known as the Clearfork Valley, nonprofit leaders and activists discussed what power looked like in their community. As the organizers and one of the coauthors of this book, Gabe Schwartzman, ate lasagna and prepared to have a monthly meeting about community-based economic development, they chatted about how power relations had changed in the Valley. The other coauthor, John Gaventa, had recently visited the Valley, the site of his 1982 book, *Power and Powerlessness: Quiescence and Rebellion in an Appalachian Valley.*[1] The activists and organizers were still ruminating on a question they had all discussed together: Who has power in the community now that the coal industry is collapsing? One community leader offered, "There is The Nature Conservancy owning all the land now." Another quickly responded, "But that's not necessarily where the power is today. I don't think anyone has power now. Not like the coal companies used to."[2]

This conversation in the Clearfork Valley is not unique. Around the world, scholars, activists, and political leaders are similarly asking what happens in fossil fuel–dependent communities as the world shifts from fossil fuels to cleaner forms of energy? What is the impact of this transition on places whose history, livelihoods, identities, political and social structures have been shaped by over a century of a largely fossil fuel–based economy? In particular, when local systems of power are built on a fossil fuel–based extractive economy, what happens to power relations when those fossil fuels are no longer needed? What new forms of power emerge, what old ones remain, and how do these changes affect the possibilities and strategies of popular struggles for a more just and inclusive future?

To pursue these questions, we returned to the Clearfork Valley, the site of Gaventa's earlier book, as well as more recent doctoral research by Schwartzman.[3] A rural area in the Central Appalachian Mountain region of the United States, the area was once a key site of the War on Poverty. Over fifty years later deep poverty and joblessness persist, and the inequalities between the region and the rest of the country have only deepened, made worse by the pharmaceutical-company-induced opioid crisis, deep environmental damage left by the legacy of coal, and the hollowing out of communities in the wake of coal's decline.

Once a mining valley owned and controlled by an absentee British company, the mines are now closed, with one of the world's largest environmental NGOs, The Nature Conservancy (TNC) controlling the land and bringing a contested vision of a new future based on a model of corporate conservation and the financialization of natural resources. TNC's impact investment team, NatureVest, started a private equity fund, called Cumberland Forest Limited Partnership, to purchase the land in the Valley, and other parts of the region. Now owning 400 square miles of Central Appalachia, TNC has attracted new investors with the promise of a return on investment for climate change mitigation, carbon offsets, and conservation investments.

As the mines have closed, the once powerful United Mine Workers of America (UMWA) has virtually disappeared, while the historically dominating coal industry still struggles to cling to its power. An area once voting largely Democratic, conservative Republicanism has grown in the Valley, with Donald Trump receiving over 80 percent support in the 2020 and 2024 elections. Increasing polarization around cultural wedge issues has diverted attention from the desperate economic and environmental issues the post-coal Valley faces. And yet, while Gaventa's earlier book presented a picture of political "quiescence" in the face of glaring inequalities of land and wealth, today we also see numerous examples of local communities struggling for a new future—seeking to have a voice in determining what today is called "a just transition" in the shift away from the fossil fuel economy.

We position the Valley, and the broader Central Appalachian region in which it is located, not as exceptional, but as an illustrative case study of the impacts of the predicted global transition away from economies that for over a century have been built on fossil fuel extraction, and the consequent effects on people, power, and participation. To set this broader context, in this introductory chapter we begin with a quick review of the urgency of climate change and the rise of the idea of "just transition," arguing that this inevitably carries with it considerations of power relations and political economies that shape how such transitions might occur. We then briefly describe the method and approach we have taken to the book and present the structure of the remaining chapters of the volume, before concluding with a few remarks for readers about how to approach this book.

The Urgency and Scale of the Challenge

The urgent need to shift away from fossil fuels in the face of climate change is now widely recognized. The Paris Agreement of 2015 established an international goal to limit global warming to well below 2 degrees Celsius, while aiming to remain under 1.5 degrees. Absolutely essential to meeting this goal is the need to phase out coal, beginning with Organization for Economic Cooperation and Development (OECD) countries by 2030, and all countries in the world by 2040.[4] While the Paris Agreement did not specifically mention the need to phase out fossil fuels in general or coal in particular, six years later, in the historic COP26 meetings in Glasgow, a coalition of 190 countries and organizations signed up to do so.[5] A press release issued by the United Nations Framework Convention on Climate Change (UNFCCC) boldly announced: "Coal is being consigned to history today at COP26, as countries, banks, and organizations move away from the single biggest contributor to climate change."[6]

The transition away from fossil fuels is critical for the planet, but it will have huge impacts on the communities that have long relied on fossil fuel extraction for their livelihoods. The coal-mining region of Central Appalachia in the United States is at the frontlines of this transition. Though the word "Appalachia" often conjures up images of poverty, the region is not uniformly poor. Since the late 1800s, the region has produced huge amounts of wealth, in the form of coal, largely owned by absentee corporate landowners, and extracted to fuel the national and international demand for fossil fuels. In 1984, over 68,000 miners were employed in the Central Appalachian region, producing over 224 million tons of coal.[7] By 2023, this number had dwindled to 11,000 miners producing only about 48 million tons of coal,[8] as a combination of market forces and environmental policy drove a precipitous downturn in what was once the region's main industry. Between 2005 and 2020 alone, mining employment in the region fell by 82 percent.[9] The Clearfork Valley reflected the trend.

This Valley and the Central Appalachian Region are by no means alone. In the western United States, coal-mining communities are also contending with a rapid transition away from coal mining and coal burning, notably with closures of facilities such as the Navajo Generating Station in the Navajo Nation,[10] and projected closures in Montana and Wyoming.[11] Across the United States, between 1978 and 2015, "the coal mining sector lost approximately 145,000 jobs, or about 60 percent of its employment,"[12] with widespread community effects. In 2023 almost 15 million people, 5 percent of the total population, still lived in communities affected by the closure of coal mines, despite the earlier job losses. When other fossil fuel–affected communities are considered, for example, those involved in the production of oil and gas, the number rises to 64 million people, or one-fifth of all Americans.[13]

Globally, according to the World Bank, over the last fifty years, changes in the coal industry in Europe, the United States, and China, "have resulted in as many as 4 million coal workers losing their jobs" due to a number of factors, including mechanization, competition from other forms of energy, and now the pressures to move away from coal production due to climate change.[14] The German "Coal Exit" law,[15] as well as the European Union's "Coal Exit" policy and Australia's reduction in coal-fired electricity generation, all evidence a rapid trend toward phasing out coal usage in the Global North.[16] In countries in the Global South—in places like Indonesia, South Africa, India, or Colombia—coal mine closures are also having huge impacts, and often on relatively poor populations and communities. Between 2023 and 2035, the Global Energy Monitor reports, some 100 miners a day are projected to lose their jobs, with workers in India and China particularly affected.[17] In all these countries, how to respond to coal phaseout represents a huge challenge.[18]

Oftentimes, the affected communities are what the World Bank calls "mono-industry" communities, where there are few other economic alternatives, and a closure of the mine can have far-reaching impacts locally.[19] In many mining communities, especially those in isolated rural locations, mine closures are about more than the loss of jobs—historically, infrastructures, revenues, services, politics, cultures, and identities were built around the mine. In Central Appalachia, the mining companies themselves often founded the towns, known as company towns or coal camps. "It was the coal company that built and owned the houses and provided for all the other facilities—whether schools, churches, commissaries, theaters, dance halls, bowling alleys, soda fountains, or even graveyards."[20] In such communities, when the mines go, everything else changes as well. More broadly, as an article in *Politico* magazine points out, "coal's retreat promises to reshape the world again . . . coal's social and political impact went far beyond the direct benefits and costs of coal-fired industrialization."[21]

Roots of the Just Transition Movement

Perhaps aware of these impacts, at the COP26 held in Glasgow in 2021, global leaders from fourteen countries and the European Commission passed a Declaration on Just Transition, which recognized "the need to ensure that no one is left behind in the transition to net zero economies—particularly those working in sectors, cities, and regions reliant on carbon-intensive industries and production." While the historic 2015 Paris Agreement had only once mentioned "just transition," by COP28 in Dubai in 2023, the phrase was virtually everywhere.[22]

Though the phrase has only recently become part of global discourse, the concept of just transition has been around for three decades, often with differing meanings or points of emphasis. The term originated in the labor movement in the later twentieth century, with a focus on how workers in vulnerable industries receive support for transition to new jobs. In the early 1990s, Tony Mazzocchi, the leader of the Oil Chemical and Atomic Workers Union in the USA, wrote about growing environmental concerns about toxic industries, "There is, obviously, a major contradiction to be overcome. The only way out of the 'jobs vs environment' dilemma is to make provisions for the workers who lose their jobs in the wake of the country's drastically needed environmental clean-up."[23] In a far-sighted proposal for its time, shortly after the creation of a Superfund for environmental cleanup, he called for a Superfund for Workers to assist workers to "make the transition from one kind of job to another."[24]

The initial focus of the just transition concept was on fairness and support to workers, based on a principle of *economic* justice. In the 1990s and early part of 2000, other related demands for justice were also growing. One of these was the recognition of the unequal impacts of environmental degradation itself, particularly on low-income communities and communities of color, both in the United States and around the world. In 1990, Robert Bullard published the path-breaking book, *Dumping in Dixie: Race, Class, and Environmental Quality*, often considered one of the first major books on *environmental* justice.[25] Although the focus of the book was primarily on the role of race as a factor in siting hazardous industries and toxic waste dumps in African American communities in the American South, Bullard also recognized the significance of other low-income communities, such as those in Appalachia: "Now all of the issues of environmental racism and environmental justice don't just deal with people of color. We are just as much concerned with inequities in Appalachia, for example, where the whites are basically dumped on because of lack of economic and political clout and lack of having a voice to say 'no' and that's environmental injustice."[26] Over the decades, a large literature has grown in the United States and globally on environmental justice movements "composed of people from communities of color, indigenous communities, and working-class communities who are focused on combating environmental injustice—the disproportionate burden of environmental harm facing these populations."[27] Between debates around justice for workers on the one hand and environmental justice on the other, Mazzochi's proposals to reconcile the two were important. However, over the next decade, issues of climate change were increasingly coming to the fore, and with them concerns about *climate* justice, focusing on who was most affected by the climate change, and who would pay the costs of transitions away from carbon-based forms of energy.[28]

With the rise of concerns about climate change, increasing awareness of how energy—particularly carbon-based energy—was a central cause of climate injustice also arose, along with a growing focus on limiting carbon production, use, and emissions. With this another justice concern emerged, what became known as *energy* justice, focusing on inequities in access to energy as well as the costs and consequences of its production. Within the context of energy justice, the impact of movements for decarbonization on carbon-producing communities also drew attention. As one study argued, the energy transition "will create economic winners and losers, but these winners and losers will not be limited to corporations and their investors. Instead, communities that have developed around coal, oil, and gas extraction and processing will be negatively impacted if this energy transition occurs."[29]

While conceptually interlinked, in practice campaigns for economic, environmental, climate, and energy justice often remained separate, led by differing organizations and networks. Increasingly, however, the idea of just transition emerged among labor and community activists as potentially a more overarching and integrated approach, with the "potential for uniting climate, energy, and environmental (CEE) justice to provide a more comprehensive framework for analyzing and ultimately promoting fairness and equity throughout the transition away from fossil fuels."[30] In the United States, in 1997 the Just Transition Alliance was formed, as a coalition of environmental justice organizations and labor unions, arguing that, "The principle of just transition is that a healthy economy and a clean environment can and should co-exist."[31] By 2013, another coalition, the Climate Justice Alliance (CJA) had emerged, which linked the economy and environment to the broader concerns of climate and energy production. For CJA, "Just Transition is a vision-led, unifying, and place-based set of principles, processes, and practices that build economic and political power to shift from an extractive economy to a regenerative economy."[32] Internationally, in 2015 the International Labor Organization (ILO) adopted guidelines for a just transition, which focused on building "well-managed environmentally sustainable economies and societies, decent work for all, social inclusion and the eradication of poverty."[33] By the early 2020s, across the world, at least seventy-five frameworks for a just transition had been published by non-academic groups such as nongovernmental organizations, multilateral institutions, think tanks, and others.[34] Many labor unions in the United States, however, have been reluctant, if not opposed, to adopt just transition frameworks in their organizing. The late president of the AFL-CIO, Rich Trumpka, has often been quoted as saying, "Just transition is just an invitation to a fancy funeral," while United Mine Workers of America president Cecil Roberts has often said, "I've never seen one [a just transition]."[35] Nevertheless, while not using the language of just transition, the UMWA has also recognized that "change is coming, whether we seek it or not" and has called for the need to keep "America's coal miners, families and communities whole in an era of global energy transition," largely through jobs in carbon capture, utilization, and storage.[36] Other labor organizations, such as the Teamsters Union, often seen as the most conservative North American union, are increasingly seeing no choice but to use the concept of just transition to advocate for job preservation as economies decarbonize. In 2024, their newsletter argued, "'Just Transition' is meant to guarantee that 'no one is left behind in the transition to a net-zero and climate resilient future.'" The union has filed shareholder proposals demanding companies set net-zero carbon targets, including at UPS, Amazon, FedEx, and Marathon Petroleum. In so doing, the Teamsters "have firmly put the issue of 'Just Transition' on the radars of investors. Today, investors are asking how the decarbonization strategies of companies provide for good jobs or create job-saving opportunities to retrain and financially support workers."[37]

While some actors thus are using the idea of just transition to protect jobs within the status quo, others, such as Mijin Cha, argue that "Just transition requires a holistic, comprehensive vision that moves beyond emissions reduction to addressing issues of health care, affordable housing, transportation, and others to ensure communities and workers can thrive in a low-carbon future."[38] Many social movement actors also argue that more radical approaches are needed that go beyond the language of *transition* to more fundamental forms of *transformation* and put more emphasis on challenging and changing underlying issues of control.[39] Indeed, "important gaps remain in terms of understanding the potential of transition coalitions to be transformative in shifting the political economic structures that cause, sustain, and deepen, social, economic, and environmental injustices." Without this understanding, there is a risk that "just transition efforts may merely reproduce or even deepen existing inequitable systems and practices, despite rhetoric and stated objectives to the contrary."[40] Given this, Dimitris Stevis calls for distinguishing "transformative" transition strategies, which address underlying structures of inequality and power, and others that are more reformist in nature.[41]

Types of Justice and Pathways to Change

While important debates have thus emerged on the depth, breadth, and ambition of just transitions,[42] other debates focus on the meanings of the term "justice" and how it is obtained within this process.[43] As Stevis writes, "Just transition centres justice—and thus (in)equality and power—and envisions abandoning, rather than modifying, ecologically harmful practices."[44] The social movement organizing entity Movement Generation puts it this way: "An economy based on extracting from a finite system faster than the capacity of the system to regenerate will eventually come to an end—either through collapse or through our intentional re-organization. *Transition is inevitable. Justice is not*."[45]

One notion of justice within the just transition debate focuses on issues of *distributional* justice, that is, who wins and who loses, who bears the costs and burdens of change. A second pays more attention to questions of *procedural justice*, involving who participates and whose voices are heard. Closely related to procedural justice are issues of *recognitional* justice: whose values and identities are recognized? Whose knowledge shapes the process of debate? Finally, there are also issues of what some call *restorative or reparative* justice, which involve how to restore or compensate for past damages, and how to rectify historic injustices.[46] In a given place, across the many actors and stakeholders involved, we often see conflict and competition for which of these forms of justice are considered most important.[47]

Others warn that this polyvalent approach risks reifying different forms of justice or treating them in isolation, rather than focusing on how they are shaped by broader "historical relations of power and inequality."[48] Alternatively, we can distinguish between those proposals that "fall largely within weak environmental justice, reflecting the hegemony of neoliberalism and associated crisis management," and those that "point in the direction of strong environmental justice and even stronger ecological justice."[49]

The movement toward just transition has evolved from different groups and sectors, and with differing understandings of justice; so too are there many debates on the pathways by which transition can be achieved.

In their book on the *Politics of Green Transformations*,[50] Ian Scoones, Melissa Leach, and Peter Newell neatly summarize four narratives for how this change will occur. There are those who focus on a *technology-based* approach. In this approach the challenge is simply one of replacing one form of energy technology for another, for example, renewable sources of energy over fossil fuel–based ones. A second approach involves aspects of *commodifying and marketizing nature*, leading to what are often private-sector led "nature-based" solutions. This approach involves, for instance, the sale of carbon credits or for-profit conservation as a solution to planetary protection. A third approach puts more emphasis on *state-led* solutions, through, for instance, stronger state regulation, investments in and support for new technologies, as well as support for workers and communities who are adversely affected by the process of change. Finally, there is a more *citizen-led* pathway,[51] with a focus on bottom-up forms of action through grassroots innovations and social movements.

Each of these strategies is reflected in the case study in this book. And though each of these pathways may be analytically distinct, in practice, in a given locality or region, they coexist and are often in competition and conflict with one another, as we shall see in the case of the Clearfork Valley. And for fossil fuel–dependent communities like the coal towns and coal camps of Appalachia, where the economy, social and political structures, and identities have all been built around the process of extraction, transition clearly implies much more fundamental and contentious issues of transformation.

Where Does Power Come In?

Each of the ideas of justice discussed above—whether around the distribution of benefits, whose voices are heard, whose knowledges and identities are recognized, or how to reckon with the past, and on whose terms—all involve fundamental questions of power. Which pathways to justice predominate are also questions of power. For instance, as Scoones, Leach, and Newell ask, "whose rules rule, which institutions define visions of change and terms of change, and which relations of power shape different pathways" to change?[52] With this in mind, growing attention has been paid to feminist, antiracist, Indigenous, and postcolonial thinking about energy and transition, and with these approaches a consideration of power is always critical.[53] Moreover, as others argue, transition takes place in broader political economies, which in turn shape what strategies of change are possible, requiring both a historical and a contextualized view of how power relations play out in different contexts and periods.[54]

While there is now growing theoretical and conceptual literature on the links between just transitions, power, and broader political economies, there are few empirical studies that seek to ground these relationships and dynamics in a single place over time. By extending Gaventa's earlier study on the rise and maintenance of power in an Appalachian valley to the study of how power changes when coal declines, we hope to help fill that gap. In so doing, we will ask three broad questions: How do the coal industry and absentee landowners who have exercised such domination for decades seek to hold on to power when coal mining, the economic base of their power, declines? As the power of dominant actors recedes and as the energy landscape changes, which new actors emerge and with what forms and sources of power? And what do these changes mean for the power and participation of previously marginalized voices, especially workers and communities on the frontlines of energy transition, as they struggle for a more inclusive and just future?

The Place-Based Study of Power and Transition

To focus discussion on one place immediately locates the debate on power and just transition in a particular context, with its own histories, structures, and cultures of domination, as well as struggles to overcome them. And as we have argued, particularly in communities that historically have been based around a dominant single industry like coal and its extraction, the loss of that industry affects much more than jobs: it is deeply intertwined with other issues and inequities, including poverty, drug abuse, environmental destruction, and more. Understanding the impact of coal's decline on power and transition then requires going deeply into the history and present of that place, focusing on these intersections. It also means taking a bottom-up view of what these national and global transitions mean in everyday life, and the concrete impacts on those at the frontlines of the shift to a post-carbon future.

In order to understand the intersections of power and transitions, we also explore both empirically and theoretically how power relations shift as political economies change. In Central Appalachia, a key transition, documented in depth in Gaventa's original book and developed further in chapter 3, covers the initial encounter of an agrarian-based area with the fossil fuel industry, as industrialists took over land and developed coal mining to feed the industrial revolution around the end of the nineteenth century. This was followed by a second much longer period of coal industry hegemony, which involved the maintenance of the system of corporate extractivism while reshaping its power at various key moments when it weakened, due, for instance, to economic crisis or political interventions. We argue that we are now in the midst of a third distinct period, shaped by the decline of the coal-based economy, and this is where we concentrate our new empirical research. By examining how a coal-based system of power emerged, how it was maintained and reenforced, and finally how it shifts as the coal industry declines, we bring a historical, comparative perspective on power and transitions over a period of more than a century.

The study builds on the small but growing number of in-depth studies of the impact of decarbonization on single places over time. For instance, Andrew Curley's *Carbon Sovereignty: Coal, Development, and Energy Transition in the Navajo Nation*, focuses on the role of coal in tribal sovereignty, and contestation over a coal-fired powerplant and mine and their ultimate closure.[55] Another is Huw Beynon and Ray Hudson's *In the Shadow of the Mine*,[56] although as an account of the political legacy of British coal mine closures in the 1980s it does not closely follow climate politics. Another is Tom Hansell's *After Coal*,[57] based on the documentary film of the same title, which chronicles a series of exchanges between mining communities in Appalachia and Wales, as they faced mine closure.

To take our in-depth, grounded view of the dynamics of power and transition over time, we combine several approaches. For one coauthor, Gaventa, this represents a "revisit" approach, building on a long history in anthropology and community studies of returning to the earlier site of one's research. For instance, in the United States, the famous community study by the Robert and Helen Lynd in 1929 of "Middletown" America was followed only eight years later by a further study,[58] as well as numerous subsequent studies by others since. In the field of community power studies, Floyd Hunter's study of urban Atlanta in 1953[59] was followed up again by Hunter in 1980.[60] Cynthia Duncan's 1999 study of three remote rural areas in the United States—Appalachia, the Mississippi Delta, and New England—was followed by an updated study in 2015.[61] But, as Michael Burawoy writes in his review of these methods, the revisit is a challenging approach, as not only has the original site of study changed but so too has the perspective and lens of the researcher, inevitably requiring a more "reflexive" approach.[62]

In this case, as Gaventa began his revisit, he quickly became aware that this by itself was inadequate. Not only was there a need to revisit an earlier story in light of recent changes but indeed a new story of fundamental transformation was rapidly occurring that also needed to be told. While Gaventa had maintained some contacts in the community over the fifty years since he had finished his original work, a more in-depth contemporary view was also required. This is found in the contribution of the other coauthor, Gabe Schwartzman, who was just finishing his dissertation in the same valley, based on several years of in-depth ethnographic fieldwork, participant observation, and active engagement with the community. Schwartzman's work followed community institutions in the Clearfork Valley as they worked to create a just transition in the very moment when the last coal mines closed. By combining perspectives, as well as our empirical research, we offer a collaborative intergenerational approach to understanding changes in power relations in this community over time.

In doing so, we employ a number of methods. We draw on in-depth interviews, focus groups, and oral histories done separately by the authors—some thirty such interviews by Gaventa in his revisits during 2022–23, and over 100 by Schwartzman in his fieldwork from 2020 to 2024, both within the Valley and with policy makers and activists in the region more broadly. We also draw from the now extensive literature on Appalachian Studies, a field that has grown enormously over the last five decades. In addition, we use an array of statistical sources, as well as primary sources from government agencies, community organizations, and activist groups, drawn from extensive internet trawls, as well as visits to physical archives.

Throughout this work, both authors have played the role of scholar-activists, engaging in and supporting processes of change with local community organizations, while also studying the process of change over time. This approach—variously referred to as action research, participatory action research, scholar activism, or community-engaged research—has now developed a long tradition in the region and elsewhere. In the 1970s, Gaventa helped to mobilize some of the actions that he also studied. Fifty years later, Schwartzman spent hundreds of hours between 2020 and 2024 supporting a local group struggling for environmental and economic justice, volunteering time as a grant writer, helping organize meetings, and spending time on the various events and tasks that arose. Activist in orientation, and based on engagement and participation with others, this approach also requires attention to ethics, being clear and transparent on roles and positionality, and taking care to not put others at risk through our research. For this reason, we have usually not included the names or identities of those whom we interviewed, though some were happy for us to do so, unless we thought that this was particularly important for the meaning, or unless these were already public figures.

Structure of the Book

Overall, our hope is that this study will speak to and contribute to a wide variety of literatures: Appalachian Studies; the study of power and community studies; the rapidly growing field of climate and just transition politics, including the study of working-class and community-based social movements for economic, environmental, and climate justice; and the broader field of poverty and working-class behavior, especially in the United States. The case of this one Appalachian valley, we argue, has relevance and implications more broadly about the challenges of moving away from fossil fuel–based development in other similarly affected parts of the world, as well as the potential to offer more conceptual insights to longstanding debates on the changing nature of power.

In chapter 1 we locate the study by looking at the economic context of the Clearfork Valley itself, particularly in the wake of coal's decline. Despite the expenditure of billions of dollars on the economic development of the region since the 1960s War on Poverty, intersecting inequalities in the Valley remain, including the persistence of poverty and joblessness; massive environmental inequalities because of more than seventy years of strip mining and mountaintop removal; and health inequalities, experienced in particular through the targeting of these communities by the pharmaceutical industry for the marketing of opioids, leading to massive addiction. All of these are deeply intertwined with an extractive coal economy, which took wealth away from the region, while leaving the land destroyed, workers in poor health and in pain, and communities with little infrastructure.

Since the publication of Gaventa's earlier text in 1982, a whole field of Appalachian Studies has emerged, from which we learn a great deal about the impact of absentee land ownership and resource extraction, the domination of the coal industry, as well as the history of resistance and opposition to its hold and destructive practices over time more broadly beyond the Valley. Chapter 2 will draw on this literature, as well as our own research to further set the context for this study, highlighting changing gender and racial dynamics in the region as well.

In chapter 3 we become more conceptual, reviewing more theoretical debates on how power shifts amid transitions. In particular, we examine and link three theories of power and transition. The first, often referred to as the Multilevel Perspective (MLP), comes out of the field of transition and sustainability studies. Though often critiqued for not including power in its analysis, we argue that it offers a useful framework of the relationship between "landscapes" (broad structures), "regimes," and "niches," and how they interact. This approach can be expanded and deepened by drawing on more structural theories based on the thinking of Antonio Gramsci, and other neo-Gramsci thinkers, who look at transition in terms of changes in hegemonic orders and the interregnums between them. Finally, however, we suggest that both approaches can be strengthened further by revisiting the work of Steven Lukes on the three dimensions of power and Gaventa's subsequent elaborations of this, arguing that the framework also contains within it a theory of how less powerful actors can mobilize for "empowerment," especially when fissures in domination emerge.

With this context in mind, chapter 4 then moves on to focus empirically on how power changes in the midst of energy transition. In this case, in the face of climate and market pressures to move away from fossil fuel, rather than support and prepare for transition, the coal regime has fought back, redoubling its efforts to maintain its hegemony and to cling on to power, including through a heavily funded and clever "Friends of Coal" public relations campaign, followed by a subsequent campaign directed against those perceived to be waging a "War on Coal," particularly environmentalists and the Obama government.

The campaign to Make Coal Great Again between 2004 and 2012 fed naturally into the Make America Great Again (MAGA) movement in the form of Trump's campaign for the presidency in 2016, and the rise of right-wing conservatism in rural communities, which we explore further in chapter 5. Between 2004 and 2024 an area that once voted primarily Democratic became overwhelmingly right-wing Republican country. The phenomenon was not only seen in presidential elections—the movement targeted local and state institutions as well. Although a great deal has been written on the appeal of Trump to the white working class, this chapter will examine this shift through the lens of the deindustrialization and dispossession of Central Appalachian coal communities over time, looking at the interplay and manipulation by elites of class, race, gender, nostalgia, and fear.

With the decline of fossil fuels, and with the pressures for more "green" economies around the world, including in this Valley, we have seen a trend toward new investors entering the field, with a philosophy of "nature-based solutions," driven by "green" forms of capitalism, through dynamics we explore in chapter 6. In particular, we explore how in 2019 The Nature Conservancy came to control these and other lands, purchased through a private equity investment project, the Cumberland Forest Project. The project represents a new post-coal business model, one based on selling carbon credits on the California carbon market and operating sustainable

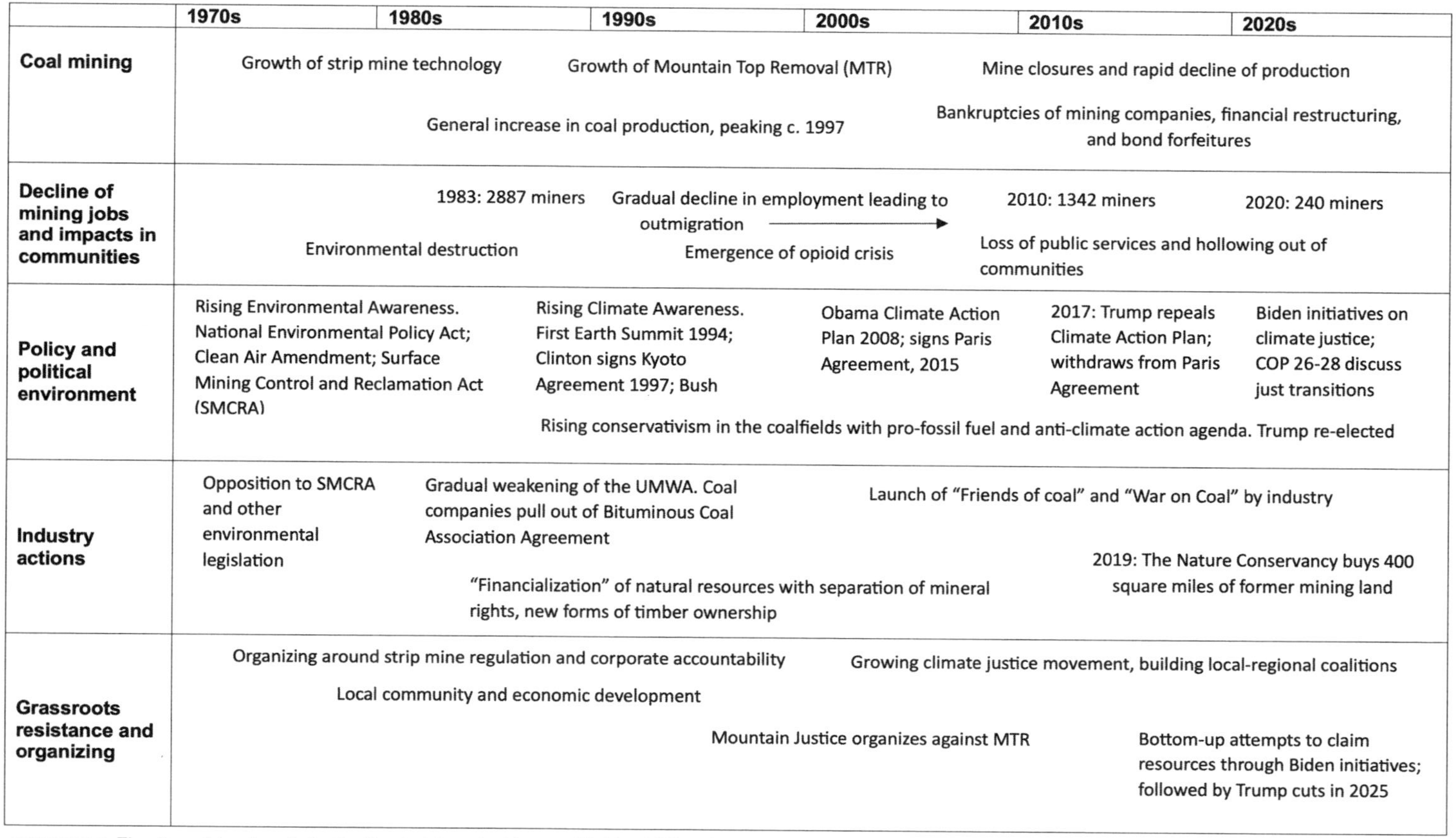

FIGURE 0.1. Timeline of key trends in the Central Appalachian coalfields, 1970s–2024 (Compiled by authors)

logging operations, as well as recreational tourism. The Valley became the testing ground to scale up the model, along with similar projects in other "bio-diverse hot spots" in the Amazon, Borneo, and Kenya.

While the previous three chapters thus show how the power of the coal industry, the political environment, and the forms of extraction have shifted over five decades, in the midst of all these changes grassroots organizing and resistance were also present and gaining their own strength. Chapter 7 begins by reminding us of the ongoing legacies of barriers to participation in the Valley, as outlined in Gaventa's earlier book, but then traces how over time these began to break, with the emergence of multiple, intersecting forms of community-led action, each of which laid the seeds for a larger movement toward just transition. Over time, these local initiatives began to come together to build regional alliances, which in turn helped to bring previously excluded voices and issues to the national agenda, including fighting for repair of the decades of damage done to the region.

In 2020, the national landscape on transition issues changed dramatically with the election of President Joe Biden, who brought a new commitment to address climate change and to support transition for energy communities. John F. Kennedy and Lyndon B. Johnson had introduced a War on Poverty in the 1960s. The Biden administration adopted the new language of environmental and economic justice, backed by programs such as the Justice40 Initiative, which prioritized funds for disadvantaged communities, as well as mandating that frontline workers and communities were to be consulted as stakeholders in the transition process. Two significant budget bills—the 2021 Bipartisan Infrastructure Law (BIL) followed in August 2022 by the Inflation Reduction Act (IRA)—released huge amounts of funds targeted for developing a clean energy sector, reclamation of mine lands, and economic transition, representing the largest investment in the region since the War on Poverty. Chapter 8 explores the power dynamics as bottom-up visions and movements for just transition met more neoliberal agendas in this top-down-created policy space—a space which Trump's 2024 election abruptly brought to a close.

The conclusion reviews the contributions of this extended case to our questions about power—how it is maintained, what new actors and forms emerge, and how this affects grassroots struggles to achieve just transitions in a post-carbon world. The chapter will draw conceptual and theoretical conclusions about power and transition, arguing that one affects the other. We end by discussing the relevance of this work to the broader contemporary challenges of achieving a more just, equitable, and sustainable transitions to a post-carbon future.

We conclude with a few notes to the reader on how to approach this book. Although the book picks up where Gaventa's earlier book on *Power and Powerlessness in an Appalachian Valley* left off in the mid-1970s, it can easily be read on its own. Throughout the book, we remind readers of the earlier findings and what has shifted since. There are also some important differences in the two books. In particular, while the earlier book focused mainly on the dynamics of "power over," that is, on how domination and hegemony of the coal industry were created and maintained over time, this book focuses much more on how grassroots opposition to this power emerged, and the multiple ways in which local groups are working for a new post-coal future.

Rather than to try and give a history of the Valley chronologically, we tell the story around particular themes, for example, how the coal industry works to hold on to its power. This means, however, that other parts of the story, such as resistance to that power, are told in other chapters, though this might have been going on at the same time. In each chapter we will cross-reference to other chapters to make these links. We also encourage the reader to refer to the timeline presented in figure 0.1 to locate what was happening at one point in time in relation to what was happening in other spaces and levels.

Although we focus on the Clearfork Valley to examine what happens to power relations as the coal industry declines, we also draw upon literature and information from other parts of the Central Appalachian region. From this perspective we link to broader studies around the themes that we consider, attempting in so doing to present the Valley not as an exceptional place, but one that shares many characteristics with other rural places shaped by the decline of industry, the rise of right-wing conservatism, and new forms of financial and extractive power. The literature we touch upon is massive—with a rapid rise in recent years of studies and theorizing on just transitions, as well as a large literature on age-old questions of the nature of power, its relationship to the broader political economy, and how these shift as capitalism itself changes. We cannot do justice to all these debates—rather our modest attempt is to engage with them by starting from the experiences of one small place in rural America, recognizing that what happens here is also shaped by broader social and economic forces.

In telling this story through the lens of one place, we hope to offer some insights into how power changes in the midst of economic and energy transition. We learn that even though the material base of the economy changes, as we move from one form of energy production to another, old actors struggle to cling on to their power. As the material control of land and labor by these incumbent actors diminishes, new discursive forms of power become more important, often attempting to control the agenda and terms of debate through shaping narratives around climate, energy, and the centrality of fossil fuels to our collective futures.

As transition occurs, some of the actors from the old order also try to reinvent themselves, while other new actors and investors also enter the scene, all vying with one another to fill the vacuum left in the process of change from one order to another. While in the past direct control of jobs and infrastructures at the local level were most important, epitomized by the coal camps and company towns, now the emphasis is more on how to profit not only from the extraction of nature's resources, but from their financialization and through strategies of accumulation through restoration and repair.[63] New forms of power may emerge, but they may involve transition from one elite to another, rather than more fundamental forms of transformation. However, as older actors and forms of power weaken, and as fissures in the previous order grow, previously suppressed voices may also emerge, which offer a more transformative vision of a post-coal future.

1

Intersecting Inequalities and the Failed Promises of Development

> And that was sad. The day that they pulled all the [coal] trucks out. And they all was in a line and they blowed their horns for the last time. You know it reminded me a lot of when my brother passed away. . . . that was exactly how it was that day.
>
> —Clearfork Valley resident, 9 September 2021

> The coal industry is collapsing, and you'd expect there to be more of an exodus [out of here].
>
> —Economic development practitioner, 10 October 2021

While struggles for a just transition away from fossil fuels inevitably involve issues of power, they also must confront a web of compounding inequalities and injustices that the legacies of the fossil fuel economy leave behind. In this chapter, we examine the impacts of the decline of the extractive economy on the quality of life in the Clearfork Valley, including exacerbating poverty and joblessness, creating fertile ground for pharmaceutical companies to profit from a drug addiction epidemic, and leaving behind significant damage to the land and environment. Any approach to creating more just and equitable futures, we argue, must begin by addressing these legacies of intersecting inequalities left by decades of coal extraction. We must also learn from the failures of past development models.

When Gaventa researched his previous book in the Clearfork Valley in the early 1970s, the Appalachian Region had loomed large in public debate around the War on Poverty, launched by President John F. Kennedy and later championed by President Lyndon B. Johnson. The Clearfork Valley exemplified the issues of poverty that Michael Harrington's 1962 book *The Other America* had revealed.[1] The 1970s brought an energy boom that theoretically should have helped to alleviate the poverty situation. But as Gaventa's book showed, the boom scarcely benefited local communities, as an absentee-owned, extractive economy continued to drain wealth from the region, leaving behind poverty and inequality.

Many residents in the Clearfork Valley left the area in that period and found work in the industrial cities of the North, such as Detroit, Michigan, or in Toledo, Akron, Cincinnati, and, importantly in the story of the Valley, Dayton, Ohio, to which many families migrated. As one middle-aged resident explained, "Everyone in my dad's generation . . . I reckon about everybody moved out of here and went North. Dayton. A bunch of them came back and when they retired. . . . They came home."[2] This man also had left, moving to a town just outside the Valley, but came back. "I hated it," he said. The Valley, with its proximity to forests and family, was home to him.

Many of those people that moved back to the Valley after working in auto plants and similar industries found their community transformed. As coal-mining jobs continued to dry up and no other industries replaced them, by the 1980s and 1990s many of the services and economic amenities, such as stores, restaurants, and schools in the Valley were disappearing. On a chilly January day, Schwartzman interviewed a woman in her mid-sixties about her life in the Valley. She too had grown up there and left, coming home to raise children. She reflected on that choice: "I brought my kids back here because I thought it would be safe, the safest place to raise them without that influence [drugs and violence]. No, it's not. It was the easiest and the only thing they had to do in this holler, because there was nothing for them to do, no place to go, no place to hang out."[3] Now she was raising her grandchildren, as her children struggled with opioid addiction.

She lived in an uninsulated trailer home with no heating or cooling, sometimes using the oven to warm the home. Despite receiving payments from the federal Social Security Disability Insurance program, she frequently struggled to pay the electric bill—failure to pay could be life threatening as she desperately needed power for her supplemental oxygen machine for the treatment of chronic obstructive pulmonary disease (COPD). And the absence of electricity could justify the state's taking her grandchildren from her. Despite these economic and personal pressures, she loved her home and had been an activist against coal strip mining. In many ways, her life illustrates the compounding effects of coal extraction and its decline on the Valley and places like it, as she fought for a future beyond coal, while surrounded by the poverty, environmental damage, and addiction that coal's decline left behind.

Building on stories such as these, in this chapter we examine what happens to communities that have been based on an extractive economy when the extraction ends. We begin by analyzing the impact of the decline of coal on jobs and the loss of services in the Valley. We then look at how this links to other measures of disadvantage, including persistent poverty, lower life expectancy and drug addiction, and environmental degradation. At the same time, we show that even amid these intersecting crises, many people remain rooted to the Valley, valuing what it has to offer.

The Place of the Clearfork Valley

In their 2023 book, *The Injustice of Place*, Kathryn J. Edin, Luke Shaefer, and Timothy J. Nelson remind us that poverty is best understood in relationship to place, for it is in a single place that the multiple intersecting disadvantages and their interrelationships may be seen. Going beyond metrics based largely on income, they construct a more wholistic Index of Deep Disadvantage, which combines measures of poverty, health, and intergenerational mobility. Applying this to over three thousand counties and cities, they found that the most disadvantaged places on this scale were in rural America, including the primarily white region of Appalachia, the Latinx/Hispanic populated area along the South Texas border, the Cotton Belt, often known as the Black Belt, across the southern United States, and Native American communities.[4] Their analysis found that these places had one thing in common: "a history of intensive resource extraction and profound human exploitation not seen to the same degree elsewhere in the United States." As they wrote in reference to the Cotton Belt and Central Appalachia, "one industry linked to national and global markets came to dominate the economy, a pattern that held, broadly, into the 1960s, when King Cotton, King Coal, and the others would bow to the twin forces of automation and competition from global markets."[5]

The Clearfork Valley (See figure 1.1) is one such place, historically affected by deep, intersecting, multidimensional forms of disadvantage.[6] The Valley cuts across four counties, two in Kentucky and two in Tennessee, and is home to roughly one dozen separate hamlets, most of which are former coal-mining camps and towns. One single main road, Route 90, runs thirty miles through the Valley, along the Clearfork River, with many side roads branching up into what are termed hollows, or "hollers," which wind farther up into the mountains. The towns and clusters of homes are not one single community, but a series of communities, which share a common watershed—places like White Oak, Duff, Eagan, Clairfield, Valley Creek, Pruden, and Fonde (figure 1.2.)

Home to roughly four thousand people, the Valley is far from the seats of government in each county, with some residents needing to drive up

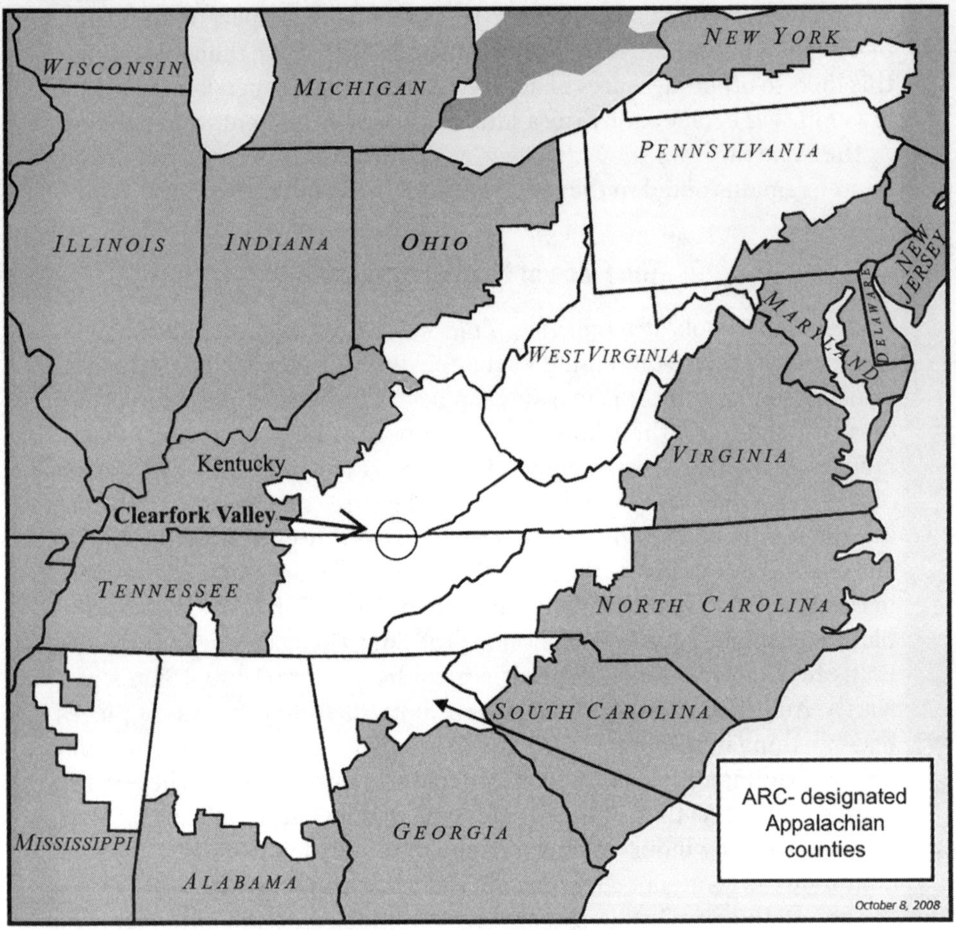

FIGURE 1.1. The Clearfork Valley refers to the circled area, cutting across the four counties of Campbell and Claiborne, Tennessee, and Bell and Whitley, Kentucky. (Adapted from Appalachian Regional Commission)

to one hour to reach their county courthouse. Those in the Valley side of Claiborne County, Tennessee, for instance, have to drive over a mountain to Middlesboro, Kentucky, and back over the Cumberland Gap to reach Tazewell, the county seat. There is one Dollar Store in the Valley, meaning residents drive out of the Valley to towns "off the mountain," as residents in the area term it, to shop for groceries and access basic amenities in places like Jellico and LaFollette.

What these communities share, in addition to their proximity, is a common history and identity shaped by coal. Even people no longer work-

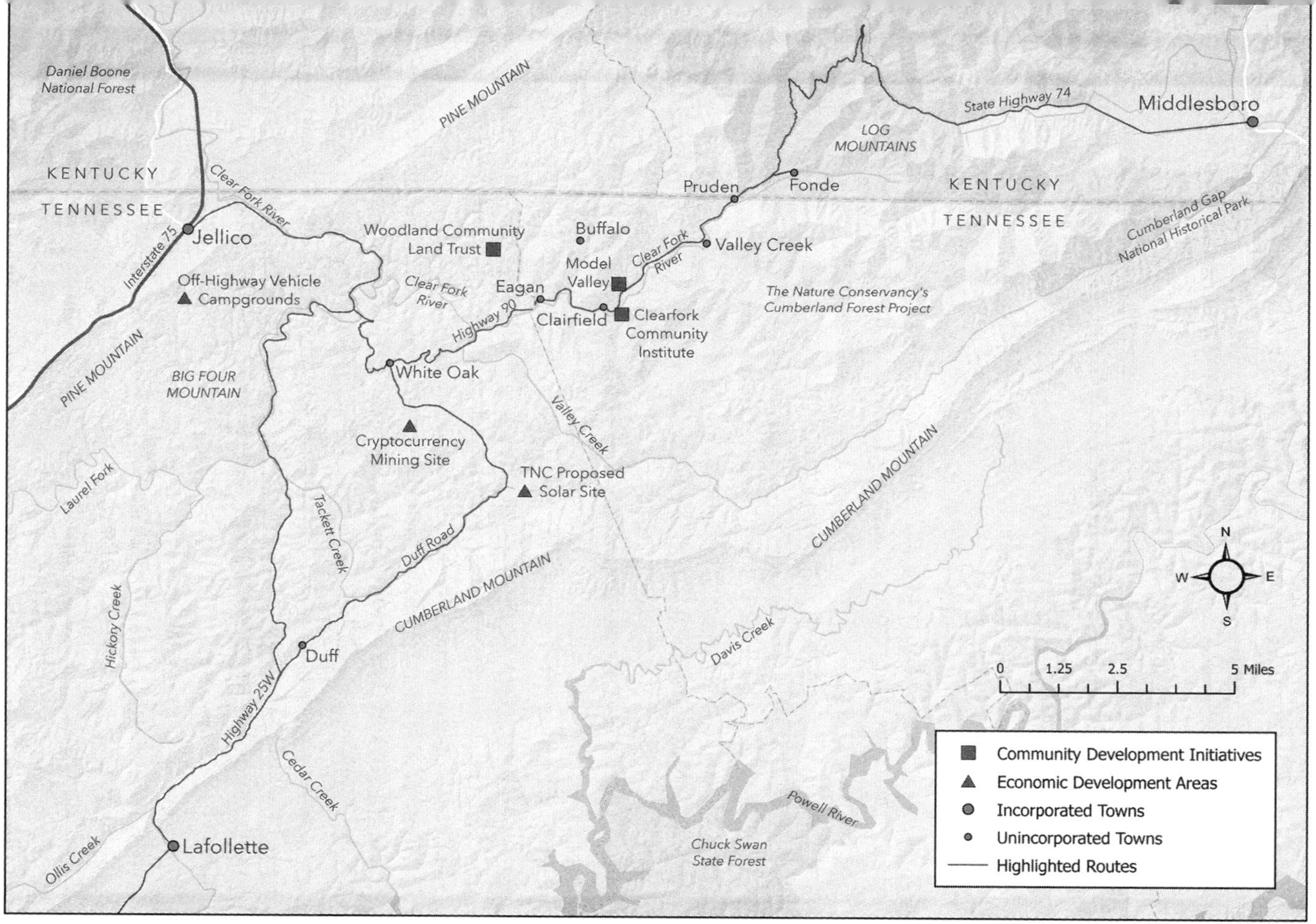

FIGURE 1.2. Map of the Clearfork Valley, with sites of economic development and community institutions (Map created by Seth Kannar)

ing in the mines might introduce themselves proudly as a "coal miner's daughter" (or son). For them, the end of the coal industry was strongly felt, signaling the end of a way of life. As quoted in the beginning of the chapter, one interviewee reflected on the sense of loss on a day in 2015 when she watched one of the last mines shut down in her community:

> And that was sad. The day that they pulled all the [coal] trucks out. . . . You know it reminded me a lot of when my brother passed away. . . . And it was even more sadder when I saw the flatbed trucks that were going up into what was Consol [Coal Company] . . . , and taking the piece of machinery and their little buildings and you see them hauling a dozer or a truck or something out of here going to other places.[7]

Consol was by far the largest mine and thus largest single employer in the area, and the last of the labor-intensive underground mines in the area. At the time of its closing the mine was owned by the Consol Energy Company, a large Pittsburgh-based energy conglomerate. The Clearfork resident mourned the loss of what had been a central part of the community for decades.

In the Valley, coal employment has declined steadily since the mid-1980s, although most precipitously in recent years. In 1987, production of coal in the four counties in which the Valley is located peaked at 10,953,364 tons. By 2022, production was down to 747,338 tons, a drop of over 90 percent. In turn, this was matched by the decline in employment. In 1984, there were 3,067 mining jobs in these four counties; by 2022, there were only 244, again a drop of over 90 percent. On the Tennessee side, there were 5 mining jobs reported, down from 953 in 1990. As of this writing (in 2024), all Tennessee mines have shuttered their operations, and only a handful remain open in the Kentucky counties.

While coal jobs in recent years represented a relatively small percentage of the jobs in these areas, they were often the best paying, especially where they were unionized. As a result, these were prized jobs, despite being notoriously dangerous, with high risks of long-term health effects from black lung disease, or coal workers' pneumoconiosis. In coal-reliant communities like those of the Valley, there are few comparable jobs in the region to which workers can easily move. Furthermore, when coal mines shut, coal workers usually "are the ones that have the means to leave" these communities, draining mining communities of their highest-earning families and community members.[8] Now, as numerous coal companies enter bankruptcy and mines close, mining communities have witnessed profound economic hollowing out. As one interviewee said of Clairfield,

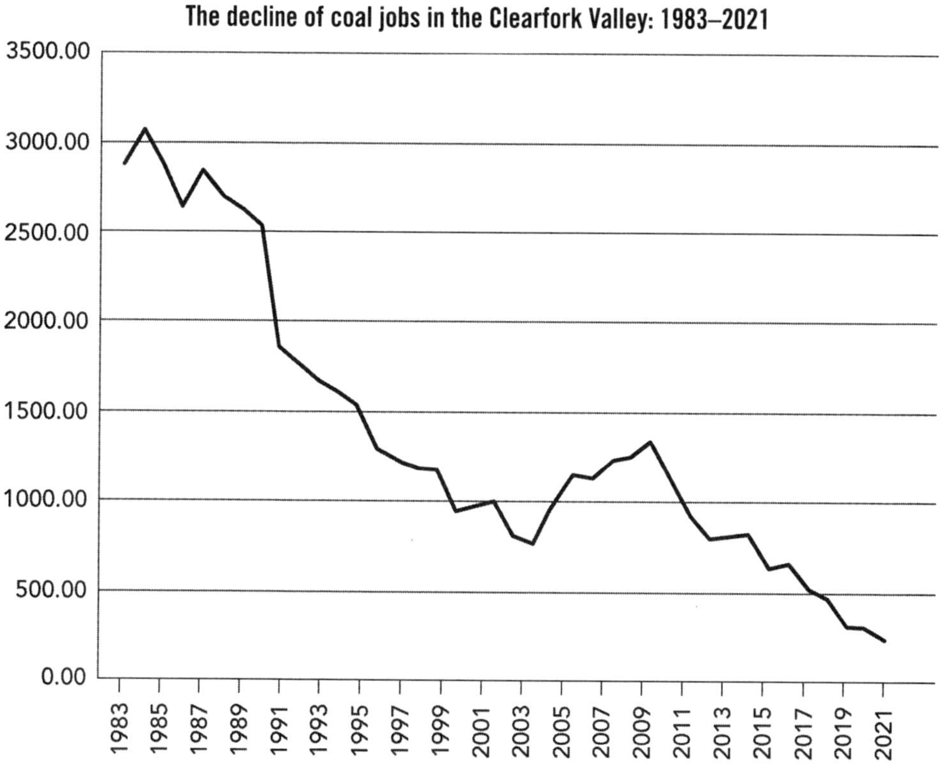

FIGURE 1.3. Data from the four counties of which the Clearfork Valley is a part, including Campbell and Claiborne Counties, Tennessee, and Bell and Whitley Counties, Kentucky (Drawn from Appalachian Voices, "OpenSourceCoal.Org," Economic Statistics, https://arlweb.msha.gov/STATS/PART50/P50Y2K/AETABLE.HTM: MSHA, 2023 1983, http://opensourcecoal.org/)

in the center of the Valley, "It's not a town for working man, because if you came in, I don't know where you'd find a job."[9]

Those jobs that are available are largely low-waged work in the service sector, or in the public sectors, such as schools. Some in the Valley commute long distances to work in regional hospitals, or thirty to forty-five minutes to work at the fast-food restaurants and motels closer to the main interstate highway. For the east Tennessee region as a whole, the largest employer in 2020 was "food services and drinking places," including fast food establishments, but the highest projected growth in jobs was in "mental health and substance abuse facilities," to help deal with the growing addiction issues linked to the opioid crisis.[10] In eastern Kentucky, the largest regional investment was for a federal prison, though this was some distance from the Valley. The congressman for the area, Hal Rogers, had already used his influence to bring three federal prisons to his district in eastern Kentucky, "giving it one of the highest concentrations of federal correctional facilities nationwide."[11]

Announcements of other new industries were few and far between, and the jobs not ideal. In Jellico, Tennessee, a cryptocurrency mining farm was developed in a former motel and another crypto mining facility was built in Westbourne, Tennessee, in the heart of the Valley, using the energy infrastructure of a former coal facility, drawn to the area by "cheap, reliable power, few zoning regulations, depressed local economies, and the opportunity to greenwash their huge electrical footprints."[12] These are noisy, use large amounts of water, and produce virtually no jobs. Across the mountain in Middlesboro, at the time of our fieldwork, the announcement of a new defense-related plant to be built on a former toxic Superfund site was generating local excitement.[13]

In 2024 there was the promise of new construction jobs from the Biden administration's clean energy investments. This included a forecast of 1,500 jobs coming in 2026 to Bell County near the Kentucky side of the Valley from a $81 million grant for a pumped-storage hydropower facility, a Department of Energy–funded, privately run project (as discussed more in chapter 8). In addition, The Nature Conservancy planned to build a utility-scale solar site in the Valley near Westbourne in the coming years, and to construct seventeen new sites nearby in Kentucky and southwest Virginia, hoping to make use of Biden administration solar tax credits.[14] These sites could generate hundreds of additional construction jobs.

A great deal of hope has also been placed on tourism in these counties as an engine of economic renewal. As one resident of the Valley said, "Something I think would help make a drastic change for good: getting a lot of seasonal tourists because of the Tackett [Creek Wildlife Management Area]."[15] As the coal mines have closed, tens of thousands of off-highway vehicle (OHV) riders have come to use a new trail system in the Valley, yet few local businesses has been established. Most campgrounds and all restaurants have located closer to the major highway and centers of commercial services. Moreover, even the few jobs that did become available in the hospitality and leisure sector paid on average less than a third of what coal miners were once paid.[16]

The compounding result has been an economic crisis in the Valley. By 2021, of the 4,292 residents sixteen and up living in the census tracts at the heart of the Valley, some 2,600, or 60.1 percent, were no longer in the labor force, reflecting the inability to perform jobs or lack of access to them. In the Clearfork Valley, 32 percent of the population reported disabilities, and many people were affected by other health issues, including drug addiction. Many young people have left the Valley to find work. The overall share of population sixty-five years or older has grown, in turn with major consequences for families.[17] There is a missing middle generation in the Valley, as the grandmother's story at the beginning of the chapter illustrates. Local interviews point out that perhaps as high as 60 percent of all children are being cared for by grandparents, with their parents either off looking for work elsewhere or unable to work due to the impact of addiction and disability.

Ripple Effects: Economies of Abandonment

The loss of jobs has ripple effects, helping to create a wider process of disinvestment, declining revenue, and loss of services. Scholars have documented similar trends in other rural parts of America, leading to what sociologist Marc Edelman calls a "hollowed out heartland": "Sacrifice zones—abandoned, economically shattered places, with growing social and health problems—are spreading in historically white rural areas, and small towns across the United States."[18]

The Clearfork Valley provides a good example. As the mines have closed, coal companies either went bankrupt or reorganized into shell companies, making it difficult to hold them to account for the toxic legacies they leave behind and commitments to worker health and retirement plans they had supported. When companies go bankrupt, states and local communities also lose "billions in tax revenue that would have gone to schools, hospitals, roads, and other infrastructure."[19] For communities already struggling to cope, this loss of funding can be devastating. Many such communities had come to rely on a tax known as the severance tax, based on the amount of coal extracted, and representing a hard-won gain from struggles for fair taxation in the 1970s. According to *Bloomberg News*, "In Kentucky, severance money paid to counties totaled $23.4 million in 2015, compared with $62 million five years ago."[20] In Tennessee the severance tax is $1 per ton, with 50 percent of taxation going directly back to roads and schools (split 50 percent each) in the county of production. In Campbell and Claiborne Counties, severance taxes brought in an estimated $1.3 million in funding in 2013, which declined to $456,000 in 2019.[21] In 2020, that figure fell to $92,000. Today, the figure is zero.[22] In the course of a decade, funding for roads and schools in the two counties that are home to the Valley disappeared.

This decrease in tax revenue coincides with a more general trend of decreasing public investments in rural infrastructure as manufacturing and other large employers shut down and rural economies contract across the country.[23] Hospitals nearby to the Valley in Bell County, Kentucky, and Campbell County, Tennessee, closed in the 2020s, Bell County's reopening with limited services in 2023, meaning residents must drive an extra forty-five minutes for health care. The community-owned water utility, the Clearfork Utility District, struggles to remain solvent, and its closure would mean that the state would force a sale to a larger district that would have to drastically raise rates or cut off customers.[24]

With the decline of services also come the loss of gathering places for socializing and maintaining community connections. Six post offices, frequent meeting places in rural communities, have consolidated or closed. The last library in the Valley closed in 2013, when Claiborne County cut its budget, supporting a mobile library bus until its funding was also cut. Driving across thirty-five miles of highway that stretches through Clearfork Valley, one sees most shops are boarded up. There are two establishments that serve hot food, but neither has a sit-down option. Some of the few places that people can gather publicly are the dozen or so churches that dot the communities.

When asked what kind of redevelopment he would want to see, one interviewee said, "Well, it'd be good to have more stores, maybe a restaurant, a bar . . . "[25] In a survey of youth, when asked what they would like to see in the community, they gave a long list, including more playgrounds, places for young people to go outside their homes, and organized activities for youth, as few at all exist. The decline of spaces for public life has also facilitated what Shannon Elizabeth Bell termed a breakdown in social capital and community cohesion. As Bell documented one West Virginia coalfield resident saying, "There ain't no bond in town like there used to be."[26]

Intersecting Inequalities

In places that have long relied on extraction, the effects go beyond disappearing coal jobs and declining public services. Rather, economic decline compounds other forms of inequity, reenforcing conditions of persistent poverty and inequality, fueling a drug addiction epidemic, and exacerbating crises of health and mortality. In addition, the loss of the coal industry, along with the corporate bankruptcies which often accompany it, leave behind a legacy of destroyed land, water, and natural resources, long a source of livelihood and identity for people living in the mountains. By looking more closely at the case of the Clearfork Valley—a place with profound persistent poverty, high levels of addiction and morbidity, and widespread environmental degradation—we see how these inequities intersect.

POVERTY AND INEQUALITY

Despite the War on Poverty and subsequent federal programs, extreme and persistent poverty still rank high across America. In his 2022 book *Poverty, by America,*[27] Pulitzer Prize–winning author Matthew Desmond observes the United States still has more poverty than any other post-industrial democracy in the world—one in seven Americans live below the poverty line, despite residing in the richest country on earth. The Economic Research Service (ERS) cites that there are 353 persistently poor counties in the United States—those that have had more than 20 percent of the population beneath the poverty line for over four decades.[28] Many of these are concentrated in Central Appalachia, as well as other distressed communities in the Black Belt of Mississippi and Alabama, Native American communities, and Hispanic communities in the American South, for example, those places also found to have multiple deprivations in the above-mentioned *Injustice of Place*. All four of the counties in the Valley—Campbell and Claiborne in Tennessee, Bell and Whitley in Kentucky—are included in the persistently poor counties as defined by the ERS.

The Appalachian Regional Commission (ARC), the federal agency created in 1965 to solve Appalachian poverty, presents a slightly different picture. The agency points to the fact that over the last five decades overall poverty of the region declined from nearly 31 percent in 1960 to 16.6 percent in 2015.[29] Yet progress has been uneven. In 2025, out of 423 counties in the region, 77 remain classified as "distressed," the majority in the Central Appalachian Region.[30] The Valley reflects these trends. In 1970, the average poverty rate across the four counties transected by the Valley was 44 percent. By 2021, this had been reduced by more than half to 21 percent. However, if we focus only on the coal area found in the Valley itself, some 26 percent of the population still remained classified as living in poverty, over double the rate of the United States as whole.[31] And when we take not only income but wider measures of "distress," we get an even more somber picture.[32] Isolated by zip code, the community at the heart of the Valley, Clairfield, Tennessee, registers in the top 99.9 percent of most distressed communities in America. The small towns nearby, to which rural residents might commute for work, health care, or other services, do not fare much better, with Jellico, Tennessee, at 99.8 percent, LaFollette, Tennessee, at 96.2 percent, and Middlesboro, Kentucky, at 97.4 percent levels of distress.[33]

Such distress exists amid growing inequality in America. A study by the Rand Corporation calculates that between 1975 and 2018, about $47 trillion in taxable income was redistributed upward, away from the poor and middle-class Americans (the bottom 90 percent) to the very wealthy (the top 10 percent), making America the most unequal country among its western counterparts.[34] This redistribution also added to the increased spatial inequality between communities. Between 2000 and 2018, prosperous zip codes gained 8.7 million jobs, generating nearly 62 percent of job growth. Zip codes that were distressed lost jobs during the same period.[35] Similarly, rural areas like those in Central Appalachia lagged behind urban areas in economic growth, increasing a more widespread rural-urban divide.

PUSHING PILLS: THE RISE OF THE OPIOID EPIDEMIC

In the spring of 2022, Schwartzman asked an interviewee from Clearfork Valley about what kind of development the area needed. Standing in the yard of a trailer home with garbage and broken furniture littering the area, the man explained that people needed cash assistance to get back on their feet and, he added, more programs that offered clean needles for injection drug users. Already sick with hepatitis C, he would die less than two months later of complications from drug use. Far from an anomaly, the man's death is one of many such deaths in recent years.

Beginning in the late 1990s, Appalachia became a hotspot in the opioid epidemic that consumed much of the United States, as surging numbers of people became addicted to pharmaceutical painkillers, and as drug overdose deaths increased exponentially.[36] The epidemic profoundly affected the Clearfork Valley. Across the four counties in 2015, an average of 241 opioid prescriptions were being written for every 100 residents, compared to the national average of 70.6.[37] In turn, this translated to higher mortality rates. For the period 2010–2014, the average mortality rate in these four counties in which the Valley is located was 49 deaths per 100,000, four times higher than in the country as a whole. In Bell County, the most heavily dependent on coal mining, the average was 77.8, or almost seven times higher.[38]

Corporate strategies promoting highly addictive pain medication to working-class patients in increasingly economically depressed communities drove the epidemic. Following changes to healthcare oversight in the 1980s,[39] a newly deregulated pharmaceutical industry found people facing pain, occupational injury, the long-term physical effects of working-class jobs, and living with increasing levels of economic distress to be highly profitable consumers of highly addictive drugs. Art Van Zee, a doctor located in southwest Virginia, warned in 2009 of the impact of the highly aggressive and sophisticated marketing techniques these companies were using, particularly targeting doctors in zip codes where pain medication was already beginning to be in use—such as rural populations like Appalachia with a long history of poor health and coal-related injuries. Sales of one drug, OxyContin, heavily promoted by Purdue Pharma, "grew from $48 million in 1996 to almost $1.1 billion in 2000 . . . and by 2004 OxyContin had become a leading drug of abuse in the country."[40]

As so-called "pain clinics" mushroomed in small towns across the region, from 1999 to 2011 the number of overdose deaths caused by prescription painkillers in Appalachia increased by 1,098 percent.[41] In her book *Dopesick: Dealers, Doctors, and the Drug Company That Addicted America*, Beth Macy wrote of this new industry as "drug diversion, the practice of using and/or selling prescriptions for non-medical purposes." Bringing new, if sinister, economic activity to the region, she argued that "pills were becoming the new coal."[42] Another commentator working in the area of substance abuse in the region referred to the trend as "pharmaceutical colonization,"[43] suggesting that it represented the latest example of a long history of corporate exploitation of the region.

The opioid epidemic, however, was also part of broader trends across the United States of increasing mortality in white working-class communities. In 2020, Princeton economists found that for the first time in recent history, death rates were on the rise among middle-aged white Americans. The fastest rising death rates were from three causes: suicides, drug overdoses, and alcoholic liver disease, which the authors labeled "deaths of despair."[44] Of these the largest number by far was death from drug overdose, in particular opioids. The trend was highly specific to a particular population, non-Hispanic white Americans who lacked a four-year college degree. The Appalachian Region, with its large population of white Americans without a college education, was at the epicenter of this new phenomenon, and once again, the Clearfork Valley reflects the trends, where nearly 90 percent of adults lack a bachelor's degree.[45]

The impact of the epidemic has been devastating, but some have fought back. A group of Valley residents joined others in a "prayer walk" to protest a pain clinic in nearby Jellico, Tennessee, in March of 2017, after residents realized what they thought was a clinic to treat addiction was also prescribing opioids in large numbers. One community group, Woodland Community Land Trust (which we will discuss further in chapter 7), hosts a harm reduction medical care group to distribute lifesaving overdose-response Narcan and clean injection needles once a month, an event that is well attended. Perhaps tellingly, though, the Land Trust is the only organization in all of Campbell County that would let the medical nonprofit use its site as a distribution point. There are no addiction treatment facilities or programs in the Valley communities, or their surrounding counties, with the exception of a Christian men's live-in rehabilitation program in Jellico, controversial for having the men work jobs, such as landscaping, without pay. One "Celebrate Recovery" program exists in LaFollette, Tennessee, and another in Williamsburg, Kentucky, a Christian version of Alcoholics Anonymous, which meets once a week. But overall, the landscape of recovery and rehabilitation in the Valley, like much of rural Appalachia and working-class communities across the country, is minimal.

ENVIRONMENTAL INJUSTICE

In 2017, residents in the Valley watched as the Kopper Glo mining company moved bulldozers past a local cemetery to begin mining a nearly fifteen-hundred-acre mountaintop removal mine on Cooper Ridge, above an elementary school, "dealing yet another massive blow to the ecology and communities of this beautiful and resilient area."[46] Since the 1960s and 1970s, the Clearfork Valley had experienced the rapid growth of surface coal mining, strip mining, which polluted water, destroyed springs and wells, and brought flooding and landslides to many in the area. As strip mines grew in number, they also increased in size. While earlier technologies carved off the edges of mountains, leaving highwalls and barren strips but the tops intact, later technology, known as draglines, enabled the removal of entire mountaintops, referred to as "mountaintop removal" (MTR). An elderly man recalled witnessing the transformations in the land that the new kind of mining brought: "We sat right here and watched them take that mountain down over there. I mean they took the top right off."[47]

Since the 1990s, the number of such massive operations using MTR technology has grown rapidly across the Central Appalachian Region, bringing new environmental risks. These included "flyrock" falling off mine sites and crashing through homes, killing a child in Kentucky in 2005.[48] MTR caused dust clouds to envelop communities below mines, and new vast mines brought flooding and landslides on unprecedented scales. Public health scholars demonstrated that proximity to these mines also brought serious health effects related to the pollution.[49] Processing the coal brought further pollution to these rural, working-class communities. Coal companies frequently disposed of liquid coal waste from coal processing, known as "sludge" or "coal slurry," behind earthen dams and underground in old mines—a waste product full of toxic compounds, such as mercury and arsenic. Slurry contaminated drinking water for numerous communities, seeping into in home wells and springs, many of these areas becoming cancer and gallbladder disease hotspots.[50]

Further issues of water contamination plague communities across Appalachia. Coal mines continue to pollute surface water, at times with difficult-to-mitigate "acid mine drainage," and with sediment and heavy metals from surface mining. Blasting frequently caused water tables to drop, making springs and wells that people have long relied on for drinking water to run dry.[51] One Valley resident reflected on the changes to her drinking water, which she now has to buy instead of getting from a spring: "We have to pay for that shit now, and it's a natural resource that we should not be paying for, and I can't even teach my kids what it tastes like, because they [the coal industry] ruined it [spring water]."[52]

As the coal industry collapses, coal companies are also increasingly leaving communities without resources to mitigate these issues of water contamination, coal waste, flooding, and the environmental safety of mine sites. Since the 1977 Surface Mining Control and Reclamation Act, coal companies have been required to reclaim strip mines to a safe standard and to purchase bonds at the start of mining to cover the costs of such reclamation. However, when companies go bankrupt, they often forfeit their reclamation bonds. Bond amounts may fall far short of what is needed, leaving the future environmental reclamation and the environmental safety of coalfield communities in jeopardy.[53]

Communities in the Clearfork Valley have experienced these environmental injustices, first through the process of mining and resource extraction, and now in being laden with abandoned mine lands, acid mine drainage, and cascading bankruptcies that slow and stall environmental restoration. An example may be found in the heart of the Valley, where the Kopper Glo mining company had continued to mine until declaring bankruptcy in 2024 and forfeiting their reclamation bonds, including on the Cooper Ridge site they opened in 2017, mentioned above. The company leaves this series of unreclaimed sites across the Clearfork Valley, posing an environmental and safety risk to nearby communities. A Freedom of Information Act (FOIA) request by the Sierra Club in late 2023 found that across Tennessee 63 percent of coal mine permits were in "bond forfeiture," with companies surrendering their bonds to the state to use to clean up the sites. Almost all of these permits were in the Clearfork Valley.[54]

With rising concerns about the combination of environmental and economic justice, the Biden administration committed huge resources for environmental cleanup and economic development in mining communities, as we shall examine further in chapter 8. With this has come a new metric for measuring the state of these communities, known as the Climate and Economic Justice Screening Tool, to help to determine eligibility of the most disadvantaged communities to receive these funds. In addition to being low income, the tracts must also be demonstrably affected by climate change, and inequities in energy, health, legacy pollution, housing, transportation, water and wastewater, and workforce development. Once again, each of the tracts in the Valley score highly on this measure of disadvantage, not only ranking high on poverty-related indices, but also scoring in the upper percentiles of communities affected by legacy pollution, largely in the form of abandoned mine lands and other climate-related risks, including flooding, agricultural loss, population loss, or building loss from natural hazards and disasters.[55]

Hard to Stay and Hard to Leave

As we have shown, the Valley ranks high in all metrics of persistent poverty and inequality, health and morbidity related to addiction, or environmental degradation. Each of these intersecting inequalities has worsened in this period of transition. Facing these realities, some people choose to stay and build community in this place, while for others, they have nowhere else to go.

On a blustery winter afternoon in the Valley in 2022, Schwartzman conducted an interview with a man in his twenties facing homelessness and making ends meet by selling wild roots, such as ginseng, and collecting scrap metal to sell. The young man was living in his car with his brother, after their late father's house that they had been living in had burned down in an electrical fire. He had spent most of his adult life as part of a salvage economy, activities in which he had lost two fingers and nearly his life when an electrical wire he thought was off turned out to be live. Having spent time in prison, the man lived for some time in a prison reentry program in Morristown, Tennessee. As he explained, "They used to bring me over here to visit, and they'd be like, you don't got much over here do you? . . . You don't have nothing." He responded, "We got a store where you can get parts for a vehicle. A store where you can buy food. That's all we need." When asked if he had ever thought of leaving to find better work, he said, "Nope, I like it . . . I wouldn't trade this for a city place never."[56]

Another interviewee reflected on the strength of community in the Valley. "It's a great place to live. I mean, it's like it can take you back fifty years, [to] the way life was. It's like that now, if your door is unlocked, you don't have to worry about stuff. "[57] Others, however, as we also discussed in the beginning of this chapter, found it difficult to leave and not come back. "I wanted to get out in the world at eighteen. But that really didn't work out. . . . I still want to get out. But, thirty years ago, I didn't really have nowhere to go. So, I came up here [to a piece of family land]. [Now]

I raise a garden and enjoy the outside of nature."[58] The tension between these two sentiments has only grown as the coal economy has collapsed.

Overall, in the recent decades, more people have left than stayed. Between 1970 and 2020, the two key census tracts that make up the Tennessee part of the Valley lost some 19 percent of their population.[59] In total, over 12 percent of the Appalachian Region's population would leave in search of work elsewhere as the coal economy contracted. At the same time, some people returned home to the Valley as they retired from careers in industrial cities. One man who worked in Dayton, Ohio, most of his adult life explained, "The city was not my home. It was just a place I existed. This is a good home . . . I come back home to die."[60] Another interviewee recounted his experience of returning from the Sunbelt. "In the early eighties, I went to Florida to work. I worked in construction. I absolutely hated it. . . . I realized it wasn't the work that I hated. . . . It was the lifestyle, the constant hustle and bustle, and nobody being respectful. And I had no money. . . . I quit that job and I was like, man, I'm ready to go home."[61] Driving back to the Valley in a breaking down car, he never left again, preferring to live a slower, peaceful life around family and closer to the nature he loved.

Others also talk about staying in the Valley because of a shared sense of community and closeness to the land. An asset mapping survey conducted in 2017 asked residents to answer "what do we love about our community?" Over half of the respondents mentioned the closeness of neighbors, followed by a love of the natural landscape and the peace and quiet of country living. Over half of respondents said they enjoy outdoor activities that the rural area offers, and a third mentioned the social activities of church, family events, visiting relatives, and hanging out. Others talked specifically about loving spending time in the mountains, collecting wild herbs, hunting, or simply walking. Despite the intersecting social, economic, and environmental crises, for many the Valley is where they want to stay.

A Top-Down Development Agenda

Longstanding efforts to address poverty and economic diversification in Appalachia have largely come up short. Since 1965 and the War on Poverty, ARC has spent over $14.5 billion for economic development in the region. Yet, as the coal economy steadily declined, the growth model it promoted failed to prepare places like the Clearfork Valley for the eventuality of a future beyond coal mining. Economic development that did occur was often uneven, with places closer to major highways and having less concentrated land ownership often benefiting. In the four counties in which the Valley sits, there are sharp contrasts between the abandoned coal communities, where populations have declined, and other parts of the county, which have attracted some industry and where populations have grown.

As a top-down approach to development, with very little room for grassroot community direction or decision-making involved in funding strategy,[62] ARC's investments have largely not met the needs or desires of coal communities in Appalachia. In the 1960s, the War on Poverty had sought to involve local residents and organizations by distributing funds through a new federal agency, the Office of Economic Opportunity (OEO), which worked directly with "community action" committees and groups. The intention was that the groups had to have "maximum feasible participation of the poor" in the governance of the groups and the distribution of the funds.[63] While fraught with controversy, and some of the most democratic elements of the funding quickly dismantled, in the early years of implementation the OEO offered a route for community institutions to directly fund projects that they considered beneficial and necessary for development.[64]

The Appalachian Regional Commission, however, had a very different aim. Created in 1965, ARC was largely an initiative of majority southern state governors to subvert the bottom-up "maximum feasible participation" policy and to secure federal funding for the impoverished white portions of their states. The Council of Appalachian Governors, what later became the ARC, in 1961 demanded that any Appalachian-focused federal aid be governable by state powers.[65] State control was partially what the OEO was aiming to circumvent, particularly in the southern United States where, in the 1960s as in the 1930s, segregationist white supremacist elites (e.g., Alabama Governor George Wallace) opposed federal aid reaching Black communities without state mediation.[66] As Al Smith, federal co-chair for the ARC from 1980 to 1982 said, "We moved power away from Washington. I cannot write a check, as I understand it, for an ARC project unless a governor asks me to."[67] Established as such, the ARC undermined Washington reformers' intentions of supporting bottom-up collective action, establishing a highly elite-controlled institution that allowed largely conservative state governors (then as now) to control where federal funds were deployed.

The ARC's top-down, elite-controlled approach quickly became narrowly focused on developing new highways, industrial parks, and recruitment of businesses and industry to certain parts of the region.[68] In the 1980s, ARC was nearly defunded during a wave of Reagan-era cuts to federal programs.[69] A concerted campaign from local and state leaders throughout Appalachia saved the ARC from the fate of many other War on Poverty programs, yet ARC came out of the process reformulated.[70] Pro-business and industry trends already present at ARC were deepened in the reorganization, part of a wider international trend that social theorists have named neoliberalism, what Jamie Peck and Nick Theodore term "state-facilitated market rule,"[71] involving the cutting of social welfare programs and institutionalization of pro-business and free market policies in government since the late 1970s.[72] In the Valley, the shift to a neoliberal development model meant loss of funds for many public projects, such as the health clinics, public water systems, libraries, schools, and community institutions. Rather than invest heavily in wellbeing or social programs, nearly three-quarters of ARC's funding in the region to date has gone toward highway construction.[73]

In this context, we can see the failure of a fifty year-long development agenda most acutely in the lack of realistic programs that planned for and responded to the long-forecasted economic transition away from the coal economy. However, beginning in 2015, ARC started operating one program to help communities contend with coal's decline: the Partnerships for Opportunity and Workforce and Economic Revitalization (POWER) Initiative, which began as a nationwide Obama administration interagency program, in 2016 became Appalachia specific and housed at ARC. The POWER Initiative has invested $421.6 million in 507 projects. Many if not most of these, however, are limited in scope and approach by the neoliberal confines of ARC development strategies, heavily funding entrepreneurship and job training programs (sometimes for jobs that do not exist), which have not improved quality of life or economic outcomes.[74]

A more recent program, the ARC ARISE program launched in 2022 specifically incentivizes investments in "energy communities" and economic development that attends to environmental justice concerns. As we shall discuss in chapter 8, these investments, from the Bipartisan Infrastructure Law of 2021 and the Inflation Reduction Act of 2022, represent the largest federal investment since the War on Poverty. Unlike the War on Poverty, however, they are aimed at decarbonizing the country and massively building out clean energy infrastructure, while also investing in communities facing environmental justice issues and bearing the burden of energy transition. Agencies implementing these pieces of legislation have mandated that recipients of clean energy funding have community benefit plans and incentivize union participation in the grant scoring metrics. These new approaches have the potential to create a new kind of more inclusive development policy, with hopes of promoting material change in Appalachian and other communities across the country. While they are promising in their intention, the jury is still out as to whether they will break with the development model of the past fifty years, and also as to whether they will survive the newly elected Trump administration, as we will explore further in chapter 8.

Conclusion

While the vision of a just transition away from fossil fuels implies commitments to fairness and inclusion, in places like the Clearfork Valley, as in so many communities historically at the front lines of energy extraction, any such agenda will have to start with the challenge of redressing the legacies of longstanding inequalities. As we have seen in this chapter, the closure of mines means much more than the loss of jobs—it deepens social, health, economic, and environmental crises. The result is that the Clearfork Valley stands among the many deeply disadvantaged communities in America. Yet, nonetheless, people remain attached to the land and place and want to imagine and struggle for a more just future.

The drivers of inequality intersect and accumulate with one another—the closure of mines affects revenues; lack of revenues affects health, education, and other services; persistent poverty and inequality affect mental well-being, compounded by pain and disability from poor health, making people vulnerable to profiteering pharmaceutical companies and individuals, and contributing to greater addiction; addiction in turn destroys the social fabric of communities. Destruction of land contributes to growing health and environmental risks, as well as a loss of access to land, which historically has been important for both informal livelihoods as well as a sense of identity for rural communities. Dealing with one aspect of these intersecting issues will not necessarily correct the other. In these communities, transition cannot be about simply substituting one job for another but must also engage with other dimensions of injustice. And, in the race to create new energy alternatives, these communities do not start on an equal playing field compared to places that have not faced such a long history of corporate control and abuse.

Such transitions also occur in broader contexts. In the following chapter, we situate the Valley in the larger political economy of the region. We examine further the social and political history of the region, including exploring the long history of resistance to corporate domination, as well the changing racial and gendered dynamics in the face of coal's decline. All of these will shape the changing nature of power and empowerment in the struggles toward a just transition, which we then interrogate in the following chapters.

2

Setting the Context

Power, Resistance, and the Rise and Decline of King Coal

The Clearfork Valley, the focus of the previous chapter, is part of the broader Central Appalachian Region, which includes parts of Tennessee, Kentucky, Virginia, and West Virginia, and historically was the epicenter of coal production in the eastern United States. From the 1880s to the 2010s, the coal industry dominated political, economic, and ideological spaces within this region. Going beyond the Valley to set a regional context, in this chapter we review that history, detailing how the industry came to power, how it held power, and the patterns of resistance to its domination. In discussing these themes, we draw on a wealth of social science and historical literature about Appalachia that has emerged since the 1970s.

We first review the political economy of the previous transition between agrarian and industrial social relations in the late nineteenth century. Second, we review analyses of the social formations through which the coal industry held power over more than a century of dominance. Third, we examine the articulations of race, gender, and class in coal communities, highlighting how coal domination occurred both through inequitable racialized and gendered formations, and how these also offered positions from which to resist coal industry hegemony. Finally, we trace the prelude to the current moment of coal's rapid decline through the mechanization and deindustrialization of the industry over the previous half century. Locating the Clearfork Valley in this larger regional and national context helps us to understand the contemporary decline of coal as a period of transition from one hegemony to a new, as yet unsettled formation of power and domination.

An Agrarian Transition

Appalachia in late nineteenth century was in an agrarian transition, a moment of widespread dispossession and enclosure that often accompanies shifts from peasant production to capitalist land and labor relations.[1] The control of land in the region had long been stratified. In the eighteenth century, colonial elites violently dispossessed Indigenous peoples of their sovereign territories, taking land from the Cherokee, Mingo, Shawnee, Yuchi, Monacan, and other Indigenous peoples.[2] English royal charters acted as legal justification for the dispossession of Indigenous communities, the king of England granting titles for vast landholdings in Appalachia to British aristocracy. After the American Revolution, many titles were transferred to elite American colonists,[3] thus concentrating landownership in the hands of relatively few individuals and establishing high levels of inequality in the mountains. Mary Beth Pudup estimates as much as 60 percent of Central Appalachians were working as landless agriculturalists in the nineteenth century, even before the concentration of land in the hands of absentee coal and timber industries.[4]

The coal industry established its hegemony in the Appalachian Mountains during the period of transition from an agrarian to a more industrial economy. In the late nineteenth and early twentieth centuries, coal, timber, and railroad tycoons purchased or stole much of the land and resource wealth across the Appalachian region.[5] Many of these new industrialists infamously tricked smallholder farmers out of land, offering contracts that mountain farmers sometimes could not read.[6] In the Valley, as Gaventa illustrates in his earlier book, the American Association, a British coal company, swindled or forced sales from small landowners, coming to own much of the land in the Valley. In addition to dispossessing smallholders of property, this period included widespread contests between agrarian elite landholders and the new corporate-industrial actors, many of whom were absentee.

Industrialists in timber, coal, iron, and salt production, among other industries, frequently used violence to seize land and resources over which agrarian elites held control. In other instances, agrarian elites themselves became industrialists, pursuing new modes of accumulation and also using violence to dispossess other agrarian elites. For instance, Altina Waller shows how the Hatfield-McCoy feud, violent episodes between 1880 and 1891 that are often depicted as backwoods (and backward) barbarousness, were in fact a contest over the control of land, a struggle between a powerful family using the forests for an agrarian economy and a family invested in turning the forests into saleable timber.[7]

The contest between agrarian and industrial elites extended to courtrooms. For example, in the 1910s in West Virginia, agrarian elites challenged the growing power of industrialists, charging that railroad companies should be liable for forest fires set by sparks from their engines. Through political intimidation (and at times courthouse wars that involved violent assaults on court employees and judges), railroad companies ultimately won a state supreme court case against agrarian elites whose agricultural operations were impacted by the frequent fires.[8]

These industrial elites not only came to control land and subsequently political apparatus through economic might and political strong-arming, but they also introduced novel ideologies that justified their control. For instance, a key discourse the American Association deployed was that there was a common purpose in building new infrastructure and a city, Middlesboro, dubbed the "Magic City of the South," out of the agrarian hamlet of Yellow Creek. The American Association and others propagated the myth that all could benefit from industrial development if they worked hard, miners and mountaineers included. Similarly, coal and other resource extraction companies articulated the ideology that "progress" was coming to the mountains through corporate investment, bringing modernity and civilization to supposedly backward mountaineers.[9]

In the Valley, the American Association promoted the idea that nature could be conquered by technology, witnessed in such feats as digging a tunnel through the Cumberland Gap and rerouting the local creek.[10] Coal and resource extractive industries deployed these narratives of "development" to garner public support and justify their dispossession of former agrarian elites and smallholders in Central Appalachia. Through political and economic coercion, at times bloody fights with existing elites, and through ideological justification, largely absentee corporate industrial elites came to own and control much of the land and resources across Central Appalachia.[11]

Coal Industry Domination

The inequities and power imbalances set in place during the agrarian transition enabled coal industry representatives to stifle resistance to their domination. As Shannon Elizabeth Bell writes, "These power relationships have been repeated and manifested throughout history so that grassroots challenges to the great inequalities many Appalachian residents face have been obstructed, time after time, by the authority and control surrounding and protecting those who benefit from the inequalities."[12] Here we examine four political economic relationships that underlay those power relations: the control of land, the organization of space in the company town, a racialized hierarchy of work and environmental risk, and a gendered labor structure.

Coal industry domination in the region relied on continued ownership of land and resources. In the Clearfork Valley, as Gaventa detailed previously, the American Association's control of land and natural resources gave the company power over communities, with the ability to intimidate some people from lodging grievances for fear of losing housing or jobs. The company summarily chose which infrastructure would be built in the area, what amenities the community could access, and who bought what parcels of land in the community. In many ways, the American Association became the arbiter of basic aspects of life through the control of land in the Valley.

Across the region, studies of landownership illustrate similar colonial-like relationship in land and resource ownership.[13] The 1979 Appalachian Land Ownership Task Force documented high rates of absentee corporate landownership in Appalachian counties with resource-extracting industries (e.g., coal mining, timbering).[14] In the study spanning six Appalachian states, the citizen-led task force found that of the thirteen million acres surveyed, "Only 1 percent of the local population, along with absentee landholders, corporations, and government agencies, control at least 53 percent of the total land surface in the eighty counties."[15] Even more striking, across seven million acres of mineral rights surveyed, "Four-fifths of the mineral rights in the survey are absentee owned."[16] Two more recent studies of land ownership in Appalachia, one in West Virginia in 2013,[17] and an ongoing decentralized study of landownership across eastern Kentucky, the Clearfork Valley, Tennessee's Wise County, Virginia, and Mingo County, West Virginia,[18] document continued absentee ownership of land into the current moment.[19]

While coal domination was based on absentee corporations owning the land and extracting wealth from the region, absentee corporations also relied on alliances with local elites to maintain control.[20] For instance, homegrown figures like former Massey Energy CEO Don Blankenship, West Virginia senator Joe Manchin, and West Virginia coal-operator governor Jim Justice rose to power in the 1980s and 1990s to make massive profits from highly exploitative coal industry practices, and as we shall see, to play critical roles as brokers of political power as well. They were only the most recent in a long line of the small, but significant, number of Appalachians made wealthy by coal industry extraction.

The alliances between absentee corporations and local elites manifested in the spatial arrangements of power in the coal company town. Company-owned towns covered the Central Appalachian landscape from the late nineteenth century to the mid-twentieth century, providing dedicated housing and services for (and control over) workers in factories, mines, mills, and lumberyards.[21] Crandall Shifflett notes that in 1920 as high as 80 percent of miners in West Virginia lived in coal towns, with lower, but comparable figures, elsewhere in the coalfields.[22] Such towns frequently included company stores, complete with company-controlled currencies, or scrip. Companies had summary power in these towns, from predatory operations of debt in company stores to the power of the company to evict workers from their housing and banish labor organizers.[23] Extensive research has also documented the ways that company towns were often constructed to facilitate control and suppression of worker mobilization with private police forces.[24]

The company towns, however, generally included a local elite that benefitted from repression and control. Doctors, bosses, and engineers were offered stately homes and high-class amenities, sometimes in separate towns altogether.[25] More importantly, company towns did not simply rely on coercion of a workforce, but also often offered novel amenities for workers, working to build an ideological consensus that company control was in the best interest of all. In the early twentieth century, this included providing electric lighting, access to doctors, and proximity to modern amenities like movie theaters and ice plants, to which neighboring agriculturalists had little access.[26] Through the provision of these amenities, and dedicated work to promote the company town as purveyor of new cultural values of modernity, civilization, and progress, coal companies worked to convince workers and local elites alike that the new spaces of control were in the interests of all.

Coal industry domination was maintained not simply through a local elite and the promotion of cultural values that justified their control but also through division and unequal distribution of benefits along racialized lines. In the period of agrarian transition, industry relied on racialized labor to bring railroads to the mountains. Black, often conscripted convict laborers from the post-Reconstruction South, frequently did the deadliest work of laying tracks and blasting tunnels through mountains, as Cicero Fain documents.[27] The folk ballad "John Henry," about a Black railroad tunneller killed by a race against a steam shovel, memorializes this era. As Scott Nelson argues, a real historical John Henry may have died digging a railroad tunnel in western Virginia, building the infrastructure necessary for the region to become an industrial coal extraction landscape.[28]

Racialized labor was also a vital part of coal mining in its early decades. Coal company towns, up until companies dismantled them in the 1960s and 1970s, were often racially segregated towns.[29] White worker housing was often superior and in more prime locations than that of segregated Black families.[30] In one example from the Valley, the coal camp of Valley Creek was segregated, with Black families relegated to living across the creek, with precarious bridges and less access to amenities.[31] Across the coal industry, Black workers were frequently paid less and did more dangerous work than their white counterparts although at much higher wages than Black workers saw in the agrarian South.[32] Racial and ethnic segregation in coal camps and towns helped divide workers and prevent organizing.[33]

In addition to segregation, threats of racialized violence and terror were a part of life in coalfield Appalachia, suppressing racial solidarity and protest. For instance, between 1878 and 1920 there were seven documented instances of lynching of Black men in the Valley counties, including four cases in Campbell County, two in Claiborne County, and one in Whitley County.[34] While the city of Middlesboro was almost one-third Black around the turn of the century, it was also known to have had a strong chapter of the Ku Klux Klan during the 1920s.[35]

Yet, despite racial segregation and terror, oral historians and memoirists have documented the ways that coal towns were at the same time spaces of diversity and prosperity for many Black families.[36] Karida Brown and William Turner have shown in detail the ways Black communities flourished in all-Black coal towns like Benham and Lynch in Harlan County, Kentucky,[37] including developing strong social institutions such as the East Kentucky Social Club.[38] The Valley also had been home to vibrant Black communities, with various Black schools in Jellico and LaFollette in Campbell County and Valley Creek and Fork Ridge in Claiborne County. In Middlesboro, Ann Matheny notes that the Black community worked with the school board in 1907 to raise funds to establish the Lincoln School, which was "to be the hub of the Black community for the next sixty years."[39] Many of these communities were also relatively integrated. For instance, in the early 1950s Middlesboro had the only integrated Little League baseball team south of Cincinnati.[40] Black communities thus found avenues to thrive in the coalfields, an example of the ways that the coal industry distributed material benefits to coal workers and their families, if within strict limits.

Coal companies additionally maintained domination through strict gendered labor regimes that largely kept women out of the paying workforce or only able to access low-wage and often precarious work. Women were not able to work as coal miners in Appalachia until the passage of the Equal Opportunity Employment Act of 1972. Even then, women miners faced widespread discrimination until an administrative complaint filed with the US Department of Labor and a campaign by women to gain the better-paying coal jobs forced coal companies to end discriminatory practices in 1978.[41] In a mono-economy where coal mining was the primary employer for much of the twentieth century, women either were dependent on men's income or worked in low-wage, "feminized" jobs.

Across industrial employment in the twentieth century, women were also expected to do "social reproductive labor,"[42] unpaid work that allowed men to concentrate on their jobs while women attended to home, kitchen, and care work.[43] These gendered relations of work enabled companies to externalize the basic costs of caring for their workers' daily needs, such as childcare, cooking, and emotional well-being, onto unpaid or low-waged women in the coalfields, putting women in positions of economic powerlessness that offered them few choices other than to rely on the wages of coal-mining husbands, fathers, and sons. In addition to laboring in the home, in coalfield Appalachia many women worked as maids, servants, and cleaners in the homes of wealthy local elites, including coal bosses. Some other women, such as in the Clearfork Valley, were able to access low-waged work in light manufacturing,[44] including textile plants in Jellico and LaFollette, Tennessee.[45]

Throughout the twentieth century, the coal industry leveraged what scholars of race, gender, and ethnicity term "the production of difference" to maintain division and control of workers and their communities.[46] The industry, as with capitalism more broadly, maintained hierarchies along racialized and gendered lines, wherein some reaped benefits from their preferential positions while others bore the brunt of labor and risk that enable coal industry profit. Yet, as we explore further in chapter 3's discussion of power, coal industry domination also relied in part on the maintenance of at least partial consensus around the shared benefits of coal industry control.

Resistance to King Coal

Despite the efforts at control, the long history of miners' militancy and everyday resistance to coal company control provide evidence that coal communities often withheld complete consent to coal's hegemony. There were always cracks and fissures within coal industry domination that allowed for resistance and contestation. These included working-class organizing, at times involving resistance to a repressive union structure, protests over living standards and environmental conditions, and contests over the terms upon which social reproduction was organized and distributed in the coalfields. Importantly, however, resistance was often met with harsh reprisal and came with significant consequence. As we illustrate, resistance was episodic, greatest when coal's field of power was weakest and waning when the industry was strongest.[47]

The early years of coal mining were rife with often violent workers' struggle for unionization, safety, job security, and higher wages.[48] One of the earliest instances of miner militancy was the Coal Creek War in East Tennessee in the 1890s, fought over the presence of convict workers mining coal in the area, almost all of whom were Black workers, incarcerated under racist laws, Black Codes (which criminalized petty offenses and vagrancy), and forced to labor through convict leasing arrangements. Organized and armed white workers fought coal company and state troops and freed the Black convicts who had been leased to mine coal, thus suppressing free workers' wages.[49] There were also widespread worker uprisings in the early 1910s–1930s, often called the West Virginia Mine Wars, during various campaigns by the United Mine Workers of America and other unions to organize the coalfield,[50] including in Paint Creek and Cabin Creek, West Virginia, in 1911–12, leading up to the Battle of Blair Mountain.[51] At Blair Mountain, West Virginia, in 1921, tens of thousands of striking miners fought a private army, hired by coal companies, in efforts to unionize the southern coalfields of West Virginia. It was the largest workers' insurrection in US history, short of the movement of Black people to free themselves during the US Civil War.[52] While the miners laid down arms after federal troops arrived, militancy continued. In Harlan County, Kentucky, in the 1930s, workers rose up in violent clashes known as Bloody Harlan.[53] In response to uprisings, coal industry repression was great and frequently led to violent crackdowns that seriously hindered union organizing efforts.[54]

Thus, widespread unionization only came to the coalfields with the passage of the Wagner Act and the subsequent establishment of the National Labor Relations Act in 1935.[55] With legal protections to unionization, the UMWA effectively took control of nearly 80 percent of the coalfields by 1945.[56] Out of a wave of postwar strikes in 1945, under the leadership of John L. Lewis, the UMWA negotiated a wages and benefits agreement with an association of bituminous coal operators, leading to a worker-industry detente. In those negotiations, Lewis first brokered the Krug-Lewis Agreement of 1946, establishing the UMWA Health and Retirement Fund, for healthcare and retirement and hospitals.[57] Subsequently, in 1950 Lewis negotiated the Bituminous Coal Operators Agreement for wages and benefits, which set the union and coal operators in a mutual agreement to not strike over mechanization in exchange for high wages and good benefits for their workers.[58] These agreements secured a relatively high quality of life for miners in the union, including establishing a series of miners' hospitals, high wages, and unparalleled benefits, with union membership peaking in the 1960s and 1970s.[59] Thus, from 1945 to the 1970s, the UMWA maintained a careful power-sharing arrangement with the coal corporations that was accompanied by a top-down union power structure.

Serving at times to challenge coal industry power, the union also became an institution that could repress rank-and-file dissent in the coalfields. Another site of resistance in the coalfields became, therefore, the numerous miners and mining community rebellions against the undemocratic, incrementalist, and at times corrupt union leadership. Barbara Ellen Smith shows how the Black Lung Movement of the 1960s and 1970s mobilized not only against the coal companies but also at times the recalcitrant and adversarial union leadership.[60] In the late 1960s and early 1970s, the Miners for Democracy movement mobilized for internal union reform.[61] In the 1970s, miners who remained outside of union representation struck for union representation including at the famous strike at the Brookside Mine in Harlan County.[62]

In the 1980s, empowered by President Ronald Reagan's conservative appointees to the National Labor Relations Board, coal operators began to break with the Bituminous Coal Operators Agreement, refusing to recognize the union and employing non-union miners.[63] Miners struck and mobilized in the 1980s and 1990s, often beyond the directives of the UMWA, frequently using violent tactics in response to the union-busting campaigns of companies such as A. T. Massey and Pittston Coal.[64] Again, in this period, coal industry responses to militant resistance were harsh and effective. Many miners served prison time for involvement in these protests, and industry lawsuits against the UMWA in the 1990s largely crippled the power of the union to organize strikes.[65]

Resistance and grassroots mobilization in the coalfields extended beyond miners' militancy and struggles over labor organizing. Many community-based groups also mobilized to demand higher standards of living, improved basic infrastructure, and responsible governance, what today is frequently termed community organizing. Community protests for improved public services became widespread during the 1960s, particularly in the early years of the War on Poverty when antipoverty programs, such as the Appalachian Volunteers and Community Action programs, organized low-income communities to demand a fair share and equal participation in the distribution of public revenue.[66] Throughout the second half of the twentieth century, protests arose at various points in many coal-mining communities over basic government services, such as poor schools, lack of sanitation, and roads that were degraded from overloaded coal trucks.[67]

Another key focus of protest and resistance in the coalfields was the anti-strip-mining movement of the 1960s and 1970s. As community groups began to question and challenge poverty and status quo inequities through War on Poverty–era organizing, they increasingly challenged the environmental and health effects of this form of extraction, which also took away jobs. Strip mining, or surface mining, had rapidly increased after the 1950s, and disproportionately affected low-income families and small farms. Known as the movement To Save the Land and the People, many scholars consider this struggle, alongside the fight against environmental racism in Warren County, North Carolina, in 1978, as one of the early environmental justice movements in the United States.[68] Groups started in that era continue to operate in the region today, such as Kentuckians for the Commonwealth (KFTC) and Save Our Cumberland Mountains (now known as Statewide Organizing for Community eMpowerment) in Tennessee, as we will explore more in chapter 7.[69]

From the 1970s through the 2000s, grassroots community organizing took on other various and diverse struggles, including fights for farmers and women workers,[70] Black inclusion in regional economic development,[71] and the empowerment of community leaders to become organizers.[72] Organizing globalized after the 1970s, as activists connected struggles for unionization in East Tennessee with workers in Mexico,[73] and coal miners built solidarity with anti-apartheid activists in South Africa[74] as well as with miners in Wales.[75]

Resistance and grassroots mobilization in Appalachia often notably involved women-led movements and actions both in labor and community organizing, which reflected changing gender roles over time. In early labor militancy, women such as the famous Mary Harris "Mother" Jones were at times leaders in strikes and during labor uprisings, using their positions as wives, mothers, and daughters of miners to push for safer mines and better pay.[76] Women's everyday practices of care and social reproduction, such as collecting wild greens, sustained long months of strikes.[77] In their roles as homemakers, widows, and pensioners, women led the anti-strip-mining protest movement of the 1960s and 1970s. In the later twentieth century, as women won greater equality in society and the workplace, they became central actors in strikes against union-busting companies in the 1980s and 1990s, leading civil disobedience campaigns that frequently landed many women in jail.[78] The tradition of women's labor militancy informed anti-mountaintop-removal mining movements of the 1990s through the 2000s, where women were key leaders of nonviolent civil disobedience campaigns.[79]

Mobilizations for union and community organizing were also frequent sites of racial solidarity. For instance, in Jellico, Tennessee, from 1892 to 1895, William Riley, a Black UMWA District 19 organizer, mobilized Black workers across the Valley, using the support of the union to fight for racial equality.[80] Union organizing in Logan County, West Virginia, in the 1940s and 1950s famously involved Latinx organizers as key UMWA leadership alongside white and Black miners, and the Mendez and Ojeda families continue to be politically significant in county politics.[81] In the 1960s and 1970s, the Black Lung Movement too brought white and Black organizers together,[82] as did union organizing of the 1980s and 1990s.

Appalachia's history has thus been one of both domination and resistance, each of which have involved changing class, race, and gender dynamics. Outside corporate entities, in alliances with local elites, have often effectively repressed dissent or efforts by workers and communities to demand improvements to working and living conditions. Yet, despite reprisals and repression, throughout the twentieth century and into the present workers rose in protest in key moments. Much of this resistance was directed against a hegemonic coal industry in Central Appalachia, as communities and workers made demands upon and protested coal industry practices. Yet, many of the protest movements and organizations that arose before the 1970s were not sustained. The conditions that shaped this episodic resistance in the past century, however, changed dramatically as the coal industry declined, as we shall explore in later chapters.

Coal's Decline in the Region

Coal's decline accompanied broader processes of deindustrialization, the decline of "employment in manufacturing as a share of total employment,"[83] across the United States. These economic shifts, mirrored around the world in industrialized economies, reproduced inequities in places such as the Clearfork Valley, as we saw in the previous chapter.

Deindustrialization occurred through both a declining number of coal workers and a drop in coal production. These two measures, while connected, have often had separate and distinct drivers. Coal industry employment in the United States peaked in 1923 at 862,536 miners, the vast majority of mining located in Appalachia or the eastern United States at the time.[84] After that peak, mines increasingly replaced workers with heavy machines, leading to a rapid growth in strip mining after the 1950s, as coal companies increasingly invested in capital-intensive strip mines rather than worker-heavy underground coal.[85] The result was an expansion in the amount of environmentally degrading strip mining across the region in the 1960s and a corresponding decline in the number of workers.

Despite falling employment, coal production in Appalachia continued to grow through the 1990s, peaking at 484 million short tons of coal produced in 1997.[86] Beginning in the 1970s, however, deregulation of the rail industry had made western coal economically competitive with Appalachian coal. This competition compounded the effects of Clean Air Act amendments in the 1990s that forced power plants to mitigate sulfur dioxide emissions, favoring lower-sulfur Powder River Basin coal in the West.[87] The growth of cleaner energy sources, such as methane gas (often called "natural" gas) and renewables, also affected the Appalachian coal economy as early as the 1990s,[88] all of which led to a declining Appalachian coal market.

Reflecting the trends we saw in the Clearfork Valley in the previous chapter, from 2000 to 2020 coal production fell by 64 percent across the Appalachian region.[89] As Eric Bowen, John Deskins, and Brian Lego report, two factors triggered this decline: "Losses in coal production stem from a perfect storm of two major national factors that have depressed demand for coal: significant reductions in the cost of natural gas—a competitor fuel to coal in the electric power industry—due to greatly enhanced productive capacity and a regulatory environment that increased the cost of burning coal for electric power generators."[90] In 2015, new emissions regulations for power plants, the Mercury and Air Toxics Standards Rule, left older and high-emitting power plants unprofitable, further incentivizing methane gas for power generation. The deindustrialization of the coal industry brought with it a hollowing out of coal communities, a closure of public space, and a drive to cut labor costs, as we saw more concretely in the case of the Clearfork Valley in the previous chapter.

Racialized and Gendered Deindustrialization

Importantly, the economic restructuring of deindustrialization was a racialized and gendered process of displacement, one that affected what kinds of jobs were available to women and people of color, while, of course, diminishing the total number of jobs available to the remaining white male workforce. Understanding the uneven social implications of this restructuring is a necessary backdrop to understanding the contemporary transition. As Karida Brown writes, in the second half of the twentieth century in Appalachia, "black people and their communities were systematically disappeared through the process of industrial decline and ruination."[91] Machines often first made redundant the frequently dangerous and lowest-paid jobs that Black workers had been relegated to in a segregated workplace. As legal segregation ended in the 1960s, union policies of seniority worked against the Black workforce. Many Black workers who had lost jobs due to mechanization found jobs at other mines, only to be fired as their new employers mechanized, while white miners with more seniority kept their positions.[92]

Black people were not only among the first to lose jobs in the coalfields; in addition, loss of work also meant the loss of their physical space. In the historically segregated coal camps and company towns, Black spaces were frequently, and systematically, some of the first to be abandoned, evicted, or torn down. Black towns and Black neighborhoods were often located on unstable hillsides,[93] closer to sites of air, noise, water, and light pollution than white neighbors,[94] or located far from town centers.[95]

Disappearing employment opportunities and environmental racism often paired with the pull of jobs, family, and connection elsewhere to reduce the Black population of places like McDowell County, West Virginia, from 30.7 percent in 1910 to 9.2 percent in 2023.[96] In the four-county area in which the Valley is located (where the percentage of Black population had never been as high as in West Virginia), the number of Black residents declined from 7,000 (6%) in 1910 to 1,295 (under 1.0%in 2023).[97] One example of how this racialized displacement occurred was when a coal company tore down the company town of Valley Creek in the late 1950s. The residents of the segregated Black neighborhood, unwelcome in the surrounding segregated white communities, had nowhere else to go in the Valley. Instead, many people moved to Jellico, Tennessee, home to a sizable Black community, or points farther away.[98] Segregation and racism meant that Black communities were displaced earlier and at greater rates than their white neighbors through deindustrialization.

The long decline of the coal industry also accompanied a gendered reordering of work and labor. Having fought to have access to mining jobs and won the aforementioned court ruling in 1979 that mandated their entrance, women began their movement to access mining jobs just as these were disappearing.[99] Furthermore, the manufacturing jobs that many women in coalfield Appalachia relied upon for income by the 1960s, such as in the textile mills and sewing plants in the towns around the Valley, left the region in the 1980s and 1990s with the North American Free Trade Agreement (NAFTA) and other free trade policies.[100] In their place, service sector jobs became more prevalent and widespread.

During this period, feminist economic geographers discuss the "feminization of labor," where more women in the Global North were working outside the home, but many of the new jobs looked more like what had been considered "women's work."[101] From data centers to a growing service economy, jobs were increasingly low waged and non-union, with inconsistent hours. Such was the case in Appalachia, as Anne Lewis's film

Fast Food Women documents.[102] Appalachian women witnessed both new opportunities for work and their incomes increasingly became necessary as coal-mining jobs, and other well-paid stable work, were rapidly disappearing.[103] While Black communities and women were particularly affected by this economic restructuring, white men also lost access to reliable and well-paid jobs. These changes had profound social and political implications, which we will discuss further in particular in chapter 5. The coal industry, however, continued production and retained a position of power and domination into the twenty-first century.

Conclusion

Understanding the current period as one of transition, in this chapter we have asked the question "a transition from what?" We have provided historical context to the contemporary period of coal's decline. We have examined the ways the coal industry came to power, how it held power, and how people resisted its domination. In summary, the coal industry came to power in large part by taking ownership and control of vast areas of land. The industry held power through economic conditions that created few other economic options outside coal mining, and it operated through a racialized and gendered labor system that stoked social division, hindered worker solidarity, and kept families dependent on mining.

After the 1960s, the industry entered a period first of rapid mechanization and rapid layoffs, and then after 2000, a period of declining production. The effects of this deindustrialization were unevenly experienced. Black communities were the first to bear the costs of deindustrialization, often losing jobs and homes before white families. Starting in the 1970s, many women in Appalachia found themselves propelled into a workforce that was increasingly low-waged and low-quality, as high-paying, unionized coal mining jobs and manufacturing positions with good benefits, primarily held by white men, also began to disappear.

These changing class, race, and gender dynamics today provide a new terrain of both domination and struggle, affecting how power is wielded and how resistance is organized. It is in this setting that we will examine the core questions of this book: How did the traditional power elites cling on even in the face of coal's decline? What new actors enter the scene and how do they exert influence? And how has this changing terrain shaped the possibilities and strategies for action of workers and communities as they face a new post-coal future? Before we do so, however, in the next chapter we will provide a more conceptual discussion on power and transition, providing the theoretical underpinnings for our later empirical analysis.

3

Power and Transitions

Any discussion of just transition, especially for places whose history, identity, social and political relations have been dominated by one fossil fuel industry, must inevitably involve an understanding of the changing nature of power. But while much has been written on the ascendancy of power and its maintenance, there is less understanding of its demise, how it changes in the midst of transitions, and what new forms of power emerge. Where this theme is discussed, it is largely in the fields of international relations or security, for instance in discussing the demise of western hegemony globally, not at the local or regional level.[1] Within the rapidly growing literature on energy transition, however, we see emerging discussion of power-related themes.[2] What is lacking is a conversation between these two bodies of work: power theory that focuses on how power shifts in transitions and transition theory that includes analyses of power. This chapter aims to contribute toward bridging that gap.

To do so, we present three frameworks that offer the basis for understanding how change happens in the process of transition. The first, what is often called "the Multilevel Perspective (MLP) framework," which emerged initially from literature on sustainability and transition, analyzes shifts between what are called *niches, regimes*, and *landscapes*. Though this framework has been widely used, it has been critiqued for a lack of attention to power in the processes of change. The second draws on the work of Italian Marxist Antonio Gramsci, whose analyses of transitions from periods of settled hegemony and "interregnums" between such periods offers a much more political economic perspective, as well as a framework to consider these periods as inherently based upon social and ideological struggle. Third, returning to Gaventa's earlier book on the Appalachian

Valley, which was based on an elaboration of the three-dimensional view of power by Steven Lukes, we will argue that within that work is also a frame that can be used to understand the multiple forms of domination, how they hold on and re-create themselves, and how new actors and forms of power might emerge in periods of change. Gaventa's later "powercube" provides us with an additional lens through which to analyze the multiple levels and spaces in which change may happen and how those levels and spaces interact.

Power amid Transition

For the last decade, as a large literature on transition in the face of climate change has emerged, so too have scholars argued that far more attention needs to be paid to questions of power and politics as part of this change. Transition scholar Peter Newell, for instance, has argued in his book *Power Shift*, "We need to understand (i) where power comes from (literally); (ii) how it is held, sustained and reproduced, and (iii) how, where and when it might change."[3]

Scholars of power and transition explore these questions in a variety of ways. One approach is to examine different types and mechanisms of power at play. Frank W. Geels, for instance, refers to the uses of instrumental, material, discursive, and structural forms of power, a framework that others have also used in various ways.[4] *Instrumental* power refers to how actors use resources "(e.g. positions of authority, money, access to media, personnel, capabilities) in immediate interactions with other actors to achieve their goals and interests."[5] In more neo-Marxist analysis, instrumental power may be seen to have largely a *material* base, such as the control of land, means of production, or other forms of accumulation. In the debates on energy transition the shifting material base, for example, away from fossil fuels to other forms of energy production, is particularly important.[6] Thirdly is the focus on *structural* and *institutional* forms of power, including market structures, as well as political institutions, and their interactions. Finally is a focus on *discursive* forms of power, including the ability to control "imaginaries" of change and the politics of knowledge, which shape the framing of the debate.[7] For our purposes, a critical question is what happens to these types of power when the material base shifts,[8] that is, when the criticality of coal and its extraction diminishes. How does this shift the types of power at play and affect their interactions?

Changing Actors

With these types of power in mind, other studies focus more on power as it relates to different actors in the process of energy transition. A great deal of work focuses on *incumbent* power: how actors within existing carbon regimes mobilize to maintain their power and domination, even in the face of the urgency of moving away from fossil fuels. Newell, for instance, examines how state and corporate power are embedded in the "global fossil fuel complex," and how "financial, material, and military power is used to secure energy access and expand the power of domestic energy industries through international relations."[9] He and others also examine the ways in which discursive power shapes the politics of knowledge production around energy scenarios and what pathways of change may be viable, through, for instance, the mobilization of expertise, media, and information exchange. In examining the maintenance of incumbency power, a number of theorists, including Newell, also draw on Gramsci's concept of hegemony to understand the interactions of material, institutional, and discursive power.[10]

Other work highlights the rise of new players in the process of energy accumulation, including, for instance, companies and investors focusing on renewables and other forms of energy production. Tobias Haas writes about two competing hegemony projects in energy politics. One, which he calls the "grey hegemony project," is "bound materially and ideologically to the old, centralistic, fossil-nuclear energy regime." The other, which he calls the "green hegemony project" is "bound to the emerging more decentralized, renewable energy regime." Both projects, however, "are linked to accumulation strategies favoring a specific form of accumulation related to the energy market."[11] This latter project often finds allies in large transnational NGOs such as Greenpeace, Friends of the Earth, World Wildlife Fund, or, as we shall see in this study, The Nature Conservancy, which also mobilize in support of a new energy regime.[12]

Another key set of actors includes the financiers in energy transitions, and the new instruments they have established, including carbon markets. In particular, as we shall see, investors seeking to establish their environmental credentials are spending vast amounts on "green" alternatives, while at the global level financing by groups like the World Bank, the International Monetary Fund (IMF), and other multilateral development banks also play a major role, through such programs as the World Bank's Climate Investment Funds and Scaling Up Renewable Energy Program (SREP).[13] The huge rise in the number of companies and financiers eager to show their "green" credentials has led to concerns about new forms of control of land and nature through "green grabbing," "whether linked to biodiversity conservation, biocarbon sequestration, biofuels, ecosystem services, ecotourism or 'offsets' related to any and all of these. . . . It involves novel forms of valuation, commodification, and markets for pieces and aspects of nature, and an extraordinary new range of actors and alliances—such as pension funds and venture capitalists, commodity traders and consultants, GIS service providers and business entrepreneurs, ecotourism companies and the military, green activists and anxious consumers among others."[14]

Outside of the private sector, another key set of actors of course involves an array of government entities, from local to national and even international levels, which are tasked with policymaking, regulation, investments, and other initiatives that can shape the possibilities of transition, and whose interests are affected by it. As we shall see in this study, while corporate power in earlier times was perhaps most visible in the control of land and labor at the local level, now it is the contestations around policy and discourse at state, national, and global levels that are particularly critical arenas for maintaining the power of the fossil industry, as well as for challenging its domination.

Many analyses of power examine competition and conflict among these various elite actors, such as between fossil fuel incumbents and emerging renewable energy actors, or between the fossil fuel political lobby and those promoting greener alternatives. However, transition from one elite to another does not necessarily redistribute power. As Benjamin Sovacool and Marie-Claire Brisbois argue, "low-carbon transitions can create, perpetuate, challenge, or entrench the power of elites."[15]

While the focus is often on the role of private and state elites in climate transition, another set of actors—or potential actors—are those relatively powerless non-elites whose futures are very much affected by the process of transition, but who rarely have a seat at the policy table. These involve the broad mass of citizenry affected by climate change, including in particular the workers and residents who live and work in energy-producing communities, such as in coal-producing areas. To understand how they act to gain power involves studying not only individual forms of resistance or protest around the fossil fuel industry but also the multiple ways in which citizens may organize for empowerment (the process of gaining power) through community groups, unions, social movements, NGOs, or alternative forms of ownership and energy production. The diversity of actors within this area is enormous, and the strategies they use are critical to the process of transformation. Newell usefully maps what he calls an "ecology of mobilizations" ranging from those that focus on developing alternative forms of production and ownership, to those engaging in and influencing policy spaces, challenging the decisions of financiers and investors, protesting the destructive practices of existing extractive industries, or trying to halt their expansion.[16]

Also going beyond a study of elites, Flor Avelino and Julia M. Wittmayer develop a useful Multi-actor Perspective (MaP) tool for mapping actors involved in transition across state, market, community, and the third sector (organized NGOs).[17] Asking the question "Who are the different actors exercising power in transition, and what are the (shifting) power relations between them?"[18] they suggest that this power typology can be used not only "to reflect on the shifting power relations *between* sectors, it can also be used for analyzing the shifting power relations *within* those sectors."[19] This might involve, for instance, the power relationships between small grassroots community groups and larger NGOs, which often advocate and work on their behalf, both of which may be considered part of the diverse ecology of civil society organizations working in the just transition field.

All of these sets of actors—energy producers, new financiers, government agencies, NGOs, unions, and local communities—will be seen to play a role, often in competition with one another, as we move later in this book to tell the story of the changing nature of power in the Appalachian Valley.

THE DYNAMICS OF TRANSITION

While the focus on the relations of power among different actors is important, it does not tell us necessarily about the dynamics of how these interact and change in the process of transition itself, or how new forms and actors emerge as older actors and forms of domination decline. Moreover, who the actors are and what actions are possible in turn are shaped by broader political and economic forces that change over time, requiring us also to examine the historical moment and circumstances in which struggles for just transition occur.[20]

As mentioned earlier, to understand the dynamic process of transition, one group of scholars have often used the Multilevel Perspective (MLP), which examines the relationship between *landscapes*, *regimes*, and *niches*.[21] Initially used in a fairly technical way, the framework is now increasingly used in a more power-oriented way.[22] In this approach, the *landscape* comprises the "structuring forces of ideologies, institutions, discourses, and political and economic trends that constitute enduring forms of socio-technical organization." *Regimes* are the "complex of practices, regulatory requirements, institutions, and infrastructures required to achieve particular societal functions."[23] *Niches* are those spaces where alternative ideas, forms of innovation, and practices can grow and develop. Within the social technical application, this model often refers more narrowly to the energy landscape and how fossil fuel regimes may give way to newer forms of energy production. But applied to the challenge of just transitions in a broader sense, *landscapes* may refer to the political economies that affect not only the fossil fuel industry and other dominant actors, but also the possibilities and strategies for action by other actors; *regimes* may refer to the particular policies, rules of the game, and configurations of power that allow certain interests to predominate, but which can include rules or politics that open new spaces for action, and *niches* may be considered in relation not only to emerging new forms of energy production but also to the variety of ways in which actors seek to develop alternative sources of power and control to the status quo.[24]

As the landscape changes, regimes are put under pressure (from above or below) and may develop "cracks, tensions, and windows of opportunity"[25] into which new actors may enter, and also grow, eventually (perhaps) toppling or replacing the old regime. "A transition is thus associated with a transformation of the regime and a particular power struggle between the current regime, upcoming niches, and landscape pressures."[26] While regimes, niches, and landscapes coexist, regimes invest most of their energy in protection of the status quo, whereas niches have the willingness and capacity to create new things and/or destroy configurations of existing resources. As niche actors develop, they can become niche-regimes that "exercise transformative power; niche-regimes have the capacity to replace old resources with new resources and to transform the current distribution of resources."[27] During periods of stability, the relationship between regimes and niches may be at equilibrium. However, during periods of instability, when landscapes are rapidly changing, niches may rapidly grow, and existing regimes may lose their power.

Introducing Hegemony, Conjuncture, and Interregnum

Another way to conceptualize the ways niches are able to grow and existing regimes lose power as landscapes shift is through the concepts of hegemony, conjuncture, and interregnum, as outlined in the work of Gramsci and subsequent neo-Gramscian theorists. As seen earlier, much of the application of Gramsci to transition literature focuses on his concept of hegemony—that is, the combination of coercive and ideological power to maintain consent or cooperation of the governed. Harald Winkler draws on neo-Gramscian approaches to argue that just transition is itself an ideology, one that should be used to secure cultural hegemony in favor of decarbonization, against the dominant narratives promoting fossil fuel–led development.[28] Others have drawn on Gramsci to investigate when and why cracks and fissures in power structures or hegemony appear, and how incumbent power responds. Newell, for instance, also builds on Gramsci's concept of *trasformismo*, that is, the ways that elites "accommodate pressures for more radical and disruptive change and employ combinations of material, institutional, and discursive power to ensure that shifts which do occur in socio-technical configurations do not disrupt prevailing social relations and distributions of political power."[29]

Gramsci understood political power, or hegemony, to be a fragile, always contested, and crisis-riven set of alliances that only temporarily suture together a ruling political coalition, or hegemonic "bloc." Even the strongest hegemonic bloc may have cracks and fissures emerge within it. Neo-Gramscian scholars have further delineated theories not only of how elites hold power through crises, but also of how grassroots actors find leverage and manifest social change, through building counter-hegemonic ideology (ideas, culture, and discourses) and action.[30] For our study of fossil fuel transition, a neo-Gramscian approach offers a capacious analysis of both elite action from above and action from below.

Less scholarship has yet taken up the question of how Gramscian theories can help periodize power relations and diagnose critical moments when power structures come together and how they break apart in moments of transition.[31] As unstable alliances, hegemonies shift with the political and economic terrain. To analyze this terrain Gramsci used the concept of the "conjuncture," the alignment of political and economic elements in a particular place in time. Gramscian scholars have since used conjunctural analysis to study the interaction among social struggle, economic arrangements, and political trajectories. For instance, Stuart Hall identified the unrolling of a new conjuncture in the late 1970s and early 1980s in Great Britain, witnessed with the rise of Thatcherism.[32] Hall defined the contemporary idea of conjuncture "as the coming together of often distinct though related contradictions, moving according to different tempos, but condensed in the same historical moment."[33]

Within this framework, struggles over hegemony are always open-ended, though shaped by the conjuncture they are within. Cracks and fissures arise when elites cease to be able to convince or coerce enough people to follow their leadership, or when a hegemonic structure "can no longer [reproduce itself] on the basis of the pre-existing system of social relations."[34] Gramscian scholars discuss these periods as "crises of hegemony,"[35] crises of legitimacy or control that signal a transition to new conjunctures, and can provoke an "interregnum," a period between clear hegemonic orders.[36] For Gramsci, "The crisis consists precisely in the fact that the old is dying and the new cannot be born; in this interregnum a great variety of morbid symptoms appear."[37] What is so "morbid" in this period of interregnum are the inconsistencies in the ideological basis of hegemony that spell the demise of once coherent hegemony. Old alliances, antagonisms, and political positions realign or stop making sense. There is a reordering of balances of power and relations of force.

In looking to understand if and when a political period is at an interregnum, conjunctural analysis prompts us to ask if political elites are facing crises of legitimacy and how political alliances are shifting in moments of transition. We need to investigate what novel and challenging entities are able to take power. Bringing the ideas of conjunctures, hegemonic crises, and interregnum into conversation with concepts of landscape, regime, and niche also helps to diagnose if the current moment is creating a new hegemony or simply recasting old hegemonic relations. Using the frame of the conjuncture helps us evaluate whether forces are fundamentally realigning and have entered an interregnum in the current moment of transition, or whether the power of incumbents has meant that while transitions in the material base of power may have occurred, a fundamental shift in the hegemonic coalitions has yet to happen. But a number of questions remain. How do regimes build their power in the first place, and seek to hold on to it as the landscape changes? How do niche actors take advantage of cracks and fissures in hegemony, and toward what ends? Where are the spaces in this process for previously suppressed voices to emerge and to demand more fundamental transformative change?

Revisiting the Three Dimensions of Power

To explore these questions, we return to the framework of power used by Gaventa in his earlier *Power and Powerlessness* volume to analyze the rise of the coal regime in the Appalachian Valley. This work built on that of his supervisor, Steven Lukes, and his three dimensions of power. Gaventa first encountered Lukes's work in the early 1970s when he was a student at Oxford University, where Lukes was based. Coming to Oxford from working as a volunteer in the Appalachian Valley that became the subject of his thesis, Gaventa landed in the midst of debates between Lukes and Peter Bachrach on the "faces" or dimensions of power. These debates contributed to the important book by Lukes, *Power: A Radical View*, first published in 1974.[38]

At the time, much of the work on community power was dominated by American political scientists, largely coming out of a tradition of pluralism, who argued that power could be seen by examining who participated, who wins and loses in relatively open policy arenas. Critiquing this approach, Lukes (1974, 2004) argued that power must be understood not only in terms of who participates, but also in terms of who does not. Power he argued, had three faces or dimensions—the public face that Robert Dahl and others had studied,[39] a hidden face, which served to keep issues off the agenda of decision-making arenas,[40] and an even more "insidious" third face, through which the relatively powerless came to internalize and accept their own condition, and thus might not be aware of or act upon their interests in any observable way. Later, more activist groups referred to these as simply the "visible," "hidden," and "invisible" forms of power.[41] Put simply:

- *Visible power* focuses on who participates and predominates in observable decision-making. Contests over interests are assumed to be visible in political institutions and policymaking processes, which in turn are presumed to be relatively open to meaningful participation.
- *Hidden power* focuses on how certain issues and voices are kept out of the decision-making process through a prevailing "mobilization of bias"[42] or rules of the game that favor certain interests over others.
- *Invisible power* focuses on the acceptance of an unjust status quo due to the internalization of certain ideologies, norms, and values.

In a more recent framing, colleagues at Just Associates (the authors of the above framing) have added to these three the idea of "systemic power": "deeply embedded logics [which] work like operating systems to shape and structure all social and economic arrangements. Dominant ones include patriarchy, structural racism and white supremacy, capitalism, and colonialism-imperialism. These logics are like the genetic codes that determine economic, political, and social relationships and permeate institutions, which in turn shape our lives."[43] In introducing systemic power, they take up a long debate in social sciences, and about Lukes's work in particular, involving the relationships between power and structure. For Lukes, power is linked to agency—it is something that actors can hold, act upon, and change. For others, who take a more Foucauldian approach, power is shaped by the broader "network of social boundaries that delimit the field of what is possible for all actors—"powerful" and "powerless" alike."[44] The concept of systemic power, then, reminds us that the options and strategies for action are shaped by these broader forces, though these boundaries change as systems change, a point that overlaps with the Gramscian ideas of hegemony discussed previously.

Lukes's work remains widely used, and as Lukes points out in the book's third edition some fifty years after it was first written, the power debate "to which it contributed shows no sign of abating."[45] Like those who study hegemony, Lukes's focus was on domination. He asked, "How do the powerful secure the compliance of those they dominate, shaping beliefs and desires, imposing internal constraints in historically changing circumstances?"[46] However, in response to criticism that this approach ignored more bottom-up forms of power, he also wrote that "power as domination is only one species of power"[47] and pointed to Gaventa's book as containing evidence of how the framework can also contribute to "reflection upon participation, empowerment, and resistance."[48]

In his earlier book, Gaventa uses this framework to ask why, in the face of massive inequalities, we did not see the visible debates of these issues in local policy spaces, as we might expect in the first dimension. He shows in case after case how grievances felt against the dominant coal companies and landowners were kept off the agenda, sometimes through force and coercion, other times simply due to perceived threat, or through mobilization of symbols, or through administrative fiat. He also shows how over time, the dispossessed groups developed an internalized sense of their own powerlessness, reinforced by control of information and establishment of dominant norms, especially the association of the coal industry with "progress" and development, that could not be challenged.

Over time, Gaventa shows, these forms of power interact. Power in the first dimension allows the powerful to accumulate resources to build and reinforce the mobilization of bias, as in the second dimension, which in turn reinforces the ability to shape norms and beliefs, as in the third dimension. Moreover, each dimension of power also has its correlated form of powerlessness, experienced as defeat at the policy table, exclusion of voices and issues, and control of beliefs and discourses respectively. Such powerlessness is accumulative, so that successive defeats in key decisions, constant exclusions through the mobilization of bias, and control and manipulation of information and discourses will lead to internalization of the sense of powerlessness over time. For this reason, Gaventa concludes, "power serves to create power; powerlessness serves to reinforce powerlessness. Power relationships, once established, are self-sustaining."[49]

While Gaventa shows us how the dimensions of power link to one another, his work also contains seeds of a theory of how these relationships may shift at key moments, when there are cracks or fissures in systemic power. Even in the face of domination, challenge may occur "if there is a shift in the power relationships—either owing to the loss or power of A or gain in the power of B."[50] Looking historically, in his book he points to

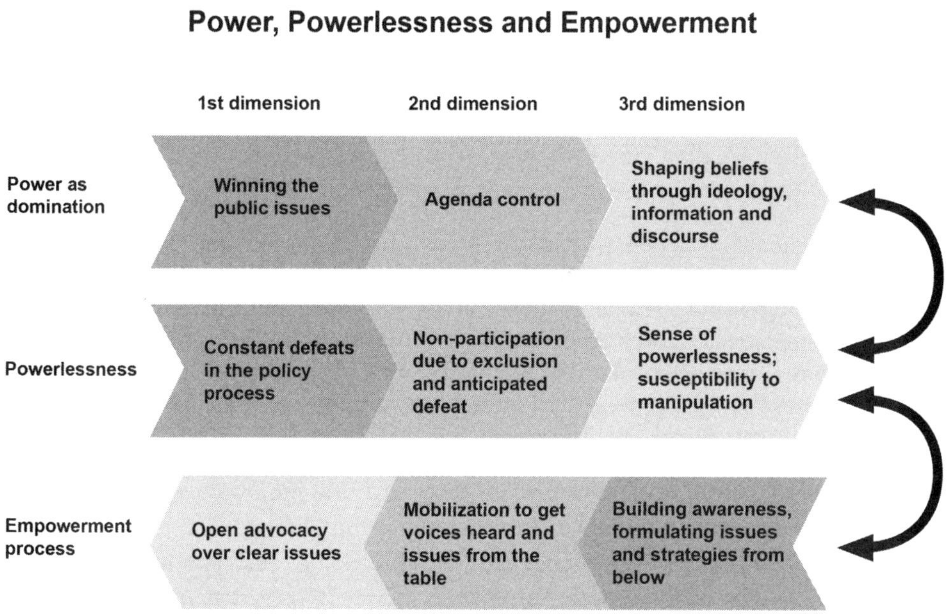

FIGURE 3.1. Power, Powerlessness, and Empowerment (Adapted from Gaventa, *Power and Powerlessness in an Appalachian Valley,* 1982, 21)

several of these moments where the domination of the coal industry in the Valley weakened, including for instance in moments of financial crisis (recessions of 1894 and the early 1930s), or the passage of new enabling legislation, such as the labor legislation in the 1930s or the "right to maximum feasible participation" language in the War on Poverty in 1960s, which created openings from above for action from below.[51]

Such moments of the shifting of power from above, however, do not necessarily mean that grievances from below will automatically and instantly become visible, due to the earlier accumulation of powerlessness. In order to enter the new openings, the historically deprived groups must also overcome the internalized sense of powerlessness, through developing consciousness and counternarratives, as well as build their own mechanism of countervailing power, before they can effectively use the new openings.

This approach has important consequences for the approach discussed earlier on the transition literature on landscapes, regimes, and niches. Once the landscapes of power shift, regimes will first and foremost attempt to shore up their discursive, structural, and instrumental forms of power, in hopes to cling on to their position of incumbent control. Even as spaces emerge, new niche actors may emerge, but for relatively powerless niche groups, this will not occur automatically. Before they can effectively enter the new spaces, they have to overcome the lingering effects of powerlessness. On the other hand, as these spaces expand due to landscape pressures and further weakening of the regime, change from below may emerge relatively quickly. As Gaventa wrote, just as

> the dimensions of power are accumulative and reinforcing for the maintenance of quiescence, so, too, does the emergence of challenge in one area of a power relationship weaken the power of the total to withstand challenges by more than the loss of a single component. . . . Once patterns of quiescence are broken on one set of grievances, the accumulating resources of challenge—organisations, momentum, consciousness—may become transferable to other issues and targets.[52]

This helps us to understand how at key historical moments or conjunctures, there can be periods of rapidly escalating change, as we shall see later in the book where we observe the rapid rise of activism in the face of the weakening of the dominant coal industry in recent years.

Toward a More Transformative Theory of Change

Though within this earlier work there is a theory of how change may happen at key moments, we still do not get a more practical understanding of where and how actors can engage to gain power. In later work Gaventa and colleagues have elaborated how at critical moments more transformative power emerges, especially from previously marginalized actors. Building on the dynamic metaphor of the Rubik's cube, he and colleagues developed what is now called the "powercube," which argues that in addition to examining the forms of power, we must also look across the levels and spaces in which they operate.[53] *Spaces* of power refer to potential arenas for participation and action and include "*closed*" spaces where decisions are made behind closed doors without broad consultation or participation; *invited* spaces where people are invited to participate in public arenas but within set boundaries; and *claimed* spaces, where less powerful people or groups create their own spaces where they can shape their own agenda. In a global world, we also need to examine these spaces and forms across levels or scales, ranging from the global, national, and local, right down to the household. These interact constantly, and changes in one part of the cube affects the possibilities of alignment in the other, as we would see in the Rubik's cube.

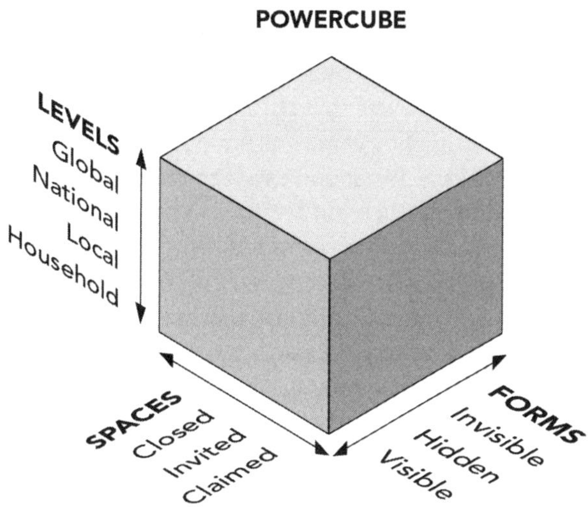

FIGURE 3.2. The Powercube: Levels, Spaces, and Forms of Power (Adapted with permission from Institute of Development Studies, powercube.net)

While the powercube approach provides a framework for analyzing power, it also has implications for strategies of change. To deal with visible power, public advocacy and political skills are needed; challenging hidden power requires mobilization and collective action to ensure that previously suppressed issues and voices are brought onto the public agenda. But to deal with invisible power, strategies of awareness building and formulation of new narratives are required.[54] These overlap with strategies for dealing with the types of spaces—opening closed spaces involves demands for transparency and accountability; being effective in "invited spaces" involves skills of negotiation and deliberation; whereas strengthening people's own claimed spaces involves supporting processes of protest, opposition, and resistance. Working across levels and scales involves processes and issues of building vertical alliances and forms of solidarity, not working at any one level alone.

Again, building on the Rubik's cube metaphor, Gaventa argues that each dimension of the cube and each of these strategies interacts with the others, opening and closing the entry points for influence and change. Power strategies that only focus on one aspect of the cube often simply displace power inequities to another. For instance, a local win may be quickly undercut by policy changes in the larger landscape. Truly transformative change happens when social actors (movements, civil society organizations, community associations, unions) work across all aspects of the cube, necessitating the emergence of networks and alliances of actors, which together address power in its different levels, forms, and spaces.

In this process, gaining power means not only dealing with domination, or "power over." Rather, it also involves overcoming the internalized sense of powerlessness and gaining what feminist scholars have often called the power *within*.[55] It involves more positive forms of agency, or what is often called power *to*, and is most effective when done collectively, involving power *with* others. And increasingly, in a world where the third dimension of power affects the ability to envision a new future, it involves what some activists have begun to call the "power *for*," or the ability to construct a new narrative and vision of possibility. As Gaventa has previously summarized,

> Taken together, these concepts give us a basis for an approach to social action that begins to transcend the often separate streams of thinking and practice on power and empowerment, and which focuses not just on power as domination, but also power as challenge to that domination. In this more unified approach, these forms of power can be seen as interrelated, such that empowerment becomes a process through which relatively powerless groups develop a sense of power within, and the capacity for power with others, in order to challenge the power over their lives, and gain the power to determine their own futures, guided by their vision of a different world, as in power for.[56]

By bringing these forms of power together, across the spaces and levels of the cube, previously relatively powerless groups can develop power that is more transformative, rather than power based on winning any single issue or resolving a particular grievance, though these gains are important building blocks of transformative change.

Conclusion

As we develop our theory of power and transition, we have argued that we can draw from three schools of thought, often considered separately, to understand how power shifts during important broader shifts in the political economy. From the Multilevel Perspective, developed by scholars of sustainable transition, we gain an understanding of the dynamic of how regimes change over time as broader socioeconomic landscapes shift and as once dominant regimes give way to newer more niche sets of actors and ideas. Gramsci understands these changes in much more structural terms as shifts in hegemonies from one conjuncture to another, and as involving class and social conflicts, rather than the evolution of one set of ideas and actors to another. We also draw from Gramsci the useful idea of the interregnum, the space in between settled hegemonic order, in which power relations are shifting. From Lukes, whose ideas of domination overlap with Gramsci's notion of hegemony, we get a more actor-oriented way of understanding the mechanisms through which powerful actors create and maintain their power, from controlling key decision-making arenas, to suppressing voices and issues, to shaping discourses and beliefs. But as in the other approaches, we also get a dynamic understanding of power, showing how weakening of dominating power at key moments can provide space for the emergence of countervailing power, or what Gramsci might call counterhegemonic forces. Finally, from Gaventa's work, we get a more concrete theory of empowerment and resistance, helping us to understand how previously marginalized actors gain new visibility, voice, and influence when the spaces and opportunities open up to do so.

The following chapters will draw upon each of these concepts to understand shifting power in the midst of energy transition in the Appalachian Valley. In particular, we will argue that a shifting landscape (e.g., changing global markets; increased pressures for moving away from fossil fuels) can threaten the existing energy regime (in this case the coal regime) creating new spaces and opportunities for niche actors and alternatives to emerge more visibly. We will ask whether this current conjuncture represents an interregnum between hegemonies, or whether it will be just another moment in which existing power relations are weakened but then restrengthened. Within this process, we will explore how incumbent powerholders seek to hold on, as well as the growing competition between niche and regime actors, as they jockey for influence in this moment of change. We also suggest that in this period of interregnum there also forms a disconnect between the ideological power of previously dominant actors who continue to promote the values of a fossil fuel–based extractive economy and the shifting material basis that no longer provides justification for these claims, leading to cracks, fissures, and openings for challenge.

In turn, we explore how in the midst of these changes, non-elite actors mobilize for change, breaking down previous elements of powerlessness to build potentially more transformative power from below. However, in order to gain power, relatively marginalized groups face numerous obstacles. They have to deal with the effects of decades of internalized powerlessness, multiple intersecting inequalities, as well as the new elites, a process that can take time, despite the urgencies that climate change brings. They must develop the skills and capacities to navigate across the forms, levels, and spaces of power, as depicted in the powercube. Moreover, in the transition from one conjuncture to another, to counter the control over narratives and discourses used by both the fossil fuel industry and the new elites, "propositional power" from below—the ability to envision and present a new transformative narrative—becomes as important as the forms of "oppositional power" used against dominant actors in the past. To influence national and global narratives and policies, new alliances and forms of solidarity that link actors across issues become critical. The opportunities and challenges for doing so will become clearer in the following pages.

4

Old Powerholders Cling On

How the Coal Industry Fights to Maintain Its Dominance

> I think the political and cultural power of the coal industry is really durable. And at some point, it became decoupled from their actual employment numbers.
>
> —Grassroots organizer in eastern Kentucky, 24 April 2023

In earlier chapters we have described in detail the decline of coal and the consequent impacts in the Appalachian Valley and the region more broadly. As the industry's direct control over jobs and production declined, increased community activism against its destructive environmental practices began to emerge, as well as growing public awareness of the impact of coal on global warming and climate change (to be explored more fully in chapters 7 and 8). But rather than invest in more sustainable ways of production and new forms of energy in the context of transition, or to engage with workers, communities, or government about an alternative future, the coal industry in the region largely dug in and worked even harder to shore up and reshape its power in the face of its own decline. Indeed, one of the key insights of this work is that a shift of the economic base on which power is derived does not necessarily lead to a simultaneous and accompanying shift of power. Rather, the legacies of historic power relations endure and are actively reenforced by incumbent power holders.

The exaggerated influence of coal even as its economic power recedes has been noted by others. In 2015, for instance, an article in *Politico* observed that "while eastern mines have been losing market share to western mines for decades, the coal industry continues to dominate the economy and politics of the traditional mining areas, especially West Virginia and Kentucky. This has given coal disproportionate power over national politics, with sometimes sweeping consequences."[1] An article in the *Atlantic* magazine referred to the "special power" of coal, which "creates communities, even ones that outlast its death,"[2] citing historical examples from the UK where mining communities continued to vote Labour in otherwise conservative regions even when the mines are closed, or in Germany where coal-aligned soccer clubs mourn the loss of coal in pregame ceremonies, or, as we shall see here, where Appalachian communities continued to be pro-coal, even as coal mines were closing, leaving a legacy of destruction on land and people. The result of such incumbent power led one author to describe the period from 2009 to 2019 (primarily in reference to West Virginia) as "the lost decade," in which politicians "aligned themselves with the interests of the coal industry to the considerable detriment of the citizens and the economy in the state." Rather than provide leadership to manage the transition away from fossil fuels, they "doubled down on coal."[3]

Where does such exaggerated power come from? How do powerful actors maintain and re-create their power, even as they lose their material base? Returning to the three-dimensional conceptual framework outlined in chapter 3, in this chapter we shall examine the strategies the industry has used to shore up its power in the face of decline. In the first dimension of power, the industry sought to strengthen its influence in political institutions and processes, especially at the state and federal level, as part of an overall strategy of protecting its own interests and those of the broader fossil fuel industry in the face of growing concerns about carbon emissions and climate change. It also sought to limit the potential of countervailing forces to bring alternative voices and issues to the table, as in the second dimension of power. This included undercutting the historic United Mine Workers of America union and its collective power in the region, as well as discrediting or otherwise weakening the voices of environmentalists or other activists seeking to raise concerns about the industry and its economic, environmental, community, or climate impacts. And finally, in the face of weakening hegemony and growing opposition, it sought to create a new pro-coal consensus, as in the third face of power. Through public relations campaigns and manipulation of information and cultural symbols, it attempted to shift the narrative from one of coal's exploitation of workers and communities to one in which companies, workers, and communities were all "friends," collectively under attack from external forces. In this regard, the industry focused in particular on President Barack Obama and "outside" environmentalists, or "tree huggers" (youth environmental justice activists) as scapegoats for the industry's decline and as targets for blame, resentment, and political action.

While the focus of this chapter is largely on how the industry sought to maintain its "power over" in the face of these challenges, such control was not complete. As in any political system, the hegemony of coal still had within it cracks and fissures,[4] which would widen as the industry's narrative of the common good gradually began to weaken in the face of the local realities of loss of jobs, destruction of land, and the growing movement to combat climate change. The gradual rise of countervailing power and counternarratives will be examined in more detail in later chapters.

The First Dimension: Power in the Political Arena

As described in chapter 2, for over a century the coal industry has been a dominant force in Appalachian politics. Much of that was based on control of land and the dependency of coal communities on jobs and coal camp amenities, as well as through strong alliances with local political elites. As the industry began to decline, control at the local level began to weaken. At the same time, issues about the environmental destruction of the land, the future of the industry, and the need for alternative forms of employment and energy in response to climate change became all the more apparent. In the face of this, the industry sought to reassert its power at the political level, its focus largely moving from control at the local level to the state and national levels, which had the greatest potential to pass new legislation that would deeply affect its interests.

An early salvo in this fight to protect its interests was found in the 2000 elections, when the industry felt threatened by the potential of Al Gore, the Democratic presidential candidate and strong advocate for the need to address the climate agenda. The industry poured millions into the campaign of his rival, George W. Bush, and succeeded in shifting West Virginia, the largest coal-producing state in Appalachia, until then a reliably Democratic state, to the Republican column. "Bush soon came out against the Kyoto Protocol climate treaty and mountain top mining restrictions. A representative of the West Virginia mining industry called it 'payback' from a grateful president who knew that 'if not for us, he wouldn't be president.'"[5]

Despite the political support, as observed in chapter 2, coal production in Central Appalachia continued to decline, falling 64 percent between 2000 and 2020.[6] But conversely, even as coal production declined, the political contributions from the coal industry to candidates in national elections soared, peaking in 2012 with $15.3 million total contributions, over twenty times higher than at 2000 levels (see figure 4.1). Though the level of contributions declined slowly after that year, they still remained higher in every year from 2012 to 2022 than any time during the previous twenty years, soaring again in 2024. The donations were overwhelmingly to Republicans. Most of this money came from mining companies operating in Kentucky and West Virginia, in the heart of Central Appalachia. The coal industry donations were not alone in their attempts to buy national influence. In the 2017–18 election cycle, lobbying and campaign donations from the oil, gas, and coal industry were thirteen times greater than spending on behalf of renewable energy.[7] In addition to campaign giving, lobbying by the coal industry also increased. In 2000, the industry spent $2.47 million on registered lobbyists. By 2008, when Obama came to office, that number had grown ten times, to $24 million.[8]

The 2012 presidential elections, featuring Obama versus Mitt Romney, were a watershed moment, in which the industry's campaign contributions peaked. By then, the battle lines over critical legislation on carbon emissions, water pollution, regulation of mountaintop removal, and climate change had been drawn. As the West Virginia's *Charleston Gazette*, one of the major newspapers in the region, posed:

> Faced with the clear science about power plant pollution, global warming, water quality damage, black lung disease, and the mounting science about public health concerns related to mountaintop removal, the obvious question for politicians—especially those who want to be president—is exactly what are you going to do about these challenges? Important follow-up questions are things like: What is your plan for ensuring a clean, safe, and sustainable energy system for our country? How will you diversify the economy and otherwise improve the lives of the people of our nation's coalfields, especially at a time when the mining industry is in the midst of a major downturn?[9]

The coal industry's response was to do everything it could to try to defeat President Obama's attempt for a second term, establishing a Republican coal industry PAC named COALition Romney to depict the Republican candidates as the only pro-coal options.[10] Indeed, since 2012, the proportion of political contributions from the coal industry going to Republican members of Congress has continued to increase, reaching 97 percent of its total contributions by 2022.

With key legislation around climate and environment on the table, congressional as well as presidential influence was very important. While the industry gave to a number of members of Congress, its power was magnified by strong links to two long-time coal allies, Senator Mitch McConnell, a Republican from Kentucky, and Senator Joe Manchin, a Democrat

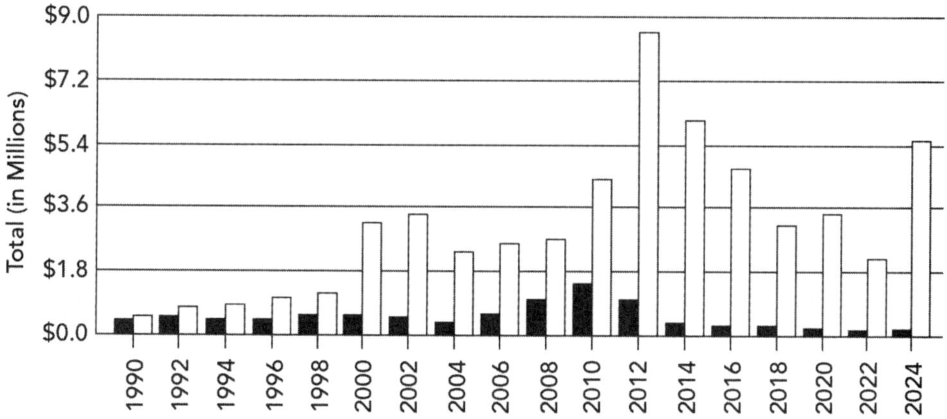

FIGURE 4.1. Coal mine industry political contributions by election cycle. White = Republican; Black = Democrat. The figures represent "contributions to all Members of Congress, including the campaign committees of sitting members who run for President." (Coal Mining: Long-Term Contribution Trends, https://www.opensecrets.org/industries/indus?ind=E1210.)

from West Virginia, both of whom held powerful positions in Congress. In Kentucky, the influential McConnell, the state's longest standing senator, has constantly been a pro-coal and fossil fuel industry supporter, and he has been well supported by the industry in return. Between 2009 and 2019, he received $3.1 million in contributions from fossil fuel interests. At the same time, since McConnell was first elected to the Senate in 1984, mining jobs in Kentucky diminished 88 percent, from 29,801 to 3,449 in 2019. During the same period, however, rather than support programs for economic diversification, McConnell has "propped up a coal industry as the economic engine of the region, instead of going all in on supporting economic diversity that could provide for a future for communities."[11] When Donald Trump became president in 2016, McConnell was a key ally in the efforts to roll back regulations on the fossil fuel industry and stall any efforts to fight climate change.[12]

Another well-positioned national ally for the industry in the region for many years was the Democratic senator Joe Manchin from West Virginia (who retired from the Senate in 2024). A former governor of the state, Manchin was elected to the US Senate in 2010 and quickly gained a prize spot on the Energy and Natural Resources Committee, the key committee on issues regarding climate change and the coal industry, and one that he would later chair. From that position he consistently frustrated attempts to regulate coal over several administrations. He attacked Obama administration attempts to regulate carbon emissions and the environmental impacts of mountaintop removal. He praised and supported the Trump administration's decision to withdraw the United States from the Paris Agreement on Climate Change. Becoming a swing vote in Biden's extremely narrow Senate majority following the 2020 elections, he gained even more influence, and used that power to weaken or sabotage key Biden initiatives relating to climate change and industry regulation, for instance, attacking a proposal to limit the emission of greenhouse gases by fossil-fuel–fired power plants or funds to support a shift to more renewable forms of energy as a "radical climate agenda."[13] Meanwhile, like McConnell, he benefitted enormously from the coal industry, having received over $5 million from coal company Enersystems (of which he was founder) between the time he joined the Senate in 2010 until 2022.[14] According to the website Open Secrets, he was also the top congressional recipient of contributions from the oil and gas industry in 2022.[15] Though Manchin stepped down from office in 2024, the new senator from West Virginia, the former governor Jim Justice, also had made a fortune in the coal industry, leading him to be sometimes referred to as the state's only billionaire.[16]

While the coal industry, along with the fossil fuel industry more broadly, worked to protect its agenda at the national level, it also has exerted inordinate power at the state level. One lawyer and former Kentucky state legislator explained that while in earlier years there was recognition "that the coal industry could control local courthouses. . . . Today, you know where the power is? The influence of the coal industry is at the state level."[17] As another environmental activist said, shaking her head, "It's very discouraging. . . . We really just don't go to the state level anymore . . . its [the coal industry] legacies are still there."[18]

For instance, in Tennessee, where much of the Valley is based, the coal industry has always had a relatively small role in state politics, as only a handful of counties are coal producing. Even so, coal industry interests were able to push Tennessee state house legislators to pass a bill in 2021 to spend a minimum of $1 million a year in making regulatory conditions more favorable for a Tennessee coal industry, despite there being a total of only four coal employees left in Tennessee that year (a potential boon to coal industry actors seeking lenient regulators to oversee potentially costly environmental reclamation).[19]

In Kentucky and West Virginia, the grip on the state legislature also has been and continues to be high—again even in the face of declining jobs and revenues for the state. One example is seen in the way that the industry has used its influence to keep coal-fired power plants open, despite having cheaper and less polluting options available. Across the country, most states now generate less than 30 percent of their electricity from coal, but in West Virginia in early 2023 the figure was 90 percent, the highest in the country, and in Kentucky it was about 70 percent. Rather than accept the need for transition, in 2023 both states passed new rules making it harder for these plants to be closed, against the expressed wishes of other large companies and consumers who are seeking to purchase their electricity from cleaner, greener sources.[20] As a seasoned activist in Kentucky described, "Even though there's all this federal money available [for transition to noncoal sources], the intention of it [the bill] is to prevent the transition from coal to anything cheaper. That's wild."[21]

Campaign funding and lobbying are important ways in which the coal industry fought to assert political control and maintain its agenda over key issues that were emerging in decision-making spaces, as in the first dimension of power. To do so it drew not only on its financial resources but also on longstanding political alliances and loyalties that had been built over decades. Such loyalties were unlikely to shift easily, remaining a key mechanism through which the industry maintained exaggerated political power, even though its economic base was failing.

The Second Dimension: Weakening the Countervailing Power of the Union

While trying to maintain control over the issues and debates in the political arenas was important, the three-dimensional framework of power teaches us that an equally important form of power is to ensure that certain issues or grievances do not reach the political agenda at all. One way of doing so is to weaken or destroy key sources of collective power, thereby limiting the ability of relatively powerless groups to raise their concerns effectively. In the Central Appalachian region, over time, this took the form of undercutting the United Mine Workers Union, historically the only large-scale source of countervailing power against the hegemony of the industry.

In chapter 2, we saw the important union battles in and around the Valley in the 1930s, as the miners worked to gain their collective power at the workplace, and then how the union became a key source of support in the community as well, establishing retirement funds and hospitals and clinics. At its height at the end of World War II the UMWA members were responsible for 85 percent of coal production in the United States. District 19, where the Valley was located, had over 20,000 unionized jobs. By 2000, a little over fifty years later, there were no unionized coal jobs in the Tennessee side, and only 638 across all of eastern Kentucky. By 2022, these were also gone. District 19 had been amalgamated into District 17 in West Virginia, and the last remaining miners' local union halls, which in earlier days had been found in almost every coal community in the region, were now shuttered. The sole remaining local, based in Middlesboro, Kentucky, consisted of about five hundred retired miners. For these miners, the union continued to play an important role advocating for health care, black lung treatment, and pensioners' rights.

In part the decline in bargaining power of the union reflected national trends under neoliberalism, in which union membership across the country declined from some 35 percent of the workforce at the end of World War II to 10.7 percent in 2017, with only 6.5 percent in private industry.[22] In the coalfields, these trends were magnified during the same period by structural conditions, with increased mechanization and a shift from underground to strip mining, which was often nonunionized. During the 1970s, the rise of massive mining operations in the western United States also weakened the bargaining power of miners in the East. In 1977–78, a bitter contract negotiation further weakened the union, with leadership backing away from "long-standing traditions of refusing to cross picket lines, rejecting work without contracts, and engaging in mass strikes."[23] Against this backdrop, the industry became more aggressive, resorting to a variety of tactics to weaken the union further. Responding to national political landscape, notably the anti-union decisions of Ronald Reagan's appointees to the National Labor Relations Board,[24] these more aggressive coal companies saw opportunities to operate without labor negotiation and relied on increasingly violent and militarized tactics to engage the UMWA.

In West Virginia, "the notoriously anti-union Massey Energy took the union's malaise as an opportunity to start buying unionized mines, laying off all the mines' workers, and then reopening the mines as non-unionized operations."[25] Others reorganized, creating small nonunion companies to mine their coal more cheaply. As Barbara Ellen Smith observes:

> "Vulture" capitalists began circling the eastern coal industry, stripping assets from larger coal operations, selling off mines one by one, and sometimes declaring bankruptcy, a legal maneuver that typically allowed them to shed contractual obligations to pay unionized miners' retirement and health benefits for life. Throughout the 1980s and 1990s, even as coal nationwide became more concentrated in ownership, the central Appalachian coal industry became increasingly fractured, unstable and non-union.[26]

In one of the last major union campaigns in the area, the Pittston strike (1989–90) in Virginia used nonviolent civil disobedience tactics, with large-scale support from across the region. Despite the nonviolence, unfavorable National Labor Relations Board rulings forced the union to pay what the leadership deemed unaffordable penalties for militant strike tactics.[27] Since the Pittston battle, the rates of unionization have continued to weaken.

In terms of a loss of collective power, the decline of the union had enormous consequences for miners and their communities. First, at the workplace, without union presence, those miners who remained were being asked to work in more and more dangerous conditions, without the force of their union health and safety committees to help them face "the bare-knuckled power that many coal operators now exert in the workplace."[28] The incidence of black lung disease began to increase, which some argued was a consequence of mining coal with higher silica content, but which others have argued was about the changing political economy of the industry, which "enabled the persistence of smaller operators who sought to profit, regardless of the consequences for their workers' health," as well as the loss of their union, which "left miners vulnerable to relatively unfettered exploitation and longer work hours."[29] Between 2005 and 2023, for those miners who were still working, there was a tenfold increase in the incidence of severe black lung.[30]

Secondly, in addition to the loss of workplace power, the decline of the union meant there was little organized regional force to promote policies for a more just transition for the workers who were losing their jobs. Unlike in some countries, such as Germany, where unions and companies worked early on to think about transition policies that would help preserve jobs or create new ones, the UMWA, on the defensive, did little to think about or support policies that would create alternatives for the future. As a result of the earlier failure of the reform movement, and the weakened position of the union, one study said, the UMWA became "cold to labor environmentalism and the notion of just transitions because the union does not possess the institutional leverage necessary to implement and facilitate a just transition."[31] The UMWA remained steadfastly committed to organizing coal miners, rather than branching out to other sectors, unlike other industrial unions, such as the United Steelworkers, which faced the decline of steel jobs with an organizing push into service sector fields, such as nursing.[32] But by 2021, faced with continued loss of jobs, the union belatedly issued a statement saying "change is coming, whether we seek it or not . . . we can look away no longer." It offered to work with Congress, the Biden administration, NGOs, community groups, and others to protect UMWA jobs, to create new jobs in renewables, and to support training, health, and infrastructure, while still advocating for carbon capture and clean coal technology to make up the bulk of future jobs.[33]

Thirdly, the weakening of union power in Appalachia was linked to the shifting and environmentally destructive practices that also put mining communities in increasing kinds of risks and amounted to new forms of enclosures of public spaces in the mountains. Nonunion mining operations relied heavily on strip-mined coal production, which required many fewer workers per ton of coal.[34] As the Appalachian coal industry then expanded to mega-mines termed mountaintop removal mining, the number of miners needed decreased exponentially as well, and few of these jobs were unionized.

Fourthly, while the loss of the union weakened both economic and political power, it also helped to set the conditions for what we see next—the shifting of a narrative around class to one focused much more on cultural politics, which in turn would contribute to a rise in populist authoritarian politics under Trump. For all of its difficulties, the union in Appalachia had created a space for workers and communities to come together around class and race lines. Its *United Mine Workers Journal*, which at one time had over 800,000 subscribers and was printed in multiple languages, provided an alternative understanding to the world than that fed by corporate news and right-wing Christian radio stations. Its union halls were community spaces, providing local opportunities for interaction and building of comradery. As Sylvia Ryerson points out, "Where UMWA miners gained critical information, analysis, and ideally protection in union meeting halls, at conventions, and on picket line protests, by the 2000's, these spaces were largely gone."[35] The absence of public spaces and alternative forms of information, along with the restrictions of countervailing power, not only meant that the coal industry could more easily control and influence the political agenda but also create the conditions in which the industry could concentrate on the third dimension of power, building and promulgating a new narrative about the decline of coal and its possible future.

The Third Dimension: Shifting the Narrative to "Friends of Coal"

Although protecting political power and weakening the possibilities of countervailing power are important, the work of Steven Lukes reminds us that perhaps the most insidious form of power rests in shaping how people think and what they think about.[36] As coal production continued to decline and as the environmental and climate justice movements were growing, the industry launched a deliberate and costly propaganda effort to strengthen its hegemony in the coalfields through the use of symbols, memes, social media, and events all designed to create a new narrative about the future of coal.

In the late 1990s and early 2000s, the protest movement against mountaintop removal was rapidly growing (see further discussion in chapter 7). In the face of such opposition and following a series of controversies involving overweight coal trucks, the West Virginia Coal Association created the "Friends of Coal" in 2002, "dedicated to informing and educating West Virginia citizens about the coal industry and its vital role in the state's future."[37] Though allegedly grassroots, the movement was heavily funded by the coal industry. One of the first steps of Friends of Coal was to hire a professional PR firm, Charles Ryan Associates, to help develop its public relations and marketing campaign to improve its image. The movement quickly spread to other parts of the coalfields including Kentucky and Tennessee.[38] In addition to Friends of Coal, other related organizations sprang up, such Count on Coal, "to ensure a future with reliable coal power and jobs for thousands of Americans," the American Coal Foundation, which distributes teaching materials to schools "to positively influence children's perception of the extractive energy industries,"[39] and a Friends of Coal Ladies Auxiliary, which "was established to educate the public about the importance of coal in our daily lives and to support coal miners and their families."[40]

As recounted by several studies, the Friends of Coal movement deployed a number of cultural tactics to build support for the industry. First was the strategic appropriation and use on social media and elsewhere of cultural icons—popular football players and coaches in the state, a racecar driver, a retired Air Force general, a bass fisherman. With a series of commercials fronted by these spokesmen, coal miners were depicted as "champions," as American heroes, defenders of jobs and nation, and conservationists, concerned about the outdoors. As Shannon Elizabeth Bell and Richard York point out, "it is no coincidence" that this archetype "is clearly constructed to be a man." As we noted in chapter 2, male miners were overwhelmingly losing their jobs in this moment, and in this context, it became important to reestablish masculine hegemony. "Because of this ideological connection between the male provider and the male coal miner, it is necessary for the coal industry to convince residents that men are still the breadwinner of the family if it is to convince them that coal is still the backbone of the economy."[41] By sharp contrast, a website of the Friends of Coal Ladies Auxiliary features none of these images, but has sections dedicated to shopping, children's activities, and events, including the Friends of Coal golf tournament.

Secondly, Bell and York point out, Friends of Coal employed the strategy of making their identity visible "virtually everywhere," to give proof of coal's support throughout the region through "visual solidarity."[42] Friends of Coal bumper stickers and license plates became widely seen, logos appeared on hats, buttons, yard signs, and social media throughout the region. The images used were symbolic. The Facebook site for the Tennessee chapter of Friends of Coal, for instance, has an iconic picture of an underground miner wearing a hard hat, with the slogans "We Support Coal!" "DIG it or STRIP it," "America RUNS on Coal," alongside the logo for "Friends of Coal." Another logo shows a male miner with a pickaxe with a female figure (presumably his wife), both kneeling in front of a cross, thus linking coal to God as well as to country. Another is an iPhone cover with the slogan "COAL KEEPS THE LIGHTS ON."[43]

The coal industry also articulated the idea of coal mining as Appalachia's central contribution to the nation. As Rebecca Scott notes, coal industry entities popularized discourses that valorized mining communities as having sacrificed bodies and environment for American industrial might.[44] In a jingle that the West Virginia Coal Association produced and was ubiquitous on television and radio media across West Virginia in the early 2000s, the all-male choir chants that "When we *go down deep* through the dark today, we *come up* with the light *for America*," the chorus chanting, "Coal is West Virginia."[45] Such popular messaging became normalized in how people talked about identity and the way they saw meaning in their work.

The industry also created and occupied public spaces through sponsoring sports events, organizing a Friends of Coal Auto Fair, attending and funding coal-related festivals, funding "Friends of Coal" soccer fields, and contributing money to local charities, such as a local hospice. As Ryerson points out, "Where the UMWA once played a central role in the community life outside the mines in addition to inside them, FOC events created new spaces for people to come together in the act of building, celebrating, and belonging to community." In raising funds for hospice and human society, coal becomes a benevolent community contributor. Attending FOC events thus becomes an act of participating in this benevolence.[46]

Such messages clearly took hold at the local level. As one organizer put it,

> [T]he coal industry did just a masterful job of saying "Your fate is our fate," creating a solitary narrative that there's one side—it's you're a friend of coal, or you're, you know, a tree hugger who wants to kill your jobs. . . . So where there once was this triangle—coal industry, workers, communities, and the interests of communities often aligned with the interests of workers who lived in those communities—suddenly the industry

found ways to articulate narratives that just lead workers and many in our communities to think we've got to be friends with coal at all costs.[47]

Building a sense of community and pride around coal was one way to attempt to restore legitimacy of a declining industry, and yet it was not entirely successful. As we see further in chapter 7, despite the campaign, resistance to the industry's environmental practices, as well as questions about the loss of employment, continued to grow. A further industry strategy then was to weaponize the "community economic identity"[48] which the Friends of Coal offered, to attack and scapegoat others who challenged the industry, again using the manipulation of cultural memes, populist rhetoric, and deliberate disinformation tactics. As the organizer quoted above continued: "The industry that has never been a friend to coal miners themselves suddenly positioned itself in this like, you know, very intensely weaponized and polarized way. . . . They did this very effectively as well."

The form this took was seen as the industry rhetoric gradually shifted from the more inclusive Friends of Coal campaign to a far more aggressive attack on what it perceived to be a "War on Coal" by the Obama administration, environmentalists, and the Washington establishment. In particular, they took aim at the Environmental Protection Agency (EPA), which was tightening emissions regulations, and on Obama's expressed desire to tighten greenhouse gas emissions, through a cap-and-trade program.[49] According to one source, "Between 2010 and 2013 alone, the National Mining Association (NMA) spent more than $50 million on marketing, advertising, and lobbying efforts intent on fighting this new 'War.'"[50] In one famous campaign ad, Senator Joe Manchin, a close ally of the Friends of Coal movement, was seen shooting a copy of this bill with a rifle, not only showing his support for the coal industry, but also his support for the powerful National Rifle Association.[51]

Industry rhetoric also put the blame for industrial decline on outside environmentalists, or "tree huggers," strategically capitalizing on an increasingly visible wave of youth climate activists who, along with coalfield environmental justice community groups, were increasing their protests against coal extraction. It employed a number of tactics similar to those of Friends of Coal, but more aggressively. First it upped the rhetoric that the Obama administration was out to destroy miners' jobs, as well as to undermine energy security that depended upon coal. Bumper stickers and slogans declared the region as "Obama's no job zone," and EPA as the "Equal Poverty Agency."[52] Mass rallies were organized. At one rally on a mountaintop removal site in West Virginia on Labor Day 2009, to which the industry claimed more than 100,000 people came, key speakers included Sean Hannity of Fox News, the country music star Hank Williams Jr., and Lord Christopher Monckton, a former science adviser to Margaret Thatcher and climate change skeptic. Going beyond the normal "save our jobs" message, the rhetoric also promoted a more nationalistic, populist fervor. The rally was named "Friends of America," and thousands shouted back and forth the chants,

> Whose coal, our coal!
> Whose mountains, Our mountains!
> Whose freedom? Our Freedom!
> Whose America? Our America.[53]

The chant cleverly equated ties to coal and to region with freedom and country. Interestingly, in another narrative that one activist recounted as being very effective in eastern Kentucky, the region was declared the "Saudi Arabia of coal." "So the 'we're the Saudi Arabia of coal' really built this sense that you have this eternal resource that is being taken away from us, and it clouded over any actual conversation about the actual forces that were affecting the coal industry and the utility industry."[54]

In addition, the War on Coal focused anger over lost jobs not only on growing regulations but on anyone who dared to question the industry, moving from building a community consensus to attacking those who threatened it. "While industry-sponsored car shows, sporting events, and school curriculum incorporated primarily positive emotions, the War on Coal incorporated the opposite: Anger, blame, resentment, and fear."[55] As Rich Kirby, a long-time musician, researcher, and activist, wrote at the time in an article entitled "Wars and Rumors of Wars," "Wave after wave of layoffs brought real pain, and real anger. The community turned tense and polarized, and the whole place felt like a fortress that was indeed besieged by a vast army of shadowy enemies. Public hearings became public theater, as hundreds of coal workers (transportation provided by their employers) swore fealty to coal and vowed vengeance to its enemies."[56] One bumper sticker that appeared in eastern Kentucky, Kirby observes, caught the spirit: "Save a coal miner, shoot a tree hugger."

At a time when dialogue about the future of coal was desperately needed, the effect of this campaign was to shut down space and to polarize communities. "You are either for coal or against it," became the battle cry. Even to speak of a post-coal future was to be seen as questioning the hegemony of coal. An example of the closing space, recounted by Kirby, was the case of WMMT, a community radio station run by Appalshop, a local cultural organization in eastern Kentucky. Though WMMT had tried hard to maintain a space where anyone could share their views, at the height of the controversy, one of its volunteer DJs, who himself worked as a strip miner, declared WMMT as anti-coal for even broadcasting a story about Appalachia Rising, a national demonstration against mountaintop removal in Washington, DC. As a result, the station received dozens of messages from miners and others saying they would no longer support the station, and some with even more hateful and vengeful threats.[57]

The campaign to silence debate in the media and invoke fear in others was skillful and well executed. One veteran organizer suggested that there may have been some sophisticated bots helping out. As she said, when "an article was posted on the website of the *Herald Leader*," the paper that covered eastern Kentucky most extensively, "within seconds there would be 100 comments, all saying 'I'm a coal miner and this is terrible.' To her, while she could understand that miners were upset, the "level and speed of the blowback" implied that something more "intense and manufactured" was going on. Another article places the War on Coal in the context of emerging "neoliberal disinformation" that was increasingly occurring globally around the climate change debate.[58]

Yet, despite being "manufactured" through massive industry-group funding, pro-coal rhetoric succeeded in mobilizing people into action. Across the region after 2010, people in coalfield communities started more grassroots groups, such as southern West Virginia–focused Citizens for Coal, that were sites where pro-coal activists planned counterprotests to anti-MTR protests. In 2012, based on rumors that "tree huggers" were plotting a protest in Blair, West Virginia, pro-coal activists used southern West Virginia Facebook groups to organize a counter-event, involving over three dozen men and pickup trucks rallying in front of a Mine Wars Museum in Blair, and confronting volunteers as supposed "tree huggers."[59]

Such grassroots mobilizations around pro-coal politics did not take root everywhere. For instance, they were less visible in the Clearfork Valley as well as the rest of the Tennessee coalfields, where Friends of Coal remained largely a bumper sticker and television advertisement publicity campaign. Nevertheless, it and the War on Coal had a chilling effect, leading one experienced organizer to think back to similar tactics used in the 1970s as the movement for strip mine legislation was growing. In that case, when the anti-strip-mine group Save Our Cumberland Mountains (SOCM) was just beginning, hundreds of miners' trucks roamed through the Valley intimidating those seen to be anti-coal, and shooting up the car of one SOCM organizer, who was given shelter by a friendly mining family for her own protection.[60]

Several analysts point to the Friends of Coal and War on Coal movements as examples of the use of culture and ideology to shape power, along the lines of the Lukes's third dimension of power and Gramsci's concepts of hegemony. Referring to Lukes's and Gaventa's earlier work, Aysha Bodenhamer details a number of the messages used, arguing that the coal industry has "constructed this pro-coal discourse to shape the wants, values, and beliefs of the powerless."[61] Bell and York argue that this is an example of "the neo-Marxian theoretical tradition, which emphasizes the roles ideology and legitimation play in maintaining elite rule."[62] "When the number of jobs it provided declined due to changing mining practices, the coal industry faced a legitimation crisis that challenged its hold on political power. The industry response to this challenge has been to engage in cultural manipulation, attempting to construct a pro-coal ideology that shapes community identity."[63]

Conclusion: The Intersecting Dimensions of Power

While Friends of Coal and the War on Coal campaigns offer good examples of how information and symbols can be mobilized and manipulated to assert ideological control, we must remember that this third dimension of power intersects with the other strategies of the coal industry to maintain power in the face of decline, which we have discussed earlier. The decline of the union, as well as its cooptation into the protect-coal rhetoric, meant that there was little source of countervailing power to push back against the propaganda war or offer other narratives. As Ryerson argues, "Absent a union counternarrative and support, in an education system inundated with pro-coal curriculum, pro-coal rallies, under the banner of the War on Coal, offered a clear explanation, solution, and protection."[64] And, as a grassroots organizer we interviewed described,

> One of the benefits of a union is they're a machine for creating solidarity . . . for getting people to focus their political organizing on material conditions, in a way that creates natural bonds between people who are different. I think when you recognize your liberation as being tied up with the Black folks who you work with, for instance, then all of a sudden . . . you're more likely to stand with them. So it is a very obvious picture of how like the decline of unions has contributed to culture war and fragmentation.[65]

The Friends of Coal campaign served also to buttress the political power of the industry, as in the first dimension of power, providing rhetoric that policymakers could use to strengthen their influence. With research showing that for every 100 mining jobs lost there was a 1.2 percent-point gain for Republican politicians, the War on Coal was widely used as a Republican campaign issue in the 2012 elections.[66] The phrase was also "used by Republican Congressmen 100 times in the House of Representatives and Senate between 2013 and 2014"[67] to try and stall legislation on both climate and coal. The rhetoric was long lasting. In 2023, a decade later, Kentucky senator Mitch McConnell, now the majority leader of the Senate and still a staunch fossil fuel supporter, would write in an op-ed piece for the *Louisville Courier Journal* about Biden's plan to revive the Clean Air Act (which had been mothballed under Trump), "Sadly, this is a story Kentuckians know all too well. For eight years under the Obama Administration, they watched the 'War on Coal,' kill jobs and cripple communities across Appalachia. . . . Now President Biden is picking up where he and President Obama left off. The Obama-Biden War on Coal has come in many different forms, but the same basic disdain for Middle America keeps showing its face."[68]

By polarizing communities around coal, the War on Coal contributed to a deepening politics of partisanship in the United States more generally, particularly around climate change. As Adam Mayer observes, "Concerted and well-funded efforts from think tanks and PR firms supported by fossil fuel industries successfully shifted public opinion in the U.S. to the extent that a sizeable portion of conservatives (or Republican voters) do not believe that climate change is happening, question its seriousness, and even engage in conspiracy theorizing about climate change science."[69] Echoes of this campaign continued to be heard in the 2024 presidential elections where the future of coal and fossil fuels more broadly continued to be a live and divisive issue. What was happening in America was not unique. Rather it reflected the broader global trend involving "how intersecting inequalities are coded into the cultural politics of coal, and how this shapes efforts to pursue a just transition."[70] In turn, these politics fed into and were reenforced by the growing conservative Republican movement in rural America, as we discuss in the following chapter.

5

Protecting the Hegemony of Coal

The Rise of the Conservative Right

> I'm a Republican. My daddy would've voted for a rattlesnake before he voted for anybody Republican. I'm just the opposite. . . . I'm gonna say this as a born-again Christian, I don't see how any Christian voted for Democrats. If you are a Democrat, I think there's no way you can convince me that you're saved and voted for someone that supported homosexuals, abortions, murders, everything that's going on and tell me that you're a born-again Christian but voted for man like Joe Biden. That's me. That's my belief.
>
> —Campbell County commissioner raised in the Clearfork Valley, 7 June 2021

Sitting in a rural county courthouse, a local county commissioner representing parts of the Valley arrived early at the monthly commission meeting to do an interview. When Schwartzman asked him what the government could do to support communities that are impacted by the decline of coal, something his district had acutely experienced, the elected official, himself raised in the Clearfork Valley, balked at the idea. To him, the government was the problem, treating coal transition as an issue of individual's "personal responsibility," not that of the state, and saying the following: "The people is what needs to change, not the government. The only thing I would say the government needs to do is, you know, they ought to separate the church and state. The state needs to stay out of the church, but the church needs to stay in the state. You need Christian people, good moral people running your business, running the state, not the state running the churches." These views echo some of those found across the country, reflecting the rise of the conservative Christian movement within the Republican Party, one often courted by and linked to the rise of Donald Trump and the Make America Great Again (MAGA) movement.

In the Valley, as in much of Central Appalachia, the change of political allegiance of many of the residents over the past decades is striking, as reflected in the quote above, where the commissioner reflected on the generational shift in views between his and those of his father. Once a Democratic stronghold, over the last two decades the region has become deeply conservative and Republican. In the 2016, 2020, and 2024 presidential elections, voters gave overwhelming support to Trump and his MAGA agenda, with increasing levels each year. In the 2024 campaign, the emergence of JD Vance as a vice-presidential candidate from the region also brought renewed national attention to the area, picking up on views of his best-selling book, *Hillbilly Elegy*,[1] which spoke to the themes of individual responsibility while often ignoring the underlying structural economic shifts that affected life in the rural coalfields.[2]

For our study of the politics of energy transition, the rise of this movement has major implications. While in power from 2016 to 2020 Trump withdrew the United States from the Paris Climate Agreement to the United Nations Framework Convention on Climate Change (UNFCCC). He rolled back President Obama's 2015 Clean Power Plan and scaled back on other regulations affecting coal production and coal-fired power plants. He appointed allies of the fossil fuels industry and climate change skeptics to key positions. Despite these moves and the promises to "Make Coal King Again," under the Trump administration coal-fired power plants continued to decline at a faster rate than in any previous presidential term, including under Obama. Nationally, coal production dropped by another 34 percent, "the largest four-year drop in production since at least 1932" and over five thousand more mining jobs were lost.[3] In the Valley production declined by almost 60 percent, halving the few mining jobs still available. Nevertheless, the support for Trump in the coalfields continued to grow, undergirded by this conservative, right-wing ideology. In the 2024 elections, as in those of 2016 and 2020, the future of fossil fuels was again high on the agenda, with Trump's rhetoric of "Drill Baby Drill" proclaiming the need to give free rein to the fossil fuel industry, continuing climate change denialism and deregulation of the industry.

How do we explain the rise of these right-wing conservative politics in the face of massive inequalities and economic crises faced by communities like those in the Valley?[4] Scores of observers have asked this question, or ones like it, in attempts to explain the appeal of the conservative right to working-class voters and communities. Engaging with this literature, we will use the lens of changing political perceptions and behaviors in the Valley and surrounding area to examine which explanations ring true.

Looking closely at the patterns of voting in the Valley and how they have changed over time, we argue that the Trump phenomenon should not have come as a surprise—rather the slow rise of right-wing conservatism at the grassroots had long been in the making and growing steadily since the 1990s, as seen in the growth of Christian right movements, antigovernment organizations, and conservative talk radio and other media. Moreover, the phenomenon was taking place not only in the Appalachian region, but also across the country, as seen particularly in the reelection of Trump in 2024 with support from a broad base of constituencies.

Drawing from qualitative interviews, we will examine some of the dominant explanations in the literature for this rise particularly among rural, working-class voters, including arguments about the importance of identity politics, the role of anger and resentment around economic and political abandonment, and the role of race and whiteness. We suggest that the answers may be found in the interactions of all three of these perspectives. Finally, moving away from national politics, we will turn to the impact of the broader phenomenon of right-wing conservatism on local politics and institutions, suggesting that perhaps its greatest power is its ability to divert attention from issues of economic and environmental inequality to issues of culture, race, and the protection of a nostalgic past. At the same time, with increasing polarization of communities came a new kind of fear, arising not from intimidation by coal companies for challenging their economic and political power, but from attack by the right if one dared challenge its increasingly tight grip on a host of cultural wedge issues.

Voting in the Valley

When Gaventa did his fieldwork for the earlier *Power and Powerlessness* book, the Valley had been a predominately Democratic-voting area for many decades. Presidents John F. Kennedy, and Franklin D. Roosevelt (as well as the famous mineworkers' union leader John L. Lewis) were popular heroes, with their pictures on the walls of many homes. By 2016, this Democratic allegiance had overwhelmingly shifted—with Trump receiving approximately 80 percent of the votes in Valley precincts, and Trump posters replacing the earlier figures of Roosevelt, Kennedy, or Lewis. Across the region, 400 of the 420 counties in Appalachia voted for Trump in 2016.[5]

The support for Trump by poor, white working-class voters in his election in 2016 seemed to come as a surprise to many, provoking a great deal of attention in the nation's media and dozens of academic studies, many of which focused on Appalachia. As writer Elizabeth Catte described:

> During the 2016 presidential election, the national press branded Appalachia ground zero for America's "forgotten tribe" of white working-class voters. . . . Appalachians were often used as both the abstract and real beneficiaries of Donald Trump's promise to "make America great again," and media outlets and prestige publications—from the *New Yorker* to *Vanity Fair*—sent reporters to Appalachia to extract profiles and images of the people they assumed could demystify our fractured political moment. Their output came to form a distinct genre of writing—what I call the "Trump Country" piece—that saturated news cycles and fatigued readers with stories of complacent white woe and toxic politics. Podcaster Jayme Dale, originally from North Carolina, described 2016 as the year "the US collectively pointed a trembling finger of accusation at the Appalachian region."[6]

Such singular attention on Appalachia was misguided for a number of reasons. First, Trump's success wasn't just in the coalfields, but across much of rural and small-town America. As the *Washington Post* pointed out in a post-election analysis, "in the 2,332 counties that make up small-town and rural America, he swamped his Democratic rival, winning 60 percent of the vote to Clinton's 34 percent. Trump's 26-point advantage over Clinton in rural America far exceeded the margins by which Republican nominees had won those voters in the four previous elections."[7]

Second, very few of the journalistic explanations put forward by the media for the rise of Trump focused on longer-term structural and political forces that were affecting the coalfields and other rural communities. Rather, they tended to focus on more individualistic explanations, hearkening back to earlier "culture of poverty" type explanations of political behavior, arguments reenforced by popular books like Vance's *Hillbilly Elegy*. However, in general, studies have pointed to more underlying reasons for this support. "Trump's average over-performance was higher in more economically, socially, and health-distressed counties," and in areas with a high percentage of residents without a four-year college degree—places like the Valley.[8] These were also places facing economic loss and downward mobility. As Shannon Monnat and David Brown found, "The places with the largest shifts in 2016 are not all among the poorest places in America (though Appalachia certainly holds that distinction) but they are the places that are generally worse off today than they were a generation or two ago. In these places there are now far fewer of the manufacturing and natural resource industry jobs that once provided solid livable wages and benefits to those without a college degree."[9] Also facing a "hollowing out" of infrastructures and public services, such places became a "breeding ground for regressive authoritarian politics."[10]

Third, those who judge the political behavior and views of rural Appalachia on the basis of participation in national elections also ignore another important fact. While rural white voters may have voted proportionately higher than other groups for Trump, they also had higher rates of *non-participation* (e.g., voter absenteeism) than elsewhere. A map of the predominantly white counties with low voter turnout in the 2016 elections shows their concentration in a geographic belt following the Appalachian chain, from upstate New York to Tennessee, with the greatest nonparticipation in the Central Appalachian mining regions.[11] In almost all of these counties, less than 55 percent of the population turned up to vote, and in many, including many in the Valley, the number was below 45 percent. Although absenteeism at the polls was strong throughout the region, it was not unique. Across the country, the white working class stayed home in large numbers. In the Rust Belt, "of those earning less than $50,000 a year, the decline in Democratic voting from 2012–2016 was 3.5 times greater than the rise in Republican voting."[12]

In the Valley, such patterns of nonparticipation in national elections were not new. Gaventa's earlier work noted the lack of engagement in the 1972 national elections, which seemed distant and removed from everyday life: "Despite the headlines in the city's television and newspapers, very few of the Valley's residents talked of the election or its issues. There were no campaign rallies held; no literature was distributed. In national politics, this community neither gives nor receives much attention."[13] The key point is that nonparticipation can be equally important as an indicator of behavior as participation. For this reason alone, we must be cautious of generalizations about Central Appalachia as Trump country. In 2016 at least, in these communities, more people chose not to participate at all than to vote for Trump.

Finally, it is also important to note that while the nation's media seemed surprised by the election of Trump, the shift in the coalfields toward Republicanism and away from a Democratic base had been underway for some time (as may be seen in figure 5.1). In the 2000 elections, featuring Gore versus Bush, Gore won 71 percent of the votes across the four precincts that make up the Clearfork Valley on the Tennessee side, despite the fact that he was also an environmentalist, and the coal industry campaigned heavily against him. While Gore lost in other non-coal areas, and surprisingly the state as a whole, his home state, this former mining valley defied the trend. Gore had been endorsed by the UMWA, came from a long-time Democratic family (his father was a Tennessee senator), and the Valley maintained its support.

On the other hand, Gore lost in West Virginia, the largest coal-mining state in the region, shifting this historically Democratic state to the Republican column for the first time in many years. In that state, the issue of protecting coal jobs, especially in the face of growing opposition to mountaintop removal, played a major role in the election, and indeed, the head of the West Virginia Coal Association was charged with leading the opposition to Gore by a key political kingmaker, who was also a key coal executive. Nationally, Bush championed the protection of jobs through what was called the "cars and coal campaign" in an attempt to gain the support of autoworkers and coal miners in the Ohio Valley and in Appalachia.[14]

Since 2000, the support for the conservative Republican agenda has grown in every election, often by substantial margins, as we see in figure 5.1.[15] The 2004 campaign featured the Republican George W. Bush versus the Democrat John Kerry, a climate change advocate. Once again, the Valley remained Democratic overall, again going against the trend in the

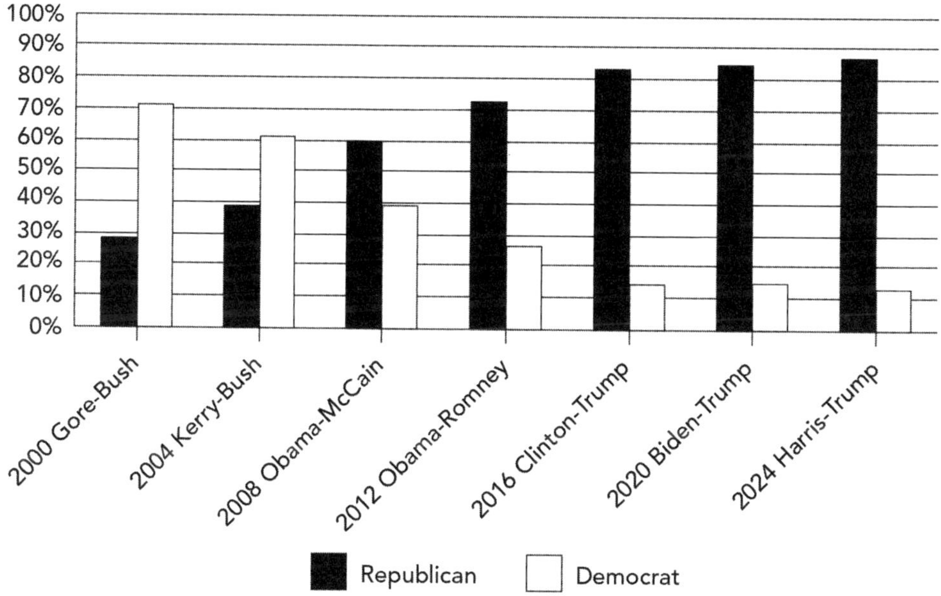

FIGURE 5.1. Voting in the Clearfork Valley: Presidential Elections, 2000–2024. The data represents precincts in White Oak, Habersham, and Clairfield, Tennessee. Complete data was not available for the two precincts on the Kentucky side. (Secretary of State, "Tennessee State Historical Election Results," https://sos.tn.gov/elections/results)

state, though the Republicans saw an 11 percent increase their column, with a 39 percent Republican and 60 percent Democrat split. But in the Obama versus John McCain election in 2008, we saw this trend escalate even more, with a 21 percent shift to the Republicans, and a 60–39 percent Republican versus Democrat split overall (a mirror image of the pattern in 2004). In every presidential election since then, the Republican share of the vote has continued to increase such that by 2016, 80 percent of those voting in the Valley voted for Trump, rising to 87 percent in 2024, a gain of almost 60 percent over the twenty-year period. These patterns were similarly seen across the Central Appalachian coal-mining regions. In 2024, Trump's margins continued to increase, not just in Appalachia, but across the entire country. Appalachia was no longer the exceptional case the press had once made it out to be.

Interrogating the Shift

There are several factors that help to explain this gradual shift from a Democratic to a Republican voter base in the coalfields. As we saw in the previous chapter, throughout the early 2000s, the coal industry had been building a grassroots campaign around the Friends of Coal and War on Coal movements, which made fertile ground for Trump's pro-coal messages. With messages linking coal to patriotism, it was an easy shift from Make Coal Great Again to Make America Great Again. Moreover, fearing greater environmental regulation and facing greater pressure from environmental accountability from organized groups in the region, through heavy funding and well-executed campaigns politicizing debates about fossil fuels, the Republicans converted the issue of job loss in the coalfields to one of political gain. One study, for instance, has shown that for every coal-mining job lost between 2012 and 2016, five people shifted their vote toward Republicans, particularly in areas of significant job loss, where there were few other jobs available and where income levels were low, such as in these counties in Appalachia. Moreover, job losses had spillover effects, affecting voting preferences in neighboring counties as well.[16]

While it is tempting to reduce the explanation for the rise of the right to be just a direct response to the loss of coal jobs and the inordinate influence of the coal industry, this explanation is too simple. First, as we have seen, the trend wasn't only in the coalfields but found across America in the 2016 elections, and in an even more pronounced way in 2024. Moreover, although Trump emerged on stage as the visible national symbol of this trend, in fact, for many years, the conservative grassroots Republicanism movement had been growing across many areas of the country, fanned on by the Tea Party movement, the rise of the Christian right, and white supremacist movements.[17] Rather than overly focus on Trump, what is perhaps more important to understand is why these movements took root in such a dramatic way over time, especially in rural communities like the Valley.

A number of academics and others have focused on the rise of "rural authoritarianism" in America and in other parts of the world, considering factors related to anger and resentment from economic precarity, the disillusionment with existing political leaders and institutions, the role of religion and patriarchy, as well as the role of race and immigration, threatening people's perceived status and identity.[18] As Ian Scoones and colleagues argue in their work, "Forms of dislocation, prolonged and widespread neglect, challenges to identity, and the undermining of rural communities and livelihoods" can have profound consequences.[19]

Many of these arguments are of course interrelated, and no one explanation will likely suffice. In her insightful ethnographic work on conservative populist politics in rural Maine, for instance, Claudine Pied says that "people's ideas about economic decline, race, immigration, and government responsibility cannot be easily separated."[20] She argues for the importance of using a more conjunctural analysis, drawing on the work of Stuart Hall and others (see chapter 1), such as that done in the United Kingdom "to explain the intersecting influences of political power, class politics, and nationalism on the Brexit vote" or similar work on the rise of neo-nationalism in Finland.[21] Moreover, she considers that in all of this work, we must go beyond "collecting opinions and perceptions of conservative populist supporters"[22] to examine how these are shaped by the social and political context.

Of course, the key factors for the rise of the right may vary from place to place. In the Central Appalachian Region, several factors seemed to emerge from our interviews (which occurred before the 2024 elections). First was the sense of distance and abandonment by more traditional national parties, which Trump's anti-establishment rhetoric could easily exploit. Second was the manipulation of anger and resentment around economic loss; and third was the role of race and the political construction of whiteness, which mobilized fears against "the other." Within the context of the region, each of these had particular sway.

In talking with people in the Valley, one quickly picks up the sense of distance from and abandonment by traditional national parties. In earlier eras, the popularity of key presidential figures—Roosevelt and Kennedy—can be explained by the fact that they paid attention to the difficult issues facing the region, and backed this with important sets of public policies—

the New Deal in the 1930s, with a number of programs for rural jobs and rural development; and the War on Poverty in the 1960s, which also had special elements focused on the region. Since that time, until Trump, both national public policies and attention directed toward the circumstances of rural Appalachia had waned. While workers saw their jobs disappear and their communities hollowed out, there was an ideological vacuum of coherent explanations for their condition. Stepping into that vacuum, the Christian right built an ideology that blamed government and immigrants for their economic decline, while the progressive Left and Democratic Party failed to offer a compelling counternarrative.

For instance, politically, after the presidencies of Kennedy and Johnson, the Democrats had largely sought their base elsewhere. When Hillary Clinton did visit the region in the 2016 campaign, she showed little understanding of the plight mining communities were facing. As we saw in the previous chapter, the decline of coal had become far more than a jobs issue. Rather, the Friends of Coal movement had made the issue about protecting identity from outsiders who were threatening a way of life as well. Inadvertently playing right into these concerns in a Democratic town hall meeting in Ohio in March 2016, Clinton said,

> Instead of dividing people the way Donald Trump does, let's reunite around politics that will bring jobs and opportunities to all these underserved poor communities. So, for example, I'm the only candidate who has a policy about how to bring economic opportunity using clean renewable energy as the key into coal country. Because *we're going to put a lot of coal miners and coal companies out of business* (emphasis added).[23]

While she went on to add, "we're going to make it clear that we don't want to forget these people . . . we've got to move away from coal and all the other fossil fuels, but I don't want to move away from the people who did the best they could to produce energy that we relied on," the damage was already done. The one sentence about putting miners and companies out of business was widely shared for months on local radio, press, and social media, and reinforced the worst fears of mining communities that had been well stoked by the War on Coal campaign. (Even seven years later, while doing field interviews for this book, the statement was still recited back to us by coalfield residents as a key factor in the lack of support for Clinton's candidacy.) In her post-election book, *What Happened*, Clinton herself would devote an entire chapter to this failure to connect to the coalfields, saying that that the comment was the one "that she regrets the most from the entire race . . . I wish more than anything that I could have done a better job speaking to their fears and frustrations. Their distrust went too deep, and the weight of history was too heavy."[24]

By contrast, Trump offered a vision very much in the perceived interest of the working-class voters in this region—one based on the revival of "King Coal," upon which much of the regional identity politics rested on at this point (as discussed in chapter 4). In one campaign stop in Virginia, for instance, "he stood before a crowd in Virginia with 'Trump Digs Coal' signs and declared that he was the 'last shot for the miners.'"[25] Rather than talk about a vague abstraction like transition, Trump promised a return to the past. As one woman in the Valley said,

> They believed him, they believed he was a person they could trust. And he was not a politician. They were tired of listening to the politicians, the same people with the same stories. And I think they thought it was just time for a change. And well, they got a change. You know, and I think that's really what it was that he was just somebody who was they'd seen on TV, you know, just when he spoke that they could believe in him that he was gonna do, you know, bring back America.[26]

Although a sense of abandonment and distrust of politicians may have been one factor affecting Trump support, the loss of jobs, combined with other forms of hollowing out in Appalachia, also combined to produce a deeper resentment and anger, similar to what Katherine Cramer found in her work on the *Politics of Resentment* in rural Wisconsin or what Arlie Hochschild wrote about in her work in Louisiana, *Strangers in Their Own Land: Anger and Mourning on the American Right.*[27] In *Stolen Pride: Loss, Shame, and the Rise of the Right,*[28] Hochschild shifts her attention to Pike County in the coalfields of eastern Kentucky where over 80 percent of voters supported Trump in 2016. Here she argues that declining economic conditions contributed to a loss of individual pride and a sense of shame. As Elizabeth Catte summarizes, "The ideology of individualism—taking full credit for one's successes, but also one's failures—prompts people to see structural failures as their own, which in turn disinclines them from voting for policies that might rein in the savage capitalism decimating the region."[29] Trump adeptly harnessed the resulting shame and anger, blaming environmentalists, outsiders, liberal elites, bureaucrats, Democrats, ethnic and racial minorities, immigrants, and others for keeping people from achieving their individual potential. Such blame built on the conservative ideology and movement that had been taking hold for at least two decades.

In our interviews with local activists and residents, anger more than shame was offered as an explanation for Trump support, perhaps more than any other:

> The former president recognized that there was an underlying anger and frustration with an awful lot of people, with the closing of plants, with the lack of representation in the workplace, and with a number of other things, legislation that was passed many people saw was contrary to their best interests or family's interests. There's a lot of underlying frustration and anger with that, and they tapped into it. And, you know, we still see the residual effects of that.[30]
>
> —A former academic still living in the area

> I think that Trump was able to respond to a lot of frustrations that rural people had. He taps into that anger and frustration, whereas the typical political establishment had become more elite, and distant from the popular culture. And Trump was smart enough as being a television reality TV presenter to know how to capture and to work on people's fears, their frustrations, and how to mobilize that into a support base. But then I feel that what's happening is just part of a long-term movement, created by partisanism, to divide peoples.[31]
>
> —A community activist and resident

A longtime cultural worker and teacher summarized more succinctly: "Just anger. Yeah, people were just mad."[32]

The sense of abandonment, as well as the anger and resentment, overlap in turn with a third factor at play in Trump's support—the role of race and racism. To the media the link was simplistically clear: Trump's support came from white voters. Statistically Appalachia was predominantly white; rural white voters voted overwhelmingly for Trump; so therefore race must have been a factor. Indeed, one study points "to racial resentment as the strongest predictor of voting for Trump's peculiar brand of bigotry, faux populism, and economic nationalism."[33]

Certainly, while there was already a trend toward right-wing conservatism going on in the coalfields, it would be hard to explain the even larger swing from Democrat to Republican in these communities in the first Obama election in 2008 without taking race strongly into account. As we saw earlier, in the Valley voting preferences that year reversed to 60 percent Republican, compared to 40 percent in 2004, and the pattern was similar in other coalfield communities. As one veteran organizer and retired local journalist said when asked to explain this swing, "It's racism, racism, plain and simple. Bald-faced racism. They might not admit it and say, Oh, no, we're not racist. But they are."[34] Or, as another informant, a lawyer and former Democratic legislator, described:

> We'd all be kidding ourselves if we got idealistic and tried to talk about economics, this that and the other. There's a lot of racism that underlies all of it. And although while the UMWA was alive and provided a strong moderating influence on racial issues, that's gone. And you know, back underneath it all is that struggle of poor people wanting some kind of "scapegoat." Yeah. And it happens to be the Blacks. That's always underlying. It's always there.[35]

For others, anger was directed toward immigrants, again a sentiment fanned by Trump rhetoric of blaming "outsiders" for declining social and economic conditions. As an older man in the Valley told us, "Our country right now, it's illegals that's what's wrong with it. I'm a firm believer that when the Good Lord made this world, if he had meant to have everyone together, he wouldn't have made so many countries. Now that they are joining up, like fox hounds."[36]

However, to say that racist and anti-immigrant feelings are present in the region is not to say that they are universal, nor that such sentiments were particular to Appalachia. Trump's racist rhetoric had appeal across America. Focusing on racism in the coalfields also risks ignoring the acts and sentiments of antiracism that are also present, as we saw historically in chapter 2. Even today, as right-wing rhetoric fans the rise of white supremacy and anti-immigrant sentiment, multiple examples of antiracism actions also continue. A local resident who tends the cemetery of the now gone Valley Creek coal camp, which had both white and Black sections, describes the racial divide in the graveyard: "The whites are inside the fence, but the Black graves are outside." But with a smile he added, "so I just moved the fence," offering a powerful example of antiracist action at the micro level.[37] Across the mountain, in Bean Station, Tennessee, when immigration authorities raided a factory with a number of undocumented Latinx (or Hispanic) workers, one of the largest raids in its history, white residents protested by the hundreds.[38] The Black Lives Matter protests, particularly after the killing of George Floyd and others, also extended to the coalfields,[39] with one group displaying the slogan, "No Hate in My Holler"—a slogan that quickly spread across the region.[40] In the small county town of Corbin, Kentucky, near the Valley, citizens organized the "Sunup Initiative" in support of racial justice, diversity, and inclusion. The name was deliberately chosen in direct contrast to the town's image of a "sundown" town, where Black people were not welcome after dusk, arising from the forcible expulsion of the Black population some one hundred years before.[41]

A key question, then, is how racist rhetoric, racial resentment, and even veiled racialized imaginaries get activated at certain periods and by certain groups and not others? William Isom, the director of the organization Black in Appalachia,[42] describes two concrete ways that Trumpism has made a difference. First, the Trump rhetoric, combined with the underlying economic and racial resentment, allowed and encouraged racism that had been beneath the surface to be more open. "So I think that there's some roots [of racism and racial violence] in some of these places that hasn't been exposed to the light. Some of that stuff has continued to bubble as time went on. Trumpism has definitely, like, fortified it. These people with racist tendencies—it's emboldened people."[43] In addition, Isom says that the construction of the region as "white" has helped to make it an even more attractive place for white nationalist organizations to organize, contributing to what he sees as a resurgence of white nationalism in the region, "because of the perception of the whole homogeneous ethnic makeup of Appalachian people."[44]

The use of "whiteness" to define the region in popular imaginations is important for other reasons as well. First, while it is true that the region is predominately white, the generalized portrayal of a "white region" erases the historical and present diversity in the region, making invisible the strong role of Black, Indigenous, and increasingly Hispanic communities, among others (as discussed earlier in chapter 3).[45] In power terms, the language of whiteness becomes part of the mobilization of bias, hiding nonwhite identities and silencing their voices.

Moreover, the idea of whiteness and the assumption that white people should occupy a privileged position in society can also become internalized and hegemonic, an unquestioned part of the status quo operating as an example of the third dimension of power described in chapter 3. Exposed to conservative media that is saturated with racialized rhetoric about immigrants and "making America great again," many could support Trump without directly expressing racist sentiments, a phenomenon that Eduardo Bonilla-Silva calls "racism without racists."[46] While some people certainly harbor explicit racial prejudice, many others may have connected to Trump's racial overtones and dog whistles, which are not overtly articulated as racist or even recognized as such. Playing on these internalized norms, Trump did not need to explicitly stoke racist animosity to implicitly draw on racialized imaginaries and racist nostalgia (harkening back to an imagined past of white prosperity for these poor communities).

In her Pulitzer Prize–winning book, *Caste: The Origins of Our Discontents,* Isabel Wilkerson argues that racial inequalities in America are more like a caste system, in which social groups are taught that they are confined to a certain place. Caste and race "serve to reinforce each other. Race, in the United States, is the visible agent of the unseen force of caste."[47] The sociologist W.E.B. DuBois famously argued that the white working class was provided a "psychological wage," the belief that they held certain privileges in occupying their position in a caste system.[48] Thus, when white working-class people see their places in that social order threatened—because of their own downward mobility and/or the perceived rise of other groups—previously latent racism may become more visible.

Robert Gipe, a writer and cultural worker in the coalfields, referred to Wilkerson's work in sharing his analysis of how caste plays out in the rise of right-wing authoritarianism in the region:

> People can live with being low as long as they're not on the bottom. And so when it looks like you might be on the bottom, that's when things get unruly. And that to some extent is explanation for what's going on with white people that have been economically dispossessed . . . they're perceiving themselves to be slipping to the bottom. . . . As long as white people here perceive everybody to be in the same boat, I think there's a lot of solidarity. But I think that there's a perception that . . . they're losing their privilege, and whatever privilege they had just to being white . . . and it's easy to find people who are willing to blame Black people or blame Latinos or whatever group you want to talk about.[49]

In discussing the pivotal role of the 2016 elections in American history, Wilkerson powerfully compares the moment to what happens when permafrost melts on buried toxins, releasing the pathogens that had been previously less visible. Similarly, in Central Appalachia the 2016 elections brought together many forces that had been simmering for some time, and which intersected with and reinforced one another. While these forces came together, none by itself was a determining factor. "To point to racism or 'racial resentment' as a key motivation fueling support for Trump is not to negate explanations rooted in the devastation of white working class and rural communities."[50] As Monnat and Brown also write, "Here race and class interact in important ways. After 40+ years of deindustrialization, automation, globalization, and neoliberal policy regimes, the residents of these mostly-white and formerly strong manufacturing and extraction towns and the rural area surrounding them *feel like* they're doing much worse than previous generations in the same places."[51]

The loss of livelihoods and communities contributed to the sense of political and economic abandonment, which deepened resentment and anger. Conservative ideologues, often through popular media targeted at rural communities, offered people racialized scapegoats to blame, without needing to even recognize or acknowledge the racial element, appealing to narratives of nostalgia, grievance, and loss. Those sentiments, implicitly blaming the rise of "the other" for their own fall, allowed Trump's messages to resonate.

From the War on Coal to Culture Wars

Much of the discussion of the rise of Trump has focused on national electoral politics and the impacts on policy, but perhaps even more profound has been the conservative right's impact at the local level, where it has become a cultural and political force, transforming power and polarizing communities. In doing field research for this book in the early 2020s, when we posed the question who had power now, or who was filling the gap as the influence of the coal industry and its local elites was weakening, the most common answer was "Trump," or "Republicans."

As mentioned earlier, this shift didn't begin with Trump. Conservative grassroots movements, starting with the rise of the Christian right and fights over school prayer in the 1970s, had focused on building a local base, and taking control of local institutions, be they county commissions, school boards, or election commissions.[52] In these communities, the rise of right-wing grassroots Republicanism was often in parallel or supported by the rise of evangelical churches, leading in turn to the increased prominence of what has been termed "white Christian nationalism,"[53] and growing grassroots antigovernment groups, including various armed militia organizations from the 1990s onward.[54] Additionally, this movement was accompanied by a shifting media landscape, with the deregulation of radio in the 1990s, allowing for the rapid growth of conservative talk radio across rural America, and Fox News cable television saturating rural airwaves from the end of the twentieth and early twenty-first century.[55]

At the local level, the political shift was highly polarizing. As a retired local union organizer said:

> I've been involved in the Democrat Party here for years. And then Trump comes along and you know, I mean, it's hard to even talk to folks around here anymore, because they want to argue about, you know, abortion, gay rights, guns, and all these things. And I guess if there's a leader here, it would be, you know, the Republican Party. I've watched this area go

> from voting pretty much straight Democrat, but now if you've got a D after your name and you're on the ballot, you don't have no chance of getting elected.[56]

Another man from the area put it this way: "There's people within my own family that I love, and I simply can't have a conversation with them."[57] For others, the views were even more impassioned. The county official quoted in the beginning of this chapter with vitriolic views about the anti-Christian views of Democrats went on to refer to the film series "Designated Survivor," which is about the one survivor of an attack on Washington's Capitol, killing almost all members of Congress. "They blew the building up and he was the only one survived. And they started over. So if we could get all the Democrats in one party and a few of the Republicans and blow them out and start all over. I can't wait. And start all over."[58]

Though such vitriol was focused on Washington, this right-wing cultural movement also increasingly shifted public debate toward cultural issues, such as gay rights, book banning in schools, abortion, or gun control. These highly divisive movements had an impact on local organizations, and their ability to mobilize. Organizing groups like Statewide Organizing for Community eMpowerment (SOCM) in Tennessee or Kentuckians for the Commonwealth (KFTC) in Kentucky, which for years had focused on issues of economic justice in the coalfields, extended their work to include racial justice and protection of childhood education from right-wing influence (as we shall explore further in chapter 7).

Regional right-wing movements were often fomented or strengthened by groups from other parts of the country. In eastern Kentucky in 2023, for instance, after being featured on National Public Radio for their innovative work on sex education for young people, a group called Sexy SexEd found itself under attack, with threats of violence against its leaders.[59] According to one of the group's leaders, a local mayor's office was swamped with calls, including from the Aryan Brotherhood.

> But they like doxed the mayor's office and had hundreds of calls pouring into the mayor's office from Texas threatening to march in town if they allowed any more sex ed happening. And the mayor knows me. But what was odd is like people that don't even know us have been fed these lies. And they were primed and ready for political action. They will call the mayor's office but they also will call the state police. They had hundreds of calls coming in—not from Kentucky but from these other places.[60]

In another instance of growing polarization along religious and cultural lines, a retreat of the Waymakers Collective, a network of progressive funders and arts organizations in the region meeting at the historic Pine Mountain Settlement School in Harlan County, was abandoned when a group of white local citizens rallied vehicles at exit roads and demanded that conference participants leave the chapel, claiming that some of its healing and meditation workshop symbols were "desecrating a Christian space."[61]

For William Isom, the director of Black in Appalachia, the connecting thread explaining the response to all of these issues, whether they be economic loss, rising racism, attacks on sexuality or religion, is *fear*,

> It's the fear of everything. . . . And we see it here in East Tennessee like, now it's like the fear of transgender people, fear of drag performers, fear of LGBTQ people. The fear of your children being indoctrinated, the fear of Black history. And so it continues; it's been honed. Firstly, like, in more recent times, it's like the fear of the fear of losing your job. The fear of these environmentalists taking your job away, and you're gonna have to, like plant trees on a strip mine for a job, or you're gonna have to install solar panels, or you're gonna have to learn to do coding, and the fear of socialism, then, you know, back in the day, the fear of like, Black men having sex with white women. It just continues to like, morph into whatever people are willing to swallow at the time
>
> It's a fear factory. It's like the manufacturing of fear and, you know, when one fear subsides, it's not marketable anymore, then they just turn to something else.
>
> Fear, because fear keeps people in power.[62]

By mobilizing such fear, right-wing conservative movements shape the agenda away from the rising inequality, economic restructuring, and the need for just transition to the future.

Conclusion

In the previous chapter, we saw a number of ways in which the coal industry worked to cling to power, even as it was declining. This included systematically weakening the key source of countervailing power, the UMWA, strengthening its political hold in Congress and state legislatures, and mobilizing culture and identity of the mining communities as ways of building a new consensus that company interests and community interests were similar, while simultaneously mobilizing fear and resentment against those who sought to challenge this new order by proclaiming a War on Coal.

In Central Appalachia, at least, this movement also provided fertile ground for the rise of conservative right Republicanism, which over time also has shifted the conflicts from the War on Coal and economic issues to new culture wars around race, religion, sexuality, and more, bringing with it deep polarization within working-class communities. The movement also led to the ascendancy of Trump and his election in 2016. In turn, the Trump administration helped to institutionalize anti-environmental and anti–climate change forces, and to attempt to protect and maintain coal's hegemony. As Faber and colleagues wrote in 2017: "The hegemony of the polluter-industrial complex in the United States is now on full display to the world."[63] With Trump's resounding reelection in 2024, this hegemony was once again in play, though this time focused less on coal and more on oil and natural gas production as a pathway to Making America Great Again.

But while powerful in its reach and sweeping in its effects, the hegemony was by no means complete. Across the country and more broadly, over the eight years since Trump's previous election, the environmental and climate justice movements have continued to grow. And, as noted in this chapter, while the elections of 2016 brought huge attention to the rise of Trumpism in the primarily white, working-class region of Central Appalachia, this support was perhaps overplayed—indeed, as we saw earlier, more voters in the region stayed home than voted for Trump in 2016 and absenteeism remained high in the elections of 2020 and 2024. The attention to Trump also ignored broader structural dynamics—coal was declining and new economic actors, less aligned to old configurations of fossil fuel power, also began to enter the scene, as we shall see in the next chapter. Despite the rise of right-wing cultural and political conservatism, there also were growing examples of grassroots resistance and organizing against the domination of coal and toward a post-coal future, as we shall see further in chapter 7. The election of Biden in 2020 in turn created new openings for these grassroots demands to hold coal accountable and to support a just transition agenda to gain national traction, at least for a short period before Trump's 2024 reelection, as we examine in chapter 8. It is to these changing dynamics that we now turn.

6

Financialization and the Rise of Corporate Conservation

> The whole point is to try and demonstrate that we can invest in nature at a scale of a quarter million acres, and build a case for investment. . . . If we can't make a positive financial investment, we can't enter this space of trying to leverage private equity towards conservation outcomes.
>
> —Staff member, The Nature Conservancy, 22 March 2023

With the decline of the coal industry, new types of economic actors began to enter the Valley and the coalfields more broadly. While in the past, the Valley's economy was largely dominated by coal extraction, in the 2020s, a forest carbon offset industry, conservation easements, and forms of ecotourism became key sites of value. The Nature Conservancy (TNC), the world's wealthiest environmental nonprofit organization, became one of the leading economic actors in the Valley, controlling land, investment, and emerging green economies. In this chapter, we investigate how these new kinds of investment bring with them new forms of power, using TNC's role in the Valley to illustrate the operation of power in a post-coal landscape.[1]

In 2019, TNC used "an inventive approach by [its] in-house impact investing team, NatureVest, which structured and closed a sustainable forestry fund"[2] to finance the purchase of 253,000 acres of land across parts of Tennessee, Kentucky, and Virginia, including much of the Clearfork Valley. Known as "the Cumberland Forest Project" (CFP), this is "one of TNC's largest-ever conservation efforts in the eastern United States."[3] The promise of the CFP is that for-profit investing can support conservation and climate goals.

TNC relies on carbon offsets, conservation easements, and sustainable logging to generate revenue for its investors in the CFP. In taking part in these activities, TNC resembles the many investment companies that own much of the rest of Appalachian forests.[4] Though TNC and its investors are but one in a long line of absentee landowners that have controlled land in Central Appalachia, their ability to derive revenues from conserving and selling access to aspects of Appalachian ecology and nature is new. As we will discuss, people living in the Valley see little benefit from these new economic engines and have little voice or influence in their decisions.

In what follows, we trace how the way power operates has shifted under this new form of ownership. We recount the story of how TNC, through NatureVest and multiple investors, came to control much of the land in the Clearfork Valley. We ask what their tenure has meant for people living in the valley, and how TNC's control differs from that of actors who came before. We illustrate how the three-dimensional model of power is now operating under this new structure, pointing to the ways that the new kind of value extraction demonstrates a shift in relations between landowners and communities living in the Valley, highlighting that while the coal companies had direct control over labor, the new accumulation strategies seemingly do not rely on controlling labor or people. Finally, we build on themes in political ecology literature on "green grabbing,"[5] rentierism,[6] financialization,[7] and "accumulation by restoration,"[8] putting TNC's land deal in the context of a global rush to control land and resources for environmental aims and climate change mitigation. We conclude by noting that, increasingly, the people living in the Valley are irrelevant to the value extracted there, with profound political and social implications.

Changing Land Ownership in Appalachia

The American Association, a British company, owned most of the land in the Clearfork Valley from when it accumulated (or expropriated) the land in the 1880s to the 1970s. It was a part of a secretive global network of companies, at the top of which sat a former lord mayor of London, Sir Denys Lowson.[9] Today, what had been the American Association's holdings of 45,000 acres in the Clearfork Valley, and 70,000 overall,[10] remain largely intact, continuing the practice of absentee corporate ownership of land in Appalachia. Yet, the specific owners of this tract have changed significantly.

Changes in the Valley's land ownership illustrate transformation in land politics across Appalachia, and indeed, the United States. Tracing the shifts in land ownership in the Clearfork Valley and this one parcel illustrates broad trends of financialization, a term that Greta Krippner defines as "a pattern of accumulation in which profits accrue primarily through financial channels, rather than through trade and commodity production."[11]

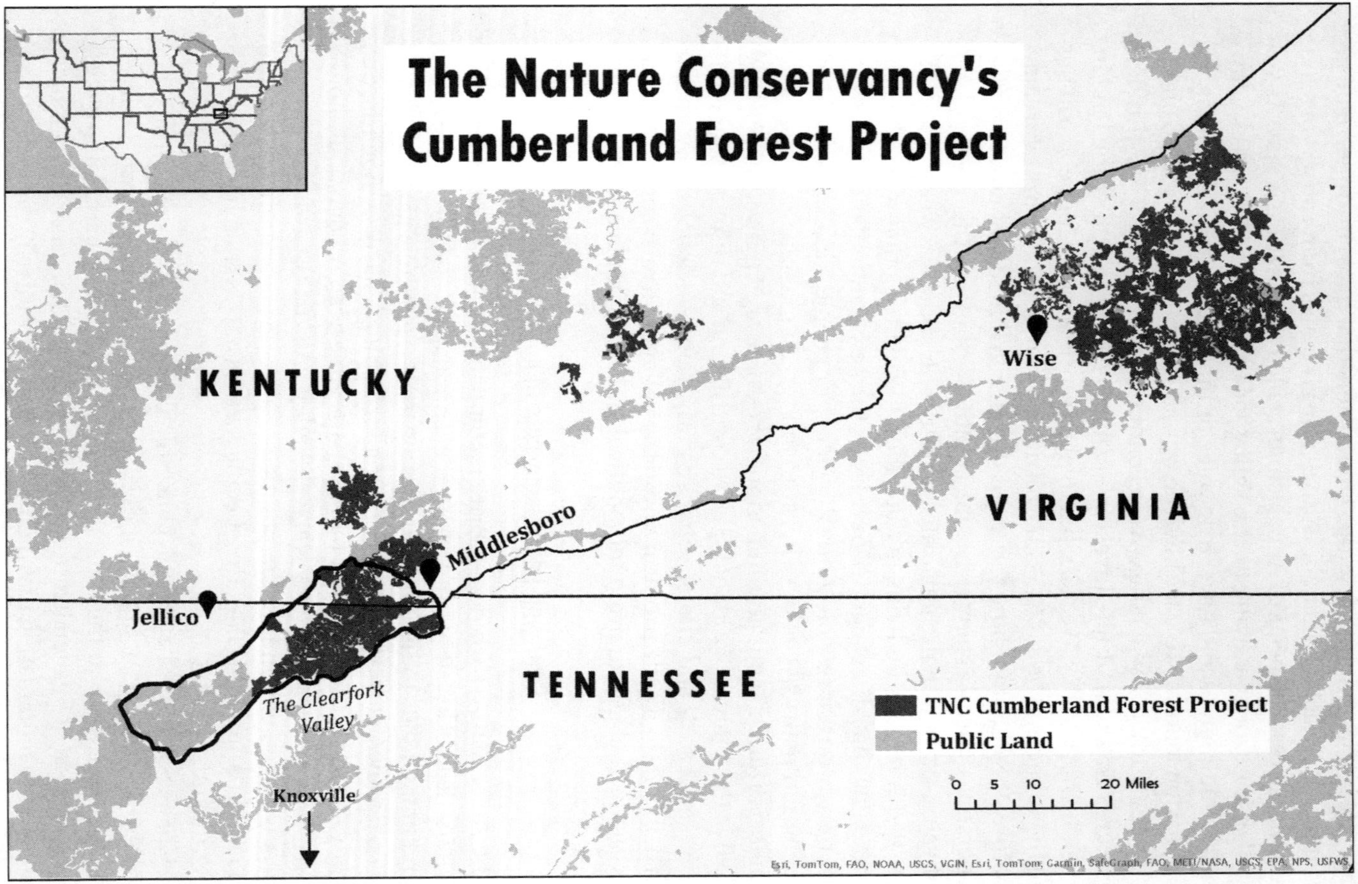

FIGURE 6.1. The Nature Conservancy's Cumberland Forest Project Covering 400 square miles across four states (Map created by Annie Liu)

In 1980, amid multinational corporations' rush to get into energy markets, the American Association land was bought by the JM Huber Corporation, one of the largest family-owned companies in North America, with its global headquarters based in Edison, New Jersey, and with holdings in over twenty countries around the world.[12] As documented in the Appalachian Land Ownership Study, JM Huber held some 227,000 acres across the area studied, with hundreds of thousands more across other parts of America, through its subsidiary Huber Resource, focusing on timberland management.[13] According to local residents, the land under Huber was more accessible than under the American Association, and Huber even donated a few acres of land to Model Valley, a local community development corporation. However, Huber also tore down the remaining housing (or camps) on the coal lands, including relocating some of the local churches, clearing the area for more strip mining.

Between 2006 and 2019, the parcel continued to change hands, moving between timber investment management organizations (TIMOs), a type of financialized investor-owned corporation now controlling upwards of 60 percent of United States forestlands.[14] In 2006 a company known as Ataya Hardwoods, LLC, a TIMO owned by the RMK Timberland Group, a North Carolina company, purchased the 70,000 acres.[15] Between 2007 and 2008, Ataya was sold again, this time to Corrigan TLP LLC, linked to the Molpus Woodlands Group, one of the largest TIMOs in the United States, based in Jackson, Mississippi. As its website states, Molpus "acquires, manages, and sells timberland as an investment vehicle for pension funds, college endowments, foundations, insurance companies, and high-net-worth individual investors. The company focuses on ensuring long-term optimal cash returns on investments while practicing responsible forest stewardship."[16] Meanwhile, in nearby Campbell County, Tennessee, in 2013, the Chinese-owned Guizhou Guochuang Energy Holding Group announced that it had raised $616 million to purchase mining lands, triggering outrage in the state legislature about foreign ownership of its assets (an outrage not seen about the British-owned American Association holdings).[17]

During this period, mineral resources were severed from the surface land, allowing financial investors in energy resources to trade mineral rights without land rights.[18] As coal began to decline, across the region, including here, the various mineral rights became more and more separated. In this case, for instance, Natural Resource Partners (NRP), one of the country's largest mineral holders, acquired the underground mineral rights for the Ataya lands. Based in Houston, Texas, the company boasts on its website that it owns some 13 million acres of mineral and subsurface rights across the United States.[19] NRP was part of a broader trend of making mineral wealth a tradeable asset separate from land; NRP trades not the mineral rights themselves, but the leases to extract mineral wealth, as NRP does no drilling or mining. Instead, entities like Kimble Companies lease access to the gas reserves from NRP to drill natural gas, while coal companies, such as Kopper Glo, leased coal rights from NRP to mine.

Thus, to make natural resources financially tradeable asset classes, landowners broke land and resources on it into component parts. NRP or other owners can earn rental income for leases to each asset, what political economists have termed "assetization," an aspect of financialization.[20] As a result, the land and the subsurface beneath often have complicated ownership and leasing structures, which can limit the economic uses because of the various entities with legal right to use and access the land.[21]

Nature as a Site of Accumulation: The Nature Conservancy (TNC)

In 2019, a new kind of ownership of these lands emerged. The former American Association lands became part of the TNC's Cumberland Forest Project, one of the first such investments to link private venture capital investors seeking significant returns on investment to the acquisition of former mine lands, for protection as well as for generating large streams of income from various nature-based assets. For the first time in over a century, the main revenue sources were not resource extraction on this land, but instead conservation and financialization of environmental services.

TNC has operated in Appalachia since the 1980s, starting with protecting the Clinch River, which a TNC staffer noted had "some of the highest biodiversity of any aquatic system in North America," and runs through Virginia and Tennessee across the mountains from the mining Valley. Gradually, TNC moved into land protection, and then into forestry—all within its biodiversity conservation mission. By the mid-2000s, however, it had identified the Southern and Central Appalachian region in the United States as one of the most important areas in the world for biodiversity conservation and climate mitigation. As Brad Kreps, TNC's Clinch Valley program director, said of the Cumberland Forest Project to the *Washington Post*, "We put the Appalachians in a very rare company along with the Amazon, the wild lands of Kenya and the forests of Borneo,"[22] as targeted regions for investment in biodiversity conservation.

Appalachia was a good place to invest in conservation for another reason. Much of the land was still owned in large blocks, given the history of absentee land ownership, not only by companies but also by state and federal governments. Linked together with private conservation corridors, these could become a critical wildlife migration corridor running up the eastern United States.[23]

Land deals at this scale require significant amounts of capital. TNC was already well-known within the conservation community as working with private investors and private companies, often to the consternation of other less profit-minded NGOs. In 2014, TNC created NatureVest, with sponsorship from JP Morgan Chase to recruit investors for conservation-for-profit–related investments. This move also coincided with the growing development of impact finance and environmental, social, and governance (ESG) concerns in the private sector and among institutions, foundations, high-net-worth individuals and other investors looking for investments that appeared to be linked to environmental or social returns, as well as profit. The mid-2010s deployment of ESG investing also coincided with the rapid rise of carbon offset markets, market mechanisms to quantify ways for companies to pay for reductions in carbon emissions through investing in carbon sequestration projects, such as improving carbon storage in forestlands, rather than reduce their own emissions.

These various trends came together with the formation in 2019 of the Cumberland Forest Limited Partnership, a stand-alone private equity fund of which TNC is a 5 percent owner.[24] In turn, the Cumberland Forest Project owns three subsidiaries: CF Ataya (Tennessee), CF Ataya (Kentucky), and CF Highlands (in Virginia). TNC (including NatureVest) manages Cumberland Forest Limited Partnership, as well as its subsidiaries. The project comprises 100,000 acres in Kentucky and Tennessee, known as the Ataya lands (the two CF Atayas), and 153,000 acres in Virginia (CF Highlands), known as the Highlands lands, formerly owned by a mining company, Clinchfield Coal, part of the Pittston Corporation.[25]

To create Cumberland Forest Limited Partnership, TNC's impact investment team at NatureVest reportedly raised "more than $70 million in equity from 27 investors (including TNC) and $40 million in debt (approximately $20 million from a state agency [Virginia Clean Water Revolving Loan Fund] and $20 million from a foundation) and used an installment sale structure to re-invest $20 million of carbon offset sales proceeds towards the purchase price."[26] (See figure 6.2) Through such a large investment, TNC wanted to demonstrate a new type of climate and conservation finance that could work at large scale. As a TNC staffer said, "The whole point is to try and demonstrate that we can invest in nature at a scale of a quarter million acres, and build a case for investment. . . . If we can't make a positive financial investment, we can't enter this space of trying to leverage private equity toward conservation outcomes."[27]

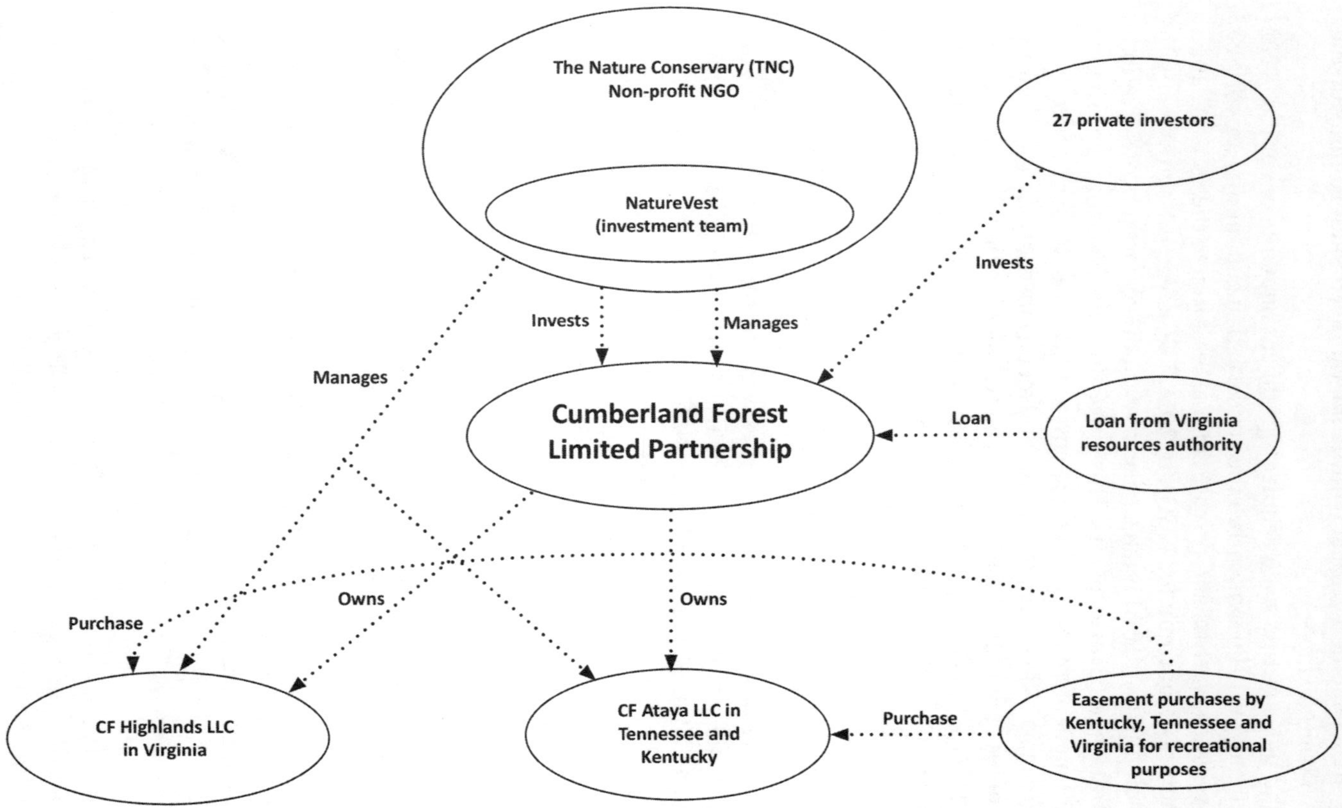

FIGURE 6.2. TNC and the Cumberland Forest Project Corporate Structure. Dotted lines represent a financial or managerial connection to various TNC-related entities. (Compiled by the authors from corporate documents, obtained in part from the Open Corporates database, https://opencorporates.com/)

To generate return on investment, the Cumberland Forest relies on four main sources of financial return. According to TNC staff, the most lucrative revenue stream comes from carbon offsets, mainly in the form of compliance (as in regulatory) offsets sold to big polluters (e.g., utilities or oil companies) on the California carbon market. Central Appalachia is, in fact, home to the second largest concentration of Improved Forestry Management (IFM) offsets outside of California in the continental United States.[28] Through this scheme, TNC uses a verifier to register the carbon credits with the California cap-and-trade program, and then companies in California can buy these "credits," the results of carbon sequestration from IFM projects. These offsets are in effect a 125-year commitment to store an amount of carbon on that land.[29] Offset sales are private (California's Air Resources Board only makes public the aggregated data on total offsets generated per quarter) and can be structured in various ways (e.g., futures contracts, installment sales), raising questions of transparency. However, it is clear from the California Air Resources Board (ARB) reports that TNC sold 4.2 million offset credits from the CF Ataya lands in Kentucky and Tennessee from 2019 to 2024.[30] One offset credit is equivalent to one metric ton of carbon. While it is difficult to know exactly how much revenue it is yielding, TNC received at least $20 million in sales of offsets in 2019 (as stated above). Prices of carbon offset sales are not disclosed, but we can estimate that the total value of the offsets from the Valley and the Kentucky TNC lands together have at least been more than $46 million since 2019.[31]

The second most profitable revenue source, according to TNC staff, is sustainable forestry on the properties. Managing timberlands and lands with resource extraction is not new for The Nature Conservancy, as it is the ninth largest timber owner in the United States, and by far the largest nonprofit owner.[32] All of the 253,000 acres of the Cumberland Forestry Project are Forestry Stewardship Council (FSC) certified, and TNC continues to manage the land for timber extraction. TNC promotes the projects as conserving "working forests," as opposed to strict-conservation forests. TNC argues that their improved forestry management will restore lands that unsustainable forestry degraded.[33]

The third important revenue stream is from payments for conservation and recreational access. At first, TNC leased the land to state agencies or public-private partnerships (e.g., trail management organizations) for use in outdoor recreation, especially for hunting lands and off-highway vehicle (OHV) trail riding. Now, recreational access is ensured as part of the permanent conservation easements on the properties. In both Tennessee and Kentucky, the Ataya lands are managed in partnership with the respective state outdoor recreation and wildlife agencies, while in the

Highlands tract in Virginia, Spearhead Trails, a public-private partnership, leases and manages the land. The Tennessee Wildlife Resources Agency (TWRA) manages hundreds of miles of OHV riding trails, which are very popular with visitors to the area, with an estimated 70,000–100,000 visitors a year riding the trails in the Valley alone.[34] For access to the land, TWRA paid significant rent until recently. In 2019, for instance, TWRA paid $95,000 for access to one parcel of 46,000 acres in the Valley.[35] In return, TWRA charged fees for riding OHVs and hunting on the land. TNC no longer collects rent for recreational access because of state-purchased permanent easements to the property.

These conservation easements constituted a sizable income stream for TNC. Often structured as one-time payments from state agencies, sometimes with the support of conservation-minded philanthropy, these easements guarantee the permanent protection of streams and habitat for endangered species and allow public recreational access. For instance, in 2021, the TWRA paid for permanent conservation of 43,000 acres of the Tackett Creek Wildlife Management Area, in the Clearfork Valley, with a "$7.98 million purchase . . . utilizing Tennessee's Wetlands Acquisition Fund."[36] In 2022, TWRA expanded that easement by 850 acres, paid in part with a "$620,000 grant from the National Fish and Wildlife Foundation's Acres for America conservation program,"[37] now making up one of the largest easements in Tennessee. Likewise, easements on the CF Highlands LLC lands represent the largest such deals in Virginia.[38]

In addition, there is now the prospect of leasing land to solar energy companies as a fourth income stream. As of the end of 2024, TNC had sold a lease to a solar developer, the company SunTribe, to build and operate a solar development in the Valley, a site called Tackett Flats, near Westbourne in the Valley. In February 2025, TNC announced it was building seventeen solar sites across the Cumberland Forest Project, totaling 360 acres.[39] The utility-scale solar operations were making use of Biden administration tax credits for solar developments in disadvantaged communities, whose status became uncertain as of 2025 under the Trump administration. These developments will take years to be constructed, yet the lease agreements have already generated revenue for TNC and promise to bring new revenue sources to the community fund that TNC operates.

Impacts of the New Ownership

TNC's promise of solid financial and environmental returns through this model has received national attention, including in *National Geographic* magazine, which described its impact-investor-based model as "one way people have attempted to reconcile conservation with capitalism."[40] TNC itself has widely promoted the Cumberland Forest Project, reported by *Environmental Finance* magazine as saying that it believed the project "is the first time a non-profit has raised a forestry-focused private equity fund at this scale," and that it could be "a model for large-scale impact investment in forests."[41] In 2020, the *Environmental Finance* magazine awarded the Cumberland Forest Project the "Impact Fund of the Year" Sustainable Investment Award, "for generating a positive measurable social and environmental impact alongside a financial return."[42]

Although the financial return on investment seems likely, whether this project is securing benefits for the climate is ambiguous and the impacts on the towns and people near the project are complicated. On the climate side, carbon offsetting has been widely critiqued for letting companies continue to pollute, while not cutting back on their underlying emissions. Additionally, there is a growing scientific consensus that improved forestry management offsets are overcredited (overcounting their carbon benefit).[43] Globally, a study from Corporate Accountability and the British newspaper *The Guardian* have shown that "some of the world's most profitable—and most polluting corporations—have invested in carbon offset projects that have fundamental failings and are 'probably junk,' suggesting industry claims about greenhouse gas reductions were likely overblown."[44]

In California, numerous "fence line" neighborhoods that are affected by ongoing pollution from companies that have bought credits are raising their concerns, while a group of academics at Berkeley and elsewhere accused the state Air Resources Board of exaggerating the value of the offsets that California polluters are buying.[45] Furthermore, in 2020, an investigation by Bloomberg Green accused the TNC of selling "meaningless carbon offsets," which had credited forests that weren't under threat in the first place, prompting TNC to conduct its own internal review.[46] Although these were not the IFM offsets on the Cumberland Forest Project (rather, they were voluntary offsets), the scandal led to further scrutiny of the model across the sector.[47]

While TNC was receiving national awards for "impact investing" in 2020, communities nearest the Cumberland Forest Project have seen mixed and at times negative impacts. One issue has to do with access to the land. Conservation easements ensure what state agencies such as the Tennessee Wildlife Recreation Agency term "public access." This means that TWRA sells permits for hunters and OHV riders to access the land. This invocation of the public, however, is complicated. As Loka Ashwood points out in *For-Profit Democracy*, many rural communities increasingly view the state as operating in the interest of large corporations.[48] This is not without reason. The operation of agencies like TWRA illustrates the point that within the neoliberalized state, agencies have witnessed decreasing tax revenues and increasing privatization of services operated through close partnership with private corporations. In the Clearfork Valley, the result is that TWRA creates a fee-to-access system on privately held land, nominally in the interest of the public, while paying TNC to access the land. Though TNC staff have said that TWRA's management does not prohibit anyone from walking onto the property, in our fieldwork we encountered many people who stated they feared that they could be ticketed or arrested for entering without proper permits.

For instance, Gaventa interviewed one resident who has restored a former coal camp house adjacent to the Ataya land. They watched a group of OHV riders drive across the little creek that divided his property from the lands now managed by the state. The interviewee said, "For three generations my family has been able to walk and use that land,"[49] but he is now concerned about entering without a permit. Schwartzman interviewed a man who digs ginseng, who reported "a lot of people won't pay to travel on it. . . . You gotta buy them permits and all that to cross over onto their property."[50] These interviews indicate that while legally the public may be able to access the land for certain purposes, many do not for fear of running afoul of the law.

The sustainable forestry approach also has unclear results for local communities. While TNC staff suggested that forest management across the Cumberland Forest Project's three states generates about sixty or sixty-five jobs, much of the work of forestry has become more professionalized in recent years, requiring credentials many residents do not have. New requirements for carbon counting and timber certification are unlikely to bolster a local wood products industry, as most forest products processing has been located outside the Valley for decades.[51]

Few jobs or investments flow directly back to the host communities, but TNC does have a "Cumberland Forest Community Fund" that invests in the area. The funds come from royalties gained from fossil fuel extraction on the lands (coal mining and gas drilling continue on the lands, as TNC claims it cannot break existing lease agreements), cash payments generated as community benefit investments from solar developers, and the fund was beginning to bring in philanthropic funding in 2024. The fund is managed through third parties in each of the three states: the University of Virginia at Wise, the Mountain Association in Kentucky, and Clinch-Powell Resource Conservation and Development organization in Tennessee. In its first round of small grants in 2021, on the Tennessee side, it gave five grants for a total of $76,062. All of the funds were invested in projects some distance away from the Valley, with the exception of $25,000 for the Campbell County Chamber of Commerce, for the construction of an elk-viewing tower.[52] A sixth grant was made to the Woodland Community Land Trust; however, it was indefinitely suspended because the trust requested to shift the focus of the grant from restoration of a roof to fixing the foundation on a building that was to be used as a small business incubator.

In 2024, however, after meeting with community members who urged TNC to fund community-led projects in the Valley, and after one of the authors, Schwartzman, gave presentations and wrote articles about the lack of funding going to community groups,[53] $75,000 in grants were made to community organizations in the Valley. These included a grant to build hiking trails on Woodland Community Land Trust property. Yet, because the grant was paid out as reimbursements, making it difficult to manage for organizations with limited budgets, the funds ultimately went to a trail-building firm based in Knoxville, Terra Strata LLC, and not to an institution in the Valley itself. In sum, most of the grants from the Cumberland Forest Project have been made outside the Valley, and the total amount of funds invested in projects since 2019 is relatively small compared to the $350 million invested in the land.

Moreover, TNC is clear that it does not intend to own the land for the long term, raising the question of what comes next? The plan is for a ten-to-twelve-year investment, in which TNC establishes a profitable model of conservation, and then sells the entire project to an investor. As a TNC staffer said, the hope is "if sustainable forestry and carbon or other ecosystem type markets continue to mature, your future owner would see the value in continued management for basically forestry and recreation ecosystem services."[54] The new owner would almost assuredly once again be a private timberland corporation, continuing the economies that leave nearby communities extraneous to the revenues generated on this land. Meanwhile, many residents in the Valley have long wanted the opportunity to purchase pieces of what was the American Association's land. In Virginia, households living adjacent to pieces of property now in the Cumberland Forest Project want the chance to create larger locally owned parcels, as the Cumberland Forest in Wise and Dickenson Counties, Virginia, are a noncontiguous parcel dotted with individual owners throughout. The possibility of breaking up land into smaller parcels for local ownership, however, may now have been preempted by the granting of the conservation easements to the state governments in each state.

Shifting Power in a Changing Economy and amid Changing Actors

How has this shift in ownership, from natural resource extraction entities to TNC, affected power relations? When discussing with residents in the Valley about how power has shifted, they are clear that in the past the fear of directly confronting the power of the company and mining industry was almost palpable. In the coal camp system of power, which shaped political perceptions and behavior for so many years, the company directly controlled aspects of daily life in visible ways. Coal companies owned housing, controlled nearly all jobs in the area, and had the ability to directly intervene in social services through its political influence around, for instance, welfare benefits. This power was often mediated through a powerful local family, who kept tabs on the local community, while being close to corporate owner and other corporate interests, described in Gaventa's earlier book "as the godfather."[55] Now, pressed to identify local powerholders in the Valley, community members responded, as we saw in the introduction, "Well, there is The Nature Conservancy. But it's not like the coal industry."[56] There is more openness to speak, and even new alliances are being shaped with elected officials, who seek their involvement around certain projects, unheard of before.

Yet, as discussed, many people in the Valley are unsure exactly who the new owners of the land are, although most interviewees were aware there were new owners. Largely, TNC's presence in the community is not felt. It remains impossible to trace the investors that own and control the land in the Valley, much like it was, if not more so, with the control of the lands by the earlier American Association. As TNC staff said in discussions, as a private equity firm, the Cumberland Forest Limited Partnership is obligated to keep investor information confidential.

At the same time, unlike the coal companies, The Nature Conservancy was happy to respond to requests for meetings, speaking to both authors. In a meeting with a TNC staff member, Gaventa was supplied with large numbers of documents. TNC staff held a community outreach meeting in the Valley at the beginning of its tenure. Following suggestions that maybe senior project staff might want to meet some of the groups directly affected by their operations several years into the project, rather than some of the more elite Chamber of Commerce, university, or local government officials with whom they had been interacting, a meeting was subsequently held in April of 2023. Dialogue continues, and the regional director has held virtual meetings about solar investments with local groups and has agreed to further dialogue with grassroots organizations across the region in 2024.

Openness to dialogue, however, does not by itself shift power imbalances. As one of the world's largest nonprofit conservation NGOs,[57] with $9 billion in assets and $1.3 billion in annual revenue in 2022,[58] operating in seventy-nine countries, with thousands of employees worldwide, and owning more than 2.5 million acres of land in the United States alone,[59] we would not expect its influence to be insignificant. How is this influence wielded?

In a 2006 article, Katrina S. Rogers uses the case of the TNC to look at the role of international NGOs in shaping and influencing the debates on climate change, drawing on the distinction made by Joseph Nye between soft power and hard power.[60] While hard power, according to Nye, draws upon tools of force and coercion, soft power pulls people toward a predefined end by making it appear desirable.[61] Groups like TNC, Rogers argues, use forms of soft power, collaboration, expertise, and lobbying to set an agenda, but through this can influence the use of hard power, for instance influencing the sanctions used by states against those that do not comply.

TNC has developed a reputation for being at the soft power end of the scale. Rather than challenge fossil fuel companies directly, it has sought to influence them through partnerships and collaboration, often to the ire of other more activist NGOs who want to confront the fossil fuel industry directly. Gregory Thaler notes that such an approach stems from "an organizational ideology of 'pragmatism,'"[62] wherein TNC justifies close relationships with companies that destroy the environment, such as timber corporations and fossil fuel companies, as offering opportunities to maximize impact. This pragmatism, Thaler notes, allowed TNC to rapidly expand and come to prominence in the neoliberal era, from the 1980s onward, as market-based solutions and probusiness approaches to environmental problems became popular.

Naomi Klein, in her book *This Changes Everything: Capitalism vs. the Climate*, calls this the "disastrous merger of Big Business and Big Green."[63] She uses by example the fact that for some years, TNC actually ran its own oil and gas operation on a property in Texas that it had acquired for the protection of a particular rare bird species. TNC also maintains an Advisory Business Council, with representatives of some of the largest companies in the world, including fossil fuel companies, and while pressing for solutions to climate change, according to Klein it actually invested over $26 million of its endowment in energy companies, including some of the largest oil, coal, and gas companies.[64] In 2003, TNC also became the subject of a major *Washington Post* exposé into its property dealings, which examined its connections to oil drilling, natural gas sales for profit, buying and selling land to board members, and more.[65] But for TNC, this was justified as a fair way of exercising influence. As the *Washington Post* observed, “Conservancy officials say their approach—which falls under a larger environmental philosophy known as ‘compatible development’—allows them to leverage corporate America’s wealth to achieve conservation on a massive scale. Instead of insisting in every case on the pristine preservation of land, the charity practices the art of the possible, its officials said.”[66]

We can understand TNC’s approach within the three-dimensional model of power. In the first dimension, not only does TNC exercise power through “coziness” rather than confrontation with the fossil fuel industry, but it is also very effective at trying to shape policies in support of its style of conservation, at both national and international levels. Within the United States, in 2021, TNC spent $2.6 million lobbying the US government, much more than any other environmental group that year.[67] Its senior leadership and board members are drawn from top echelons of the corporate and political world, including previous executives of finance and fossil fuel companies, members of Congress, and senior members of both Republican and Democratic administrations.[68] In 2023, for instance, the board chair was former Republican US Senate majority leader Bill Frist, and treasurer was Sally Jewell, former secretary for the interior in the Obama administration.

TNC uses its power quietly to influence national governments in other countries, as well as to influence the global rules of the game.[69] In 2008, for instance, it was the first international NGO to be appointed to the governing board of the World Bank’s Forest Carbon Partnership Facility, widely seen as a kickstart to carbon markets, putting up $5 million to fund them.[70] It was also seen as a key actor in promoting the controversial idea of “nature-based solutions,” persuading companies that they could invest in and profit from investments in nature—what critics term “nature-based dispossessions.”[71] As Rogers observes, “TNC has also shown an exceptional ability to work both in the halls of governmental power and in corporate boardrooms. Staffers pride themselves on being able to move smoothly between government and industry.”[72]

TNC also seeks to bolster its influence and credibility through grounding its work in “science.” While evidence may be important for conservation, the use of scientific knowledge also operates within the second dimension of power as a “mobilization of bias,” setting the “rules of the game,” deciding whose and what kind of knowledge count in environmental decision-making. “Follow the science” is a slogan used on its website, which goes on to say, “with a grounding in rigorous science, we take innovative conservation approaches from idea to impact, scaling to achieve system change.”[73]

In 2024, TNC said it employed 400 staff scientists worldwide. TNC's use of scientific expertise offers a kind of knowledge power that can serve to exclude and delegitimate local voices.[74] Indeed, as it developed its plans for the conservation and preservation of the Valley lands, at no point, to our knowledge, did it seek out local ecological or experiential knowledge from those who live in the environment it sought to protect.

The use of science as a justification for a widely contested conservation-for-profit model is a method of legitimation, and in that way, it is also part of the third dimension of power. In the earlier text, Gaventa showed how investors deployed discourses that claimed nature must be tamed to make way for progress and modernity to justify natural resource extraction. TNC's control relies on distinctly different discourses—that nature can be preserved, even improved, if made profitable. Such discourses serve to justify TNC's governance of its land based on expert scientific knowledge. TNC's claims articulate an ideology that asserts the irreproachability and inevitability of for-profit conservation and expert scientific knowledge. Such discourses attempt to shape the way communities and the larger public view options for the future, working to foreclose the possibility and legitimacy of criticism of what is presented as a progressive response to climate change.

When TNC's power is challenged, following initial signs of openness, it can quickly choose to remain aloof from local concerns. An example is found in a controversy over logging and TNC's position on sustainable forestry. In 2020, over fifty grassroots environmental organizations signed a letter to TNC's CEO, Jennifer Morris, "asking for a meeting to discuss concerns that TNC was 'prioritizing the financial interests of the industrial logging and wood products industry at the expense of solving the climate crisis, protecting nature and advancing environmental justice.'"[75] Two meetings with senior staff and various scientists, and environmental justice and forest protection groups occurred, at the end of which the alliance of local groups asked TNC to join them in making a public statement "on the importance of protecting forests from industrial scale logging as a top-tier climate priority." Six weeks later, the CEO "thanked the coalition for the dialogue" but made no offer for a public statement or further dialogue, while continuing with their existing policies. In 2022, over 150 faith, justice, and environmental groups followed up with a scathing open letter about TNC.[76] Organizers said they felt TNC had outmaneuvered them.

In the Valley, it is too early to know what will come of the attempts at dialogue that are now underway. But many residents have not seen much difference so far from those of the previous large absentee owners. Although TNC staff have high hopes for place-based conservation, opening local offices and becoming "members of the community and build ground level trust and relationships," residents of the Valley have seen little of this. As one woman put it in 2023, "They keep saying that they are talking to somebody but not us. Or no one else that I know of in the community."[77] Subsequently, in 2024 TNC staff responded to requests to inform community organizations in the Valley about the Cumberland Forest Community Fund, mentioned above, and held several meetings with community stakeholders from around the region.

Despite the new level of engagement, fundamental aspects of the project remain the same. As an experienced activist in the region put it: "We have new players coming in, but . . . we haven't seen the markets and opportunities open up to local people in the way that you would hope. . . . For carbon offset credits, it's still the fundamental problem of the land and minerals are owned by people outside of this area."[78] Across the globe, communities have expressed similar sentiments of being left out of TNC's decision making.[79] While TNC may at times meet with residents and champion "community engagement" practices, it is rarely willing to make changes that alter its larger approach in response to this consultation.

Conclusion

Unlike coal and land companies, TNC's approach does not rely on direct control of residents to maintain and build their power. In fact, TNC is rarely mentioned by residents as major powerholders. Their power grows more from decisions made in distant financial markets and in national and global policy spaces, which are helping to shape new forms of appropriation from nature.

The case is an instance of what James Fairhead, Melissa Leach, and Ian Scoones term "green grabbing":[80] the increasing global trend of appropriating land and resources for environmental ends. More specifically, TNC's Cumberland Forest Project involves a different kind of accumulation than under the coal industry. In this new nature-based accumulation, value is extracted from the land, but very little labor is needed. As Schwartzman has argued elsewhere, that kind of accumulation strategy is a form of "rentierism," a political economic arrangement that relies on increasing rents, or the income derived from the control of access to a scarce resource or asset, rather than using labor to produce commodities for sale.[81] TNC's Cumberland Forest Fund relies on making more assets out of the land, such that it can generate more investment and rental income to pay outside investors, while employing few local people.

Compared to coal mining, TNC's new revenue streams of carbon offsets, conservation easements, and sustainable timbering all require increasingly fewer people working on the ground, and some experience the easements as dispossessing them of access to the forest. The new economic activity that leaves out local people follows successive rounds of dispossessions throughout the area's history, from deindustrialization, closure of coal camps, and strip mining (as discussed in chapter 1). Many residents see the new developments as furthering these trends.

Although the projects employ few people, they appear lucrative for investors. Investor-owners, like those of TNC's NatureVest, have increasingly become the owners not just of North American forestland in TIMOs, but home mortgages, credit card debt, pension funds, personal digital data, and, in short, all aspects of life. This is financialization.[82] Kelly Kay notes that rentier relations of forestlands in North America have created a kind of "financial enclosure," as new investor-owners increase the kinds of revenue streams from forests, including the expanding conservation easements and new payments for recreational access.[83] Yet, when financiers find new sites to accumulate from nature and climate change mitigation, the actual revenue sources themselves are often drawn from public coffers and public funding mechanisms.[84] This trend bears out with the Cumberland Forest Project, as recreational leasing relies on public funds, including fees to access; conservation easements are purchased by state agencies; and carbon offsets are in effect a tax on pollution in California. NatureVest joins this trend toward financial enclosures, but with a distinct and new focus on mitigating climate change.[85] In this way, NatureVest demonstrates an emerging "climate rentierism."[86] In addition, as we have suggested above, financialization also serves to shift the arena of power and contestation from the local level, with control of labor and communities, to more opaque and distant arenas where decisions are made on financial ledgers.

Importantly, the limited benefits that communities see from TNC's fund and its inability to employ local people are indicative of the larger trend in both green-grabbing projects and climate rentierism. TNC, however, is far from alone in taking part in the new economies detailed above. Carbon offsets, leasing land for outdoor recreation, establishing conservation easements, and sustainable forestry are becoming the rule, rather than the exception across the former coalfields in Appalachia. The handful of TIMOs that own much of Central Appalachia, with particularly high concentrations in the coalfields, as discussed, have virtually all found that they can produce additional revenue streams from these nature-based assets.

Community organizations in the Valley and around the Cumberland Forest are not staying silent. The TNACE group in the Clearfork Valley, and the Clinch Coalition in Virginia, alongside several other community-based nonprofits, such as the Southern Appalachian Mountain Stewards (SAMS) and the Appalachian Citizens Law Center, have mobilized to negotiate a minimum level of community benefit from the Cumberland Forest Project. The results of this organizing are yet to be known. This coalition, however, is evidence of a much broader and longer tradition of community organizing and building community-level power in coalfield Appalachia and, particularly, in the Clearfork Valley, as we see in the following chapters.

7

Building Collective Power from Below

At one time, they did have fear, and it was passed down generation to generation. . . . Now, it's not fear anymore.
—Community leader, 27 March 2023

There was this new coming together, a new coalition building, which also corresponded with the Obama administration and preparing for any wins that we could have during this administration. And then you've got ten years of a movement moment. And so many things happened during that period, I mean, hundreds and hundreds of arrests and direct action and nonviolent civil disobedience happening across the region, regulatory changes with EPA, and lots of wins with litigation. So it was a very exciting time.
—Community organizer, 27 September 2022

Despite the industry's ideological power, the hegemony of King Coal was never complete, nor was the rise of conservative extremism. Just as the decline of coal created space for the entry of new corporate actors, over the decades it also created space for the emergence of more organized forms of opposition by citizens in the coalfield communities, demanding accountability for the industry's devastating record of damage to land, water, labor, and community. Whereas in the heyday of coal's dominance, even questioning the future of coal could be risky, increasingly over the last few decades, public discussions on a more equitable post-coal future have begun to emerge.

In his earlier book on *Power and Powerlessness*, written some fifty years ago, Gaventa argued that over time coal had created a system of domination, which included a sense of powerlessness among coalfield residents, often contributing to apparent quiescence even in the face of glaring inequalities. Though it also included a discussion of key moments of opposition and resistance, the primary focus of the book was on the problem of inaction and obstructions to action rather than on the questions of how and when action arose. However, in more recent visits to the Valley since the earlier book, we are struck less by quiescence and more by the variety and extent of actions that small groups of citizens are taking, often against enormous odds. While chapters 4, 5, and 6 outlined trends which tended to suppress or at least resist community mobilization, simultaneously to these, important movements for action were also occurring (see timeline, figure 0.1). Given this, in the next two chapters we reverse the question from the earlier book. Rather than ask why action did not occur in the face of inequalities, we ask instead, "Why and how does citizen mobilization emerge in the face of such overwhelming barriers?"

In this chapter, we focus largely on the period of the gradual decline of the coal industry, from roughly the early 1970s, when the previous book was written, up until recent years, when the industry has more or less collapsed. First, we revisit the legacies of nonparticipation and other barriers that preclude action, historically as well as today. Then, we explore how, as the industry's hold on the region weakened, groups began to take more visible action through various strategies, including mobilizing local assets to create alternative forms of development, grassroots community organizing to counter the destructive effects of the industry, and key moments of direct action and civil disobedience. Over time, these began to come together across the region, through the development of multi-issue and multisited coalitions for change, thus linking strategies for gaining power.

Revisiting the Context: The Legacies and Factors of Nonparticipation

Just as legacies of "power over" linger on, even in the face of changes in the economic base, so do legacies of powerlessness. Gaventa's earlier book concluded in the early 1970s, with a description of how emerging actions to challenge the corporate coal owners in the Valley were quickly shut down by violence and repercussions, directed not only against those who protested against the coal industry directly, but also against others who were trying to create small-scale community and economic alternatives. The book ended on a somber note: "The responses of power were effective. A general mode of fear was re-invoked. By the end of the 1975, the challenges of the community against the Company had virtually ceased."[1]

Some fifty years later, the company is gone, and the fear seems to have dissipated. Yet for some, it leaves behind a legacy of internalized powerlessness. As one community leader describes further from the quote at the beginning of the chapter: "At one time, they did have fear, and it was passed down generation to generation, and you still hear people today, you know, blame others for them losing the coal mining jobs and things. . . . Now, it's not fear anymore, I don't think. Maybe we've just become complacent and just live, you know, it's always been this way. We're just never going to speak up against anything we feel is wrong."[2] Or as another long-time male resident from a longstanding coal mining family said: "If you're taught to believe that you don't have a voice and you don't exercise the voice, then it's very easy for people not to ask for that voice or to ignore that voice. . . . I think I mentioned this to you before, [people] have no vision of their lives and what they want to do or what they want the community to be. And without it, and you can see it all around us, we're dying."[3] While the legacies of nonparticipation continue, so too do the labels that historically were used to discredit those who tried to challenge the coal industry, who were often stereotyped as "outsiders" or "troublemakers" or, as coal declined, were blamed for "stealing our jobs." For example, one community activist said that people thought of SOCM, a grassroots anti-strip-mining group (discussed later in the chapter), as "a reason that they don't have the jobs anymore . . . because of them, and SOCM. I don't think people will ever get past SOCM history in this area."[4] Even local community development groups who were careful not to confront the coal industry often got painted with the same brush. A leader of a local community center recounted that the fear of being seen like those "activists," "prevents people from walking in the door, even just coming to a celebration at the community center. It's a real obstacle for bringing folks together."[5]

In addition to these legacies of internalized cultures of nonparticipation and stigma against those who broke the mold, other barriers to participation today have to do with the sheer difficulties for people in the Valley who are facing dire economic, health, and social conditions (as we examined in chapter 1). For many, just surviving is a crucial struggle, much less having the time or resources to attend meetings. The opioid epidemic also had an impact, causing key community leaders to pull back, as a result of their own addictions or to take care of family members. In order to feed addiction, petty theft and other crimes emerged within the community, leading to breakdown of trust and of social capital. As one leader put it in a focus group discussion, "[The] drug crisis has absolutely rendered the community fabric in a way that like people are not trusting of their neighbors. People are not even, like, trusting of groups. There's so many talented people who I just know, at this point, will occasionally drop out of the organizing for months, to years at a time, because they have relapsed. . . . Everyone identifies it as a major issue."[6]

On top of the economic hardship, an aging and unhealthy population, and the impact of the drugs crisis, along came COVID. Even as groups were beginning to come together, now they had to learn to work remotely. In the Valley this was particularly a challenge, as most homes lack access to broadband internet, relying on expensive satellite internet or coming to the free wireless at the Clearfork Community Institute. As one organizer lamented, "and then COVID . . . in terms of our organizing, we went virtual for three years. It's just deeply painful, right?"[7]

When these current obstacles to collective action are combined with the historical legacies of inaction, as well as with the culture war politics as outlined in chapter 5, it is surprising that challenges to power arise from below at all. Yet, despite these historical and current obstacles to participation, over the last fifty years a variety of interesting and significant strategies for action have emerged, which we consider below.

Creating Alternatives: Asset-Based Community Development

In situations of high inequality, where there are risks to challenging power directly, one way that communities build their agency is to construct alternatives within the spaces and with the resources they have, often quietly and under the radar. In power terms, the approach claims the space that is available to build the "power to" create something new, rather than directly challenging the "power over," which dominant actors hold. This approach was made famous in the United States by John Kretzmann and John McKnight,[8] as well as in rural Canada, by the Coady International Institute, which has promoted the asset-based community development (ABCD) approach around the world.[9]

In the Valley, examples of this community development approach were already evident in the 1970s, when under the rubric of what was called the "Model Valley"[10] programs, a series of community health clinics, a small pallet factory, a crafts cooperative, and other initiatives were all part of efforts by the community to create a different type of development. While not directly challenging the corporate power holders, even these faced repercussions, struggling to get access to land for local community development projects from the corporate landowners.[11]

To counter this problem, in 1979, a number of residents launched the Woodland Community Land Trust, now one of the oldest community land trusts in the United States. Using donations and grants, Woodland was gradually able to acquire 450 acres of land for housing, small business development, food preservation, gardening, hunting and gathering, and community activities. In an area where affordable housing is a desperate need, at its height the land trust had twenty-five homes, leased long term to low-income residents.[12] When it celebrated its fortieth anniversary in 2019, a national magazine commented, "Over time, Woodland CLT has helped to restore land holding, livelihoods, and economic self-sufficiency in the area. In a place perhaps best-known for mountaintop removal mining, where the majority of the land is owned by absentee extractive companies and communities largely migrate to urban area for work, many in the local community have embraced the CLT as a tool of collective organizing to rebuild their landscapes and relationships in a life-affirming way."[13]

In 1997, the land trust was able to acquire a former school from a coal company in the small town of Eagan, once a coal camp owned by the Blue Diamond Mining Company. They converted this into the Clearfork Community Institute (CCI), to serve as a gathering place for the Valley, and a learning, training, and research center. Over the years, CCI has been a site of many activities, hosting volunteers from outside the valley, providing awareness programs for them, as well as developing training, cultural events, and festivals within the community. One of the projects hosted in the CCI building, for instance, is a local broadband project, Southern Connected Communities, offering the only publicly accessible internet across the Valley.

Meanwhile, down the road a little way in Clairfield, Tennessee, the Model Valley Community Development Corporation, now known simply as Model Valley, continues. A small piece of land has become something of a town center, with a post office, clinic, and thrift shop. Model Valley has also acquired land and then has often resold it to local residents or for local development (taking a somewhat different philosophy than Woodland, which preserves land in trust). Among its most recent successes was attracting and selling land to a Dollar General Store, a rapidly growing national chain making millions in poor rural communities across America. While the Dollar General Stores have been critiqued for taking advantage of isolated communities,[14] for this community it became one of the few local places to shop for food and other necessary items without making the twenty-mile trip to a nearby town. Among the most important accomplishments of Model Valley was the development of a locally owned water utility, providing drinking water to over five hundred families—quite a step from when in 1976, while Gaventa was doing his fieldwork for the previous book, local residents celebrated the opening of a public spigot, which offered rare access to clean, unpolluted water.

While all of these efforts may be small, in this context, they offer impressive examples of attempts at self-control and self-determination as an antidote to the outside control and dependency the area has experienced for years. And in a remote community which has very few services from the local governments, the community leaders have had to fend for themselves to develop services such as water and health care.

In an area where, historically, male miners have been the breadwinners, many of the leaders in these efforts have been women. For many years, for instance, one of the key activists was Marie Cirillo, a former nun who had lived and worked in the Valley since the late 1960s. Cirillo helped start Model Valley, the Woodland Community Land Trust, and CCI, as well as a number of other groups in the area, linking them as well to regional and national groups such as the National Congress of Neighborhood Women.[15] In the early 2000s she was joined by Carol Judy, an herbalist, root digger, and educator who traveled the region fighting for the protection of the land, water, and forests. Both women relied on a different knowledge and understanding of the land and community than those promoted by mainstream corporatist development. For Judy, who became a key, self-taught activist in many organizing efforts, development was bound up in a different relationship to the land to that of the extractive, destructive mining industry—one where land was cared for, preserved, and used in more sustainable ways. But unlike the technical knowledge of TNC scientists discussed in the previous chapter, Judy's knowledge was deeply experiential, drawn from hours of walking the woods and observing the changes in flora and fauna. As one observer wrote in her honor after she passed away in 2021, "Her understanding of the mountains, their ecosystems, and indeed, even their chronosystems, was so embedded in her everyday thought and language that even the sharpest of minds would find themselves outpaced by the scale and depth of her insights."[16]

In a region known for its deficits—enduring poverty, opioid addiction, destroyed landscapes—these community-based initiatives sought to develop a different narrative, based on starting with what people valued and the assets that they identified as important to their identity and for their future development. For instance, in 2008, CCI hosted a community economics conference, designed to hear from residents on what a more locally based sustainable economy would mean to them. In a later project in 2012, volunteer Michelle Mockbee, along with Marie Cirillo and Carol Judy, worked with young people in a six-week institute to learn skills of local participatory research, in what was described as an "intergenerational process of creating spaces, skills, and voices for change." As one of the young graduates of the program said, the process was about "moving the power of research from traditional entities into the hands of local people, enabling communities to set their own research priorities, thus overcoming negative stereotypes, preserving traditions, building relationships, and improving the opportunities for local livelihoods."[17]

Continuing this tradition, in 2018 a coalition of groups working in the Valley led an intensive listening project "to gather information about the unique assets in our community and bring people together to create new projects that address our communities' needs." Rather than focusing on the absence of local capacities, the listening project identified local skills (arts and crafts, construction and repair, outdoor gardening, hunting, etc.). Rather than name the deficits, the project asked people what they loved about the community, and overwhelmingly the answers were "people help each other here," as well as appreciation for the landscape and peaceful country living. The hopes named by participants included activities and places for youth, solutions to the drug problem, and jobs.[18] Such asset-mapping processes become a way of recovering knowledge, as well as a basis for positive action.

Although these sustained asset-based community development activities over fifty years have been impressive, they have not been without their challenges. While people will show up and mobilize in times of crisis or for key moments, like a celebration, the network of local leaders involved is quite small. For them, gaining wider participation is a key concern, one made all the more difficult by the recent trends mitigating against participation, as discussed earlier in this chapter. Of these, the opioid crisis has been particularly devastating, threatening to erode the sense of social capital the community so valued. For instance, the Woodland Community Land Trust suffered a series of fires, which destroyed many of its homes, and which appear to have arisen from petty conflicts surrounding drugs or attempts to claim insurance money to feed addictions. As one person said, "In the asset mapping, we learned that one of the reasons people stay and what they love about the community is their relationships that are more like family than neighbors. But with the drug epidemic, there's more distrust, the need to lock doors—a sense of community but also distrust because of massive opioid epidemic."[19]

Moreover, while the land trust and CCI could create their own "claimed spaces," often safe spaces for youth to learn and grow, these were not insulated from the rest of the world. As one of the leaders of the youth programs described, "The second anyone left the door, the overwhelming compression of all the boulders over everyone's head and shoulders just kind of returns. There's this safe space where people came into and felt valued, but the second they left, you know, they were seen as drug addicts or they're caring for their grandmothers, or they had no money."[20]

Despite the challenges, these groups continue to meet and respond to new opportunities. What started as the Appalachian Community Economics project in 2008 in 2012 became the Tennessee Appalachian Community Economics (TNACE) project, a roundtable of groups working in the Valley who have met regularly at the CCI building since that time, with a common mission of "preserving our culture through hands-on education for ourselves and building our community through shared knowledge and skills."[21] The group works democratically, sharing leadership, respecting each other's views and values, and continuing to create a safe space for collaboration. Such collaboration, the process of "power *with*" others, has been important to maintain the energy and work in the face of immense challenges.

> It's good to know that you're not by yourself, that there's other groups who really believe in the work you're doing and, you know, someone you can actually just talk to. . . . You know, you get discouraged that more people aren't coming, other groups aren't participating. I still think we have that sense of getting together and still being part of each other. I think we all need that. We all need that community.[22]

When asked about successes, another community leader commented, "We're good at still trying, we're still TNACE, we're still meeting—we haven't given up."[23]

Building Power through Organizing—SOCM, KFTC, and Local Protests

While asset-based approaches focus on using available assets to create alternative spaces for development, another important strategy focuses on grassroots community organizing as a means of building collective power for directly challenging and holding to account more powerful actors. In the United States, influenced by writers and activists like Saul Alinksy, organizing is widely used, with many variations on core approaches.[24] Many of these approaches have gained ground in more urban settings; yet now, building on the history of resistance we outlined in chapter 2, two well-known examples of rural organizing have emerged in the Central Appalachian coalfields, including parts of the Valley. In the east Tennessee coalfields, the last fifty years have seen the rise and spread of Statewide Organizing for Community eMpowerment (SOCM, originally called Save Our Cumberland Mountains) and in east Kentucky, Kentuckians for the Commonwealth (KFTC, originally called Kentuckians for Fair Taxation), now two of the oldest and most successful grassroots rural organizing groups in the country.

SOCM emerged as an organization in the early 1970s when a group of coalfield residents in east Tennessee came together to challenge the lack of taxation of mineral wealth in their communities, leaving their counties poor and without funding for needed services. After winning their case, they decided to stay together, as a grassroots membership-based organizing group, based in five coalfield counties.

Early organizing meetings to build local chapters were sometimes attended by company thugs who tried to intimidate the attendees and break up the gatherings. In one case in 1978, the first president of SOCM, JW Bradley, and two other SOCM members were attacked in a courtroom while speaking out in a hearing on water quality issues. In 1979 and 1980, the houses of three SOCM members were burned following their speaking out against strip-mine damage. Yet, gradually, people began to stand up against such harassment. An early SOCM organizer described one meeting in a community near the Clearfork Valley where at the end of the agenda, after the organizers had described what SOCM was trying to do, members were invited to join, which meant standing up, walking to the front of the room past the coal company thugs, and paying dues of two dollars each. She went on: "Every one of those old people went in front of those guys and went down there. Two dollars, and I saw courage I've never experienced, and it changed me. They didn't succeed in breaking up any meeting, nor did they succeed in any person leaving SOCM because of it."[25]

With examples of courage against the odds like this, gradually SOCM continued to build its base, and to have some successes in challenging the power of the coal industry. It won a statewide suit to change the assessment procedures on coal lands, which had long been undertaxed, thus generating some revenues for local public services. Through statewide lobbying it also was able to pass a severance tax on the coal that was being mined. Joining forces with national groups, they lobbied successfully to pass the first national law regulating strip mining, the Surface Mining Control and Reclamation Act (SMCRA) in 1977. Involving members as data gatherers and observers, they monitored the implementation of the act, challenging illegal practices, and succeeded in declaring some areas as unsuitable for mining.

Gradually, SOCM's membership base grew across the rural counties in east Tennessee. Yet being in only a few parts of the state limited its influence in the state capital. Increasingly wanting to build a larger, multiracial organization, it gradually began to build alliances with more Black-led organizations in the western part of the state, which demographically was far more diverse than the eastern coalfields. In the early 2000s, its board made the decision go statewide, leading to the change of name to Statewide Organizing for Community eMpowerment.

In 2021, SOCM celebrated its fiftieth anniversary. While we cannot go in depth into its rich history, what is interesting for our purposes is its approach to building power of previously marginalized groups. The organization was rooted in a chapter structure, with those local chapters deciding what issues to work on, and then with SOCM staff helping to build the capacity of local residents to have the power to have a voice in the future of their own communities. Believing strongly in involving and being led by local residents, SOCM became a "citizenship school," where members constantly learned skills of active engagement that they could use for a lifetime.[26]

In a speech in 1994 to the Appalachian Studies Association Conference, Connie White, then the SOCM president, passionately described the method: "The first thing we've learned is that we can change the world, but only if we work together. . . . But when people came together, when they figured out together how to act in their own best interest, when they supported each other and cared about each other and took risks for and with each other, then their homes and communities could be saved. They had to do it together—that's where the power is."[27]

The second important lesson for White was the need for patience and persistence "to learn how to build organizations for the long haul." The third lesson White offers is that "in changing the world, we change ourselves," with each step leading to more critical awareness: "for many of us, it's also helped us think critically about our home, about the way people are divided by class and by race, the way women are treated, about who has power and why—and how to take that power and use it more responsibly."[28]

While SOCM was one example of the empowerment of local residents in and around the Valley, across the state line in Kentucky, a similar organization also developed, Kentuckians for the Commonwealth (KFTC), founded in 1981. Like SOCM, KFTC came together around a single issue—the demand that coal and timber companies that owned most of the land in the area pay their fair share of taxes. In 1988 one of its early coal-related victories was a successful campaign to amend the Kentucky Constitution to ban the so-called "Broad Form Deed," which had allowed mineral owners to mine land under surface owners without their consent. With these successes, KFTC took on other issues, including stronger regulation of strip mining and toxic wastes, as well as other issues of economic and environmental justice. And like SOCM, it also gradually expanded its base across the state, taking on other issues of racial justice, voting rights, economic inequality, and climate change.

For Lisa Abbott, the long-time director of the organization, the process of organizing is also all about building power. It is about the power to make things happen, and to stop things from happening. It is also about shifting the power to write the rules, but ultimately, she says, the biggest contributions are in what she herself calls the "that third dimension of power, the shaping of what people think is possible."[29]

Yet despite their wins in the coalfields and across both states, while there were individual members in the Valley communities, neither SOCM nor KFTC were able to build strong local chapters in this particular area. Organizers reflect that this may be because the legacy of corporate control was particularly strong there and the ownership of land in the hands of a single owner particularly concentrated. One long-time SOCM organizer recalls working in the area: "To be anti-coal in that particular part of coal country was like you had to be a communist or something awful that you would doubt that coal was the answer."[30] It may also have been because energies were concentrated in other efforts, like the less adversarial asset-based community development strategies described earlier. Nonetheless, the organizing efforts in nearby areas did help to shift the sense of powerlessness, as well as to create the legal frameworks that enabled local citizens to take action.

At key moments, as cracks in the power of the coal industry were made visible, there also emerged examples of more spontaneous acts of resistance and protest in the Valley. These included what we might call "micro-protests"—the smaller, sometimes individual acts of organic resistance and dissent that differ from organizing as they are often divorced from larger political mobilizing and organizational infrastructure. An example may be found in the heart of the Valley, where a local resident decided he had had enough of the constant dust stirred up by coal trucks going up and down the unpaved road by his home. A descendant of coal miners in the area, he had bought one of the last remaining coal company houses, so he could remain in the area. But for years the dust was causing pollution issues, and despite complaints, nothing was ever done.

When the coal company filed for a permit for further expanded strip mine operations in the area in 2014, the resident filed a complaint, taking advantage of provisions under the 1977 Surface Mining Control and Reclamation Act (SMCRA) allowing public input. Although such hearings are usually dominated by lawyers, the resident, who was relatively low income and lacking a college degree, decided to make the case himself. Using his own knowledge of the area, taking hundreds of photos documenting the damage, he submitted reams of documents, arguing that the Office of Surface Mining Reclamation and Enforcement (OSMRE) had failed to look appropriately at potential water damage, including to his own drinking water, which came from a nearby spring; pollution from the dust stirred up by the mining traffic; and from the accumulation of air pollution from this and other surface mines. The OSMRE granted the permit anyway. Not to be deterred, and in the face of constant harassment from the local company and foot-dragging by the authorities, the local activist appealed. In 2018, the company and the county agreed to pave the road, though further remedies were denied.

While this is a case of courage and persistence against the odds, it also was made possible by the openings provided by the SMCRA legislation. As the resident later wrote, "It gives people like me, who are uneducated, and poor, a voice, that is, if they are willing to speak up. It is also a process to have grievances mediated. Let's hope and pray that it never gets pushed aside."[31]

Single actions such as these also can have ripple effects. While this case was one of a single individual against the OSMRE and the coal company, further down the Valley, in an area known as White Oak, in 2015 other residents also came together around dust and road issues. In this case, the community took a more collective action approach, led by a local minister and involving dozens of residents, but also supported by experienced organizers from SOCM and the Sierra Club. Again, the previous work of SOCM had provided an entry point for citizens to raise their demands, in the form of the severance tax that the county was now receiving from the state to help deal with the effects of coal mining. Groups of twenty or thirty residents kept showing up at county commission meetings, demanding that the road budget be allocated to deal with the coal truck/dust problem and that the county pave the road to provide adequate access into their community. At the same time, the county was proposing a local property tax increase on residents, "And so somehow this issue blew up to them, like hundreds of people coming to all these meetings. It was like standing room only. And they were separate issues, but they were related and made us appear very powerful. And that road got paved pretty quickly."[32]

Buoyed by this victory, the community then organized again when a mining firm that owned land in the area, Davis Creek Energy, announced plans to establish coal ash landfill on the property in 2013. The community was incensed, worried about the toxic effects of coal ash, how it would affect groundwater, especially on top of an area already riddled with underground coal mines. With a local leader who had already gained a lot of organizing and advocacy experience advocating for disability rights for her son, the group began to mobilize. Though the company had already applied for a National Pollution Discharge Elimination System permit, hundreds of people showed up to an opposition meeting. They were also able to take advantage of a legal opening created by SOCM's previous statewide organizing, called the Jackson Amendment, which ruled that counties had the final say-so on location of landfills in their county. Within a year, the group had stopped the landfill. Later the same group organized against a cryptocurrency mining operation in the area, though without success.

The Rise of Civil Disobedience—Challenging Mountaintop Removal

Over time then, continuing the earlier history of resistance in the region (discussed in chapter 3), grassroots organizing by groups like SOCM and KFTC gradually began pushing back against the intimidation and control of the coal industry, to get issues of the accountability of the industry on the table, and to win some concrete gains. However, as the extent of strip mining continued to grow, and as movements for environmental justice in other parts of the county began to employ more direct forms of civil disobedience to supplement the community organizing strategies, so too did this direct strategy begin to emerge in the Central Appalachian region.

The context for this movement was the enormous rise of what was called mountaintop removal, a process of not only blasting and bulldozing the sides of mountains to get at the coal seams but also removing the tops of mountains altogether.[33] As the industry was seeking ways to save costs, this technology grew enormously across the region especially from 2000 on. While cheaper for the companies, MTR had hugely negative consequences for those who live nearby, filling streams with pollutants and toxic minerals, and increasing risks of flooding. Blasting away the natural mountainous landscape caused further disturbances.

While groups across the region were increasingly fighting against MTR, a trigger moment happened in 2004, when a boulder from a blast on a strip mine in Inman, Virginia, crashed into the bedroom of a three-year-old boy, Jeremy Davidson, killing him instantly. A protest march was organized in nearby Appalachia, Virginia, joined by others across the region. Building on the momentum from this incident as well as growing youth outrage around MTR and climate change, in 2005 Mountain Justice was founded, bringing a repertoire of nonviolent direct action and civil disobedience to the fight against strip mining in the region.[34] Originally named Mountain Justice Summer, the name was chosen "specifically to reference both the Freedom Summer, the 1964 voter registration through southern states during the struggle for civil rights, and Redwood Summer, a series of EarthFirst! sponsored protests against deforestation" in California.[35] In 2005, a constellation of this and other organizations in the region began to engage in collective acts of disobedience against MTR.

Civil disobedience is not new in the struggles against strip-mining in the region, as we saw in in chapter 2. In the mid 1960s, when strip mining was just emerging, in eastern Kentucky, local residents had also blocked bulldozers, and sometimes engaged in violence—using explosives to sabotage strip-mining equipment, or exchanging gunfire with strip miners.[36] In Campbell County, Tennessee, in 1968 saboteurs reportedly had destroyed "a diesel shovel, six bulldozers, a truck, drills, and a railroad car, which together were valued at nearly a million dollars."[37] However, in the effort to pass the SMCRA in 1977, which involved local groups like SOCM, the leadership was largely from national environmental organizations, the Big Greens, which convinced local groups to accept a regulatory approach (rather than an outright ban), and which distanced themselves from more local acts of civil disobedience.[38]

The movement for nonviolent civil disobedience that emerged in the early 2000s was somewhat different. While engaging with local leaders and groups, many of the participants were college students and environmentalists from outside the affected communities, who participated in trainings and took part in the nonviolent actions. In 2005, Mountain Justice held its first summer camp, bringing together college students and regional youth to protest mountaintop removal. The growth of the Mountain Justice movement corresponded with a growing youth climate movement, with the first national convening termed Power Shift bringing six thousand young activists together in Washington, DC, in 2007. This was followed by an even larger summit attended by more than ten thousand youth climate activists in 2009 calling for an end to fossil fuels, specifically an end to coal mining and involving mass civil disobedience at the Capitol. By 2009, the anti-MTR protest movement intensified with thousands of climate protestors coming to the coalfields for more direct tactics of tree-sits and equipment scaling that sensationalized environmentalist protests across the region and the country, with ten direct action events and close to one hundred arrests in 2009 alone.[39] These protests also involved arrests of high-profile celebrities, such as NASA scientist James Hansen and actress Daryl Hannah.[40] In Campbell County, Tennessee, Mountain Justice joined forces with United Mountain Defense (UMD) and Three Rivers Earth First!, two Knoxville-based organizations committed to ecological preservation and protection, in a struggle against the Zeb Mountain Removal Coal Mining Operation, a plan to strip mine across three peaks running along a ridge, near Elk Valley, just over a mountain from the Clearfork Valley.[41] Although sympathetic lawyers had used the courts to oppose the permits for mining here, these were not effective. More unconventional methods were needed. These included "listening projects," where volunteers sought to hear the views of local residents, publication of thousands of copies of the *Defender*, a fact sheet to counter misinformation about the mine, active water testing streams around the mine, aerial photography, and most importantly direct action, including blockades, banner drops, and protests, including at the annual shareholders' meetings of National Coal Corporation, the company doing the mining. All of these actions also involved press releases and the media, bringing a great deal of public attention to the issue. While the company fought back with a Strategic Lawsuit Against Public Participation (SLAPP), and protestors at the shareholders meeting were arrested and labeled "eco-terrorists," the campaign continued.[42]

Over the next few years, activities like these persisted across the region, building a sense of a regional movement and attracting attention nationally and internationally. In 2010, more than one thousand people joined the Appalachia Rising March in Washington, DC, calling for "an end to mountain top removal strip mining and the beginning of serious investment in sustainable economic diversification in the region,"[43] where 114 people were arrested in an act of nonviolent civil disobedience at the White House.

As the movement grew, so too did the opposition to it, with counter-demonstrations and attacks organized through the Friends of Coal and War on Coal movement described earlier. In particular, the fact that so many of these actions involved outside students turned into another wedge issue, allowing the industry to blame the outside "tree huggers" for taking away local jobs. As Shannon Elizabeth Bell writes, "Although the environmental justice movement was *started* by local coalfield residents, and these local coalfield residents are *still* central to the leadership of the movement, the influx of non-local people into the region has provided an opportunity for the opposition to capitalize on an 'insider-outsider' dichotomy, effectively challenging the collective identity of the movement, so that many in the region no longer perceive it as a 'local' struggle."[44]

The intensity of counterprotests and shifting national attention to pipeline struggles meant that by 2015 the direct-action campaigns were largely over. Nevertheless, the movement galvanized both action and attention on environmental justice in the coalfields like none before. Bonnie Swinford, an early volunteer with Mountain Justice, now an organizer with the Sierra Club in east Tennessee and very involved in the Clearfork Valley, describes (as also quoted in the beginning of the chapter):

> There was this new coming together, a new coalition building, which also corresponded with the Obama administration and preparing for any wins that we could have during this administration. And then you've got ten years of a movement moment. And so many things happened during that period, I mean, hundreds and hundreds of arrests and direct action and nonviolent civil obedient disobedience happening across the region, regulatory changes with EPA, and lots of wins with litigation. So it was a very exciting time.[45]

Networks and Alliances

Although each of these strategies of action—local community development, community organizing and advocacy on strip mining, and civil disobedience and protest activity—are distinct, in practice, they represented cross-cutting networks and alliances. At the local level, individuals, especially the most active leaders, might be part of each. Within the Valley, TNACE itself has become a networking and coordinating body, linking local community development leaders with groups like SOCM and the Sierra Club, some of whom also participated in or had allied with the civil disobedience action. Rather than being separate strategies, the approaches described earlier gradually began to coalesce in their efforts to shift power. As these movements emerged, there was also increasing networking and alliance building across the region. KFTC and SOCM, for instance, became part of the Alliance for Appalachia, a network of fifteen organizations across five states in Central Appalachia launched in 2006 "to promote a healthy, just Appalachia, by supporting our member organizations in communities impacted by destructive resource extraction."[46]

The development of these networks, linking across issues and from local to regional to national levels, marked a sharp contrast to the isolated community organizing efforts of earlier years. Using in-depth mapping techniques, Robert Todd Perdue and Christopher McCarty traced the evolution of this "network of resistance" in Central Appalachia.[47] In the early 1990s, they find the key ties were between SOCM and KFTC. By 1999, other groups had entered the picture, in West Virginia and Ohio, but between 2005 and 2009, following the death of Jeremy Davidson in Virginia and the launch of Mountain Justice Summer, collaboration increased greatly. By 2010–11, the authors find a dense network of fifteen anti-strip-mining groups, who were relatively decentralized and collaborative in their approach, yet still worked closely together. Such density of organizing made a difference. As they go on to point out: "Success, in the form of affecting legislation and public awareness, is often more attainable in highly connected and dense networks, which this network has become over the last thirty years."[48]

Conclusion

In this chapter, we have traced the rise of citizen action in the Clearfork Valley and nearby communities from roughly the mid-1970s until the 2010–2020 period, when the coal industry, already slowly declining, did so more precipitously. Against the historical legacies of fear and domination and building as well on legacies of resistance in previous periods, strategies such as asset-based community development, community organizing, and direct civil disobedience gradually helped to give rise to a sense of "power within" among coalfield residents, as well as build more collective "power with" others in the Valley and across the region. With these there also emerged more direct challenges to the "power over" of the coal industry, seeking to hold it accountable for its historic practices related to the land, water, and community. In the context of the historical legacies of fear and internalized powerlessness, combined with current barriers and disincentives to participation, such actions were significant.

In terms of the model of power provided in chapter 3 (figure 3.1), these actions illustrate the steps of empowerment involved. First, small actions, focusing on building local capacities, helped to overcome legacies of powerlessness. Direct action media campaigns helped to build awareness of coalfield injustices more broadly (as in the third dimension of power). Collective organizing, legal actions, micro protests, and other tactics all helped to get these issues on the agenda, in local governments, state legislatures, Congress, regulatory agencies, and the courts (countering the second dimension of power). Through well-connected cross-regional organizing, mass actions as well as direct lobbying and advocacy led to some successful policy victories (first dimension of power), including on regulation of strip mining, unequal taxation of natural resources, and reclamation of mining lands.

Just as the dimensions of dominating power are reinforcing, so are these dimensions of empowerment, though not always in a linear fashion. Building awareness and a sense of power not only contributed to the possibilities of more direct community mobilizing, but in turn mobilizing itself helped overcome the internalized sense of powerlessness. The empowerment process spread horizontally across communities, where a victory in one place could inspire action in another, as we saw in the spread of micro-protests in the Valley. Vertical spread was also important. Policy gains at the national level, such as SMCRA, created and legitimated new entry points for organizing at the local level, in turn building more hope for change.

Of course, the growing movement for change was not without its setbacks and defeats. Though we have pointed to some successes drawn, other studies have shown how industry actions also led to successful "demobilization of environmental protest," through corporate tactics of controlling information, denying or obscuring the risks of mountaintop removal, concealing production sites, and isolating activists from community support.[49] The work by Shannon Elizabeth Bell on the challenges to micro-mobilization in *Fighting King Coal* also demonstrates ongoing issues of elite control, as well as the ongoing cultural manipulation of symbols like "insiders" and "outsiders," to delegitimate the movements' identity.[50] And as the timeline in figure 0.1 in the introduction reminds us, even as these movements were growing, so was the conservative right and the industry-led movements to protect coal.

However, as the mines began to close more rapidly in the period, and with a growing national awareness of the need to move beyond coal in the face of climate change, the issue at hand was no longer how to ameliorate the damages by the industry. It was now about what a post-coal future would be like once that industry was gone. But these groups would not start from scratch to face the new challenge. Perhaps one of the biggest contributions of this recent history of action in the coalfields was to provide a new baseline for action. From the quiescence of fifty years ago, we see well-organized, interlinked networks of actors now bringing previously suppressed issues and voices to the larger stage, and in so doing, challenging the "power over" long held by the coal industry. To face the uncertainties in the wake of coal's decline, as we shall see in the next chapter, would require a new kind of power—the "power for"—which could envision and enact a just transition. And in the context of the Biden administration which professed, unlike the Trump administration, to champion—not restrain—the struggle for environmental and economic justice, this power built from below would have the opportunity to engage even more in new initiatives from above.

8

Bottom Up Meets Top Down

A New Policy Moment?

There's more money out there than most communities know what to do with.
—Economic development staff person, 6 July 2021

Oh, it'll never make it down to the little guys like us . . .
—TNACE member, 12 January 2022

From about 2010, organizing in the coalfields began to shift from not only holding the industry accountable, but also to envisioning a post-coal future, often joining with an increasingly vocal national movement for a just transition. Partly in response, in 2021 President Joe Biden launched historic federal investments for a clean energy transition with mandates that the funding benefit communities historically at the receiving end of environmental and economic injustice. The programs specifically targeted "energy communities," including those in the Appalachian coalfields.

With hundreds of billions of federal dollars released, these initiatives brought the largest amount of federal funding to Appalachia since the War on Poverty of 1965. As discussed in chapter 1, the War on Poverty offered a set of top-down policies that, while incomplete and insufficient, provided opportunities for collective action and building power. Biden policies similarly offered top-down policies to address issues of injustice, bringing resources and mandates that grassroots groups could make use of to build power. Would communities and the institutions that mobilized against coal in the past, such as those discussed in chapter 7, be able to make use of these new political openings? Here we examine that question, illustrating the challenges and possibilities of connecting grassroots organizing from below with top-down policy initiatives, and drawing larger lessons about the difficult work of linking claimed and invited spaces, from the local to national levels.

While for many years mining had been increasingly declining, for reasons that we have seen there had been little public conversation or organizing around the transition to a more socially just and prosperous economic future. With the ideological control we saw in earlier periods, to even talk about life after coal was to admit that the coal industry and its power were waning. For communities affected by both economic decline and the destruction it left behind, there were two challenges: first, to get the issues of coal's decline and the industry's legacy on the political agenda, but also then to engage in a discursive struggle over what a new future might include. As demand for coal shifted and Appalachian coal mining contracted severely, the reality of coal's decline became unavoidably obvious, and the need for a new kind of activism followed suit. This required both mobilizing to get previously suppressed voices heard, building the "power to" as we saw in the previous chapter, but also developing a "power for," that is, to shape a vision of an alternative future (as discussed in chapter 3).

Although the language of a "just transition" away from extractive industries was being used in other parts of the country, questions of transition largely did not enter the discourse in Appalachia until the 2010s. Various nonprofit and state entities in the region have had economic diversification as their mission for decades, such as MACED (now the Mountain Association) in Kentucky and Appalachian Sustainable Development in Virginia, and notably the Appalachian Regional Commission, a federal agency. While there had also been nascent grassroots efforts in the early 2000s attempting to create political movement around the idea of a transition, many of these were peripheral to larger oppositional politics against MTR and coal industry domination.[1]

The Importance of "Power For": Creating a New Vision of Just Transition from Below

As the decline of the coal industry became more apparent to all around 2010–11, the spaces for new discourse emerged. Lisa Abbott, the director of KFTC, described the moment:

> Our members kept coming to us to say, we've got to be talking about more than just what we need to stop. We've got to be talking about the future that we need to build. And as the mountaintop removal issue became more and more polarized and weaponized, and the coal industry invested tens of millions of dollars locally in these local PR campaigns . . . the disinformation campaigns, the weaponization, the polarization.

> . . . Our members just said we have got to develop much more capacity as an organization to first help people envision the future that we want, and then figure out what are the policies that we need to go after to fight and win that can support that kind of future.

In 2011, emboldened by the direct-action campaigns against MTR, Abbott and thirteen other KFTC members had a sleep-in at the state capitol not only to protest the government's submissiveness to the coal industry but also to demand that the state start paying attention to a more diverse and sustainable future for the coalfields. In 2013, KFTC took the bold move to hold a three-day conference in Harlan County, Kentucky, the heart of Friends of Coal country, called Appalachia's Bright Future, to spark a public conversation about what a Just Transition for Appalachia might mean and what it would take.[2] That same year, they also helped to create a new national organization, the Climate Justice Alliance, a network of organizations across the country dedicated to moving "away from extractive systems of production, consumption, and political oppression, and towards resilient, regenerative, and equitable economies."[3]

KFTC joined forces with the Alliance for Appalachia, which around the same time were convening several forums to discuss its visions for a post-coal future, and also the strategies for achieving them.[4] Alliance members launched two participatory research projects, including a "listening project," to learn from some forty-five organizations in the region that were carrying out grassroots economic transition projects, and an "agency mapping project" to try and figure out entry points for engaging with state and federal agencies on policy agendas.[5]

In this way, KFTC and the Alliance for Appalachia used the capacities, networks, and awareness that opposing MTR and coal industry domination had built up to advance new narratives and counter-hegemonic discourses for a post-coal future. In turn, those movements and the increasingly blatant and rapid collapse of the coal economy pushed state policymakers to begin to shift their own discourse. Having resisted any public conversation to think about a post-coal economy, in 2013, as a response to plummeting coal jobs in eastern Kentucky and as an apparent response to the KFTC and Appalachian Alliance listening projects, the governor of Kentucky convened a gathering of business and government leaders through a Shaping Our Appalachian Region (SOAR) program. SOAR now meets annually "to help guide the flagging coal communities of Appalachian Kentucky into a new post-coal economy."[6]

As groups began to invent new discourses about the region and its future, various initiatives followed. In 2014, the Highlander Center in Tennessee established a series of Appalachian Transition Fellowships, which by 2019 had supported thirty-two emerging leaders and "88 Appalachian organizations across sectors and issues, boosting capacity for community-led projects advancing a 'just transition.'"[7] Similarly, the role of queer, LGBTQA, and nonbinary youth was critical in leading the work of envisioning a future beyond the masculinized jobs of coal miners. Spaces such as the Staying Together Appalachian Youth (STAY) Project, a group that supports young people to stay in the region and provides space for queer, Black, and other young people to find community, became infrastructures for such radical and visionary leaders to emerge.[8] In 2015, a group of donors founded the Just Transition Fund to support coal communities in economic distress, with a great deal of support going to Appalachia.[9]

With such support and networking, the region offered a rich array of civil society initiatives working for a just transition, with one source identifying ninety-eight initiatives led by seventy organizations during the 2010–2020 period in Central Appalachia alone.[10] In the absence of leadership by government or labor unions to ensure a healthy and sustainable transition to a new future, grassroots civil society organizations increasingly took on a "power for" approach.[11] The issue of post-coal and post-fossil-fuel futures, once hidden away from public debate, began to enter popular discourse and mainstream political agendas. Informed by a long history of participatory research as a knowledge and organizing strategy, the listening projects of Alliance for Appalachia, KFTC, and Highlander ensured that for the future, visions were based on local knowledge that was embedded in the lived experience of coalfield residents. As Lyndsay Tarus, Mary Hufford, and Betsy Taylor argue, "Post-carbon economic transition requires reclaiming forms of knowledge and power that are currently shaped by corporate-dominated government structures."[12]

Contested Narratives for a Just Transition

In organizing for a just transition, some of the most galvanizing campaigns around the region mobilized groups on issues of the environmental injustices of economic abandonment and fossil fuel decline. This included cleaning up the legacy pollution and devastation from coal and fossil fuel extraction, notably cleaning up abandoned mine lands (AML), dealing with mine reclamation issues, and capping "orphaned" gas wells. Many institutions also organized more expansively to envision how a post-coal future could be more just and equitable for Appalachia. Groups in the Clearfork Valley participated in both these campaigns, monitoring water quality and documenting pollution risks from coal mine sites that no longer were mining coal, as well as conducting years-long asset mapping projects to guide the priorities for development in a post-coal future.

Normative political discourse across the region also shifted to account for realities in coal employment. Through the 2010s and 2020s, economic transition became both normal political discourse and the basis for policy in Appalachia. In 2015, the Obama administration launched the Partnerships for Opportunity and Workforce and Economic Revitalization (POWER) program, providing funding to assist coal-dependent communities as the coal industry declined. By 2020, both candidates in the West Virginia governor's debate openly stated the need to plan beyond a coal economy.[13] In the senate races in Kentucky, policies for economic transition became a frequent media topic, particularly programs to support dislocated coal workers, including from long-time coal industry ally Mitch McConnell.[14]

Yet, while programs like SOAR and the POWER initiative put forward resources and plans for economic transition, these programs were frequently small and ineffective at catalyzing large changes. As Schwartzman argues elsewhere, this was largely because resources were allocated through neoliberal frameworks of supporting entrepreneurship and innovation (largely funding the private sector or ineffective worker training programs).[15] The limitations of that funding did not meet the goals and visions of community groups, who called for a different model of development. In juxtaposition, for instance, programs such as the Highlander Transition Fellowship focused on community-identified needs that went beyond jobs, to include "a concrete analysis and plan for an economic transition away from extractive industries, ecological devastation, profound wealth and health disparities, and scarcity mindsets around resources."[16]

These competing visions entailed a deeper contestation over what in fact "a just transition" means. The Highlander Center and many community-led projects across Appalachia argued that the goal must be social and economic transformation, not simply transition from one regime to another. The final report of Highlander's transition fellows program even challenges the limited usage of the term "transition" and is entitled "Beyond Transition: Appalachia's Pathway to Justice and Transformation." A note in the report explains:

> When we began the interview process, we used the term "just transition" for all of the interviews, questions, and project framing. As we moved through the interviews and reflected on the bigger picture, it became

> clear that community leaders are calling for a need to move beyond a "just transition" to something bigger, bolder, stronger, more innovative and with greater capacity for systemic change. While we refer to just transition in places throughout the text, we are also signifying the need to move beyond transition to transformation.[17]

The Highlander report points to debates in the just transition movement over the question "What forms of justice do we mean?"[18] In the introduction we defined these various kinds of justice, including *distributional* (who wins and loses), *procedural* (whose voices are heard), *recognitional* (whose values and identities are recognized), and *restorative* (how to rectify historic injustices or damage).[19] For those living in Central Appalachia, as well as other communities across the globe that face environmental damage from extractive industries, questions of restorative justice are particularly important. While planning for a future economy needs to be done, many in the region also want to see restoration of the denuded mountains and streams that decades of strip mining have left behind. As one veteran organizer described, while an earlier "movement moment" was "all around regulating the bad effects of the coal industry," now in the current moment "it's dealing with the aftereffects of the coal industry."[20]

This restorative justice approach to transition became a key feature of Appalachian community organizing following the 2014 gathering of the Alliance for Appalachia. Alliance members, around a dozen environmental justice community organizations across Central Appalachia, decided to focus energy on securing the funding and adequate federal policies to conduct widespread reclamation of abandoned mine lands, focusing on reinvigorating a federal program known as the Abandoned Mine Land fund. Established as part of the SMCRA Act in 1977, the purpose of the fund was to reclaim land and water damaged by pre-1977 mining. Alliance-led working groups pushed for reclaiming these lands as a way to create tens of thousands of jobs. The task of reclamation was no longer just an environmental issue but was also couched in the vision for just transition: "an economic transition is inevitable, and in that inevitability, communities see an opportunity to create a new economy that is sustainable and works by and for Appalachians."[21]

Taking up reclamation as a key issue, Alliance members pushed congressional representatives to craft legislation around AML and mine reclamation, drafting and promoting the RECLAIM (Revitalizing the Economy of Coal Communities by Leveraging Local Activities and Investing More) Act. In 2016, Kentucky congressman Hal Rogers introduced the bill, which, after five years of attempts get it passed, died in the Senate in 2021.[22]

Although RECLAIM did not become law, it did demonstrate the power of community groups to create visions of change located within a restorative justice framework and have them taken up and carried to the highest halls of power.

Unlike instances where failures to succeed in community organizing were often met with coal industry intimidation and worked to reinstill a sense of powerlessness, in the moment of severe coal industry decline in the 2010s, failure to pass RECLAIM did not end a growing just transition movement. One organizer from SOCM talked about mobilization around RECLAIM as one of the successes of organizing a just transition. As he said,

> This [bill] . . . literally came from the groups and the Alliance for Appalachia. And I have multiple times kind of served as the Tennessee state lead on lobby trips, helping people from communities with abandoned mine lands go and lobby in Washington on the need for this funding. And after years of keeping the pressure on in a way that I think was not community led, but definitely very community involved and coming from this plan that grassroots groups put forth through the Alliance, the infrastructure bill passed last year contained $11 billion of additional funding.[23]

The fight for RECLAIM became part of broader mobilizations around issues of restorative justice. In 2016 after years of lobbying and advocacy, this coalition was able to get some rule changes on stream protection, including rules against placing mining waste from mountaintop removal directly into streams and other key rule changes on the Clean Water Act.[24] Concerned that the rules would still not be enforced, an Appalachian Citizens Enforcement Project mobilized "citizen water testers" across the region. Despite Congress overturning the rule in 2017 under President Donald Trump, in the Clearfork Valley a TNACE water task force coordinated by the Southern Connected Communities Project still routinely monitors the pollution from mine runoff in the stream, reporting findings to authorities and demanding enforcement of broader clean water regulations.

Nonprofits and groups also mobilized around the consequences of coal industry bankruptcies across the region. The Surface Mining Control and Reclamation Act (SMCRA) of 1977 had allowed companies to post less-than-full-cost bonds, and use pool-bonds (only paying in a portion to a larger pool), and self-bonds (using their own equipment as collateral).[25] As companies go bankrupt, as they are increasingly doing, the risks that the less-than-full-cost bonds would fail to cover the extensive costs of reclaiming large areas of land were mounting. The Alliance conducted a listening project to decide what to do about the looming "bondpocalyse" and how to provide their own policy solutions, including creating jobs and economies in the region.[26]

As part of a larger fight for a just transition, alternatives to the bonding crisis illustrated the new "power for," and a commitment to a restorative justice approach. For instance, in the Clearfork Valley, members of the TNACE coalition conducted citizen inspections of strip mine sites to ensure that adequate reclamation was to be done. As one organizer with Sierra Club and part of TNACE recounted, on "the Clearfork surface mine. . . . We got a bond release denied. . . . And we did that because for years . . . the Clearfork water project has been monitoring bond releases. . . . And one outcome of engagement was the reclamation was not adequate on the site to release the bond."[27]

As Trump came to power in 2016, despite rhetoric about bringing back coal, mobilizations for a just transition were already well underway. Regional groups, like the Alliance for Appalachia and Appalachian Voices, had clearly proven the demand for transition policy, and grassroots groups had formed strong networks and coalitions around these issues. When Joe Biden was elected in 2020, the political opportunity for new funding and reforms reflected the growing demand for transition policy, and with decades of advocacy behind them, these groups were hopeful they could make use of these policies.

Linking Bottom-up and Top-down Organizing

In 2021, the Biden administration issued Executive Order 14008, "Tackling the Climate Crisis at Home and Abroad,"[28] mandating the Justice40 Initiative, "a goal that 40 percent of the overall benefits of certain Federal climate, clean energy, affordable and sustainable housing, and other investments flow to disadvantaged communities that are marginalized by underinvestment and overburdened by pollution."[29] In addition, Justice40 was committed "to center communities overburdened by pollution, on the frontlines of climate impacts, and marginalized by decades of underinvestment."[30] These policies became important first with the passage of the Bipartisan Infrastructure Law (BIL) in 2021, and then with the passage of the Inflation Reduction Act (IRA) in 2022, both laws that brought hundreds of billions of federal funding for new infrastructure that tackles climate change and a rapid energy transition, with the goal of "50–52 percent reduction from 2005 levels in economy-wide net greenhouse gas pollution in 2030."[31]

The federal provisions targeted economically "disadvantaged" communities, "energy communities," and places facing environmental justice concerns, including coal communities. As Biden said at the executive order signing ceremony, "We're never going to forget the men and women who dug the coal and built the nation. We're going to do right by them and make sure they have opportunities to keep building the nation in their own communities and getting paid well for it."[32] By the end of 2024, these investments had already begun to flow, with the Interagency Working Group on Coal and Power Plant Communities and Economic Revitalization announcing that "a massive infusion of federal investments is now beginning to flow to America's energy communities—in excess of $20.79 billion just since the start of 2021. Currently, more than $500 billion is available in open/planned funding and tax credit opportunities."[33]

The programs were potentially transformational for Appalachia, and not simply in scale of investment. Among other things, the legislation included authorization of $11.3 billion of Abandoned Mine Land Funding, which the Alliance for Appalachia had long called for, to clean up mine lands using high labor standards. More, broadly, the Justice40 order and the directives to federal agencies provided openings through which communities could mobilize to access some of these resources, as the new policies "directed Federal agencies with Justice40 covered programs to conduct meaningful engagement to ensure community members have the opportunity to provide input on program decisions, including in the identification of the benefits of Justice40 covered programs, engage 'disadvantaged communities,' generate benefits to communities, and support high quality jobs."[34] Frequently, federal agency staff directed grant recipients to create opportunities for "two-way engagement," where people affected by projects should be able to provide feedback and participate in decisions about "community benefits."

These Biden policies presented new opportunities for mobilization from below. As Jonathan Fox and colleagues found in his research on the "sandwich model" of how top-down state actors create openings for collective action from previously excluded groups,[35] the Biden agenda provided an impetus for collective action for grassroots coalitions in Central Appalachia. In this way, bottom-up mobilizations and top-down reforms worked together to build momentum for action, creating conditions that strengthened the position of various civic groups to make claims upon the new resources and put forward new proposals for what a just transition would look like.

For instance, in response to this new policy moment, novel organizations emerged in 2020, such as Reimagine Appalachia, an Ohio River Valley–focused regional coalition presenting new policy avenues for a just transition. The new policies created the conditions to strengthen organized labor, as unions mobilized around the promise that the new federal investments would engage labor organizations and use high labor standards for all work. In East Tennessee, for instance, the Labor at the Table group, a project of East Tennessee Jobs with Justice brought unions and civil society organizations, such as the Woodland Community Land Trust in the Clearfork Valley, together to make concrete plans for how to access and use the new federal investments to achieve collective goals. Across the region some civic groups were able to access substantial resources early on. These were often some of the most well-established and already well-funded organizations, such as Coalfield Development in West Virginia, which received $62.8 million from the Build Back Better Challenge in 2022.

Mobilizing around Biden Funding and "Community Benefits"

Activists saw opportunities to advance local priorities through the new Biden agenda, but there were clearly barriers to accessing the new programs for small, grassroots groups. For instance, in April of 2022 state-level officials from United States Department of Agriculture (USDA) Rural Development came to the Clearfork Community Institute to hold a public meeting about its funding. There, the state director announced that since the area had been underserved by the United USDA's Rural Development programs (i.e., received less percentages of funding than neighboring census tracts per capita), they were prioritized for USDA grants. Despite promises to follow up, however, no details were provided nor were future meetings held to facilitate or prioritize entities or individuals in the Valley for making use of these funds. No USDA Rural Development funding came to the Valley from 2022 to 2024. The experience with USDA was, in many ways, indicative of a larger shift in discourse from federal and state partners toward greater inclusion, but without fundamental changes in how grants were allocated.

Similarly, in December of 2022, TNACE members found out about and attended a public conference held at Oak Ridge National Laboratory about the Department of Energy's Office of Clean Energy Demonstration (OCED), Clean Energy on Mine Lands grant program. There, entities like The Nature Conservancy and solar firms gave presentations on successful experiences with energy projects on mine lands. OCED's energy justice liaison defined environmental justice and energy justice for the group, stating both would be prioritized in the funding. As proposals were intended to be roughly $100 million with a 50 percent match, TNACE members quickly realized they would not be receiving the funding because of this high dollar match. Despite state interests in energy and environmental justice, by design only corporations with many hundred-million-dollar or billion-dollar operating budgets would receive these funds. These invited spaces were largely ceremonial and not arenas where grassroots entities either received resources, recognition, or room to enact their plans for regional development, because decision making happened elsewhere.

TNACE members did find openings to advance their visions of just transition around the new AML funds, a provision they considered the result of their advocacy efforts over decades. They redoubled their efforts to map Abandoned Mine Lands in the Valley and put pressure on the state to have Valley communities prioritized for receipt of some of the new funds. In the summer of August 2023, TNACE organized an open-house community meeting with the Tennessee Department of Environment and Conservation (TDEC), the state agency administering AML funds in the Valley. TDEC presenting to an open forum of Clearfork residents was a rarity. TDEC shared that they were looking for new sites to reclaim, an exciting possibility for TNACE. Yet, TDEC also shared that its plan for community engagement was a new website, not future meetings or avenues for dialogue or discussion with communities, raising concerns from TNACE members that TDEC's relationship to communities would once again be unidirectional: providing information, not practicing two-way engagement. However, the new AML funding also expanded the scope of local coalitions. It came with a promise of requiring federal prevailing wage standards, which would allow well-paid union contractors to bid on the AML cleanup work. SOCM organizer Adam Hughes and other TNACE members worked with the Teamsters Union Local 519, based in Knoxville, to pressure TDEC to make the bidding processes accessible to union contractors. This work brought labor partners to join TNACE for the first time in its more than ten-year history.

Throughout 2023 and 2024, TNACE members continued to mobilize to pursue new federal funding opportunities. TNACE received technical assistance from the Recreational Economies for Rural Communities program, a federally funded planning assistance program to help communities grow their outdoor recreation economies. Through the planning process, TNACE coalition members brought together local stakeholders to draft a bottom-up plan of how a recreation economy could benefit their community and address issues that had arisen several years before in their mapping project. In 2023, many of the federal funding applications were announced with only a few months' notice, giving little time to prepare.

In 2024, however, using the planning processes they had conducted, TNACE groups applied for and were awarded a Department of Energy (DOE) SolveIt Prize of $80,000, an award for stakeholders to conduct further planning for community-based solutions for clean energy. TNACE groups, led by Woodland Community Land Trust, also applied for and were awarded a DOE Capacity Building for Repurposing Energy Assets award, bringing $100,000 for planning for new energy and workforce projects in the area. Woodland Community Land Trust, additionally, with the support of TNACE partners, received an Appalachian Regional Commission POWER grant for outdoor recreation asset planning, of $50,000, although much of it was allocated to contractors. Compared to the $20-plus billion spent in energy communities from 2021 to 2024, these were tiny awards; however, the funds made a big difference in how organizers in the Valley were able to spend their time and plan for larger projects.

Power in "Cramped" Spaces

The Biden administration funding became a site of contestation over whose voices will be heard and who will benefit—questions of recognitional and distributional justice. While the mandates from the Biden administration for community engagement and community benefit opened spaces for participation, our research found that these were also "cramped spaces," to draw on a term that Lauren Berlant uses, building upon the work of Gilles Deleuze. They were limited in who could participate and what activists and movements were able to contest or demand.[36]

A key indicator of who benefits in this contestation was evidenced in who received the funding. Appalachian coal mining communities are high on the list of census tracts that are eligible, but as we have seen in the Clearfork Valley, much of the funding was not available to organizations and civic groups based in or represented by residents of mining communities. Funds that reached places affected by coal's decline, like the Valley, were generally minuscule compared to the billions granted, loaned, or provided as tax credits to private industry contractors building clean energy infrastructure. We argue this is because of the power dynamics surrounding the BIL and IRA investments.

In the first dimension of power (introduced in chapter 3), coal and fossil fuel politicians directly intervened to ensure the clean energy investments supported some fossil fuel sectors, such as methane gas, and that the requirements of programs, such as community benefits plans, would not unsettle arrangements of elite control. The initial funding came first from the BIL of 2021, that brought $550 billion in direct investments and

$1.2 trillion in new spending to attend to infrastructure needs. This initial investment was significantly aided by the narrow passage in 2022 of the IRA, for which West Virginia senator Joe Manchin was the deciding vote, a huge bill estimated to involve $891 billion and containing a variety of budget revisions directed at climate change–related investments. Within this highly divided setting, Manchin played a pivotal role, both blocking the most ambitious parts of the Biden administration's agenda, what Manchin dubbed Biden's "radical climate agenda," while including provisions for the gas industry, such as "blue" hydrogen technology and carve-outs for fossil fuel industries to use unproven carbon capture, utilization, and storage technology.[37] Manchin, personally tied to various coal companies and interests,[38] had long served as a champion for coal and other fossil fuel interests in the US Senate (see chapter 4). His ability to shape the Biden policies, as well as those of the fossil fuel lobbies and Republican colleagues that supported Manchin, exemplified the ability of old power elites to retain power through a transition. Furthermore, Manchin and his coalition typified the kind of political strong-arming that kept Biden policies from being more focused on public and community ownership and broader participation in decision making.

In addition, the operation of the second dimension of power, the setting of the rules of the game or the mobilization of bias (as introduced in chapter 3), meant that certain actors were acceptable recipients of the funding, while many community-based grassroots groups were not. While federal mandates for environmental justice came from above, the policies were delivered through existing federal agency policies for grant-making and through state and regional offices, complicated bureaucracies that favored the large companies and nonprofits usually able to access federal funding. Furthermore, those implementing the programs often did not wholeheartedly buy into the Biden agenda, if they were not outright critical of some of the goals of environmental justice, as Jill Harrison previously found in the EPA and state environmental agencies.[39]

More importantly, the funding that arrived in the coalfields in the 2020s largely came to private sector actors. For example, the DOE's Clean Energy on Mine Lands program invested $500 million in private companies to develop clean energy on formerly mined lands. Unlike the War on Poverty's "maximum feasible participation of poor people," the Justice40 Initiative had directives that investments like the Mine Lands program *benefit* "disadvantaged communities," but no requirements that the programs allow them to participate in decision making or direction of resources. The main avenue for community engagement in the incoming funding was through "community benefits plans," required on most DOE funds.

These plans required that a grantee form a plan for how to benefit the community, informed by a process of engagement. Yet, without control of funding or ability to direct the benefits planning processes, these were narrow, limited openings for mobilization.

The third dimension of power, that is, the operation of hegemony (introduced in chapter 3) also worked to close the possibility of certain contests even arising or to narrow the imagination of what is possible. For instance, one EPA staffer tasked with implementing environmental justice mandates with whom the authors met reported seeing few applications come from areas designated as disadvantaged.[40] This may be because of limited expectations arising from years of government neglect and exclusion. The epigraph in the beginning of this chapter helps illustrate this dimension: as one nonprofit leader in the Clearfork Valley said of the Biden funding, "Oh, it'll never make it down to the little guys like us." Despite a decade of mobilizations around just transition, many people remained unconvinced that federal funding could actually reach grassroots and community-led struggles. Others feared that their institutions would not be able to put together the requisite applications to access these funds. Over time, however, as organizations in the Valley put more applications together and received $230,000 in 2024, skepticism about accessing larger resources started to shift.

The promise of new funding also propelled new alliances to emerge. The presence of the Claiborne County Commissioner for the Valley on the Recreational Economies project steering committee marked the first time a local elected official had been so involved with a TNACE project. Historically, many local officials had considered many of the activist organizations affiliated with TNACE, such as SOCM and Sierra Club, as outside environmentalists, not potential collaborators. Similarly, the work of the Labor at the Table group and the presence of Teamster representatives working with TNACE indicated new possibilities for organized labor and community alliances to grow out of this policy moment.

Overall, the presence of the new federal funds also impelled groups like TNACE to build concrete plans for how to enact a just transition. This work positioned groups like TNACE to become involved as secondary beneficiaries of the new federal investments. Within the Biden investments, as mentioned above, "community benefits" were intended to flow to grassroots groups through community benefits plans that are often required when companies receive these federal funds. These community benefit plans provided clear openings not only for community input on projects, but also more broadly as vehicles to advance community priorities. Grassroots organizations across Appalachia mobilized and demanded to be included in the growing number of community benefits plans. In 2024, TNACE members reached out to federal staff tasked with environmental and energy justice. They lodged concerns about not being included in federal funding allocations for environmental justice, which prompted federal staff to invite TNACE groups to apply for certain awards. Consultation with environmental justice staff became an invited space from which to push for further recognition and inclusion. Other groups, such as Appalachian Citizens Law Center in Kentucky, worked with private industry actors that want better community benefit plans. Appalachian Voices, a regional nonprofit, took on equitable community involvement in community benefit plans and federal funding as a key goal in 2024.

Furthermore, in addition to community benefits, some TNACE groups in the Valley saw major funding from BIL and IRA as potential vehicles to create lasting investments in community-owned infrastructure, despite the reticence that others in the Valley felt about the possibility of even receiving this funding. Accessing multimillion-dollar awards requires building large coalitions, but encouraged by their small successes, the Land Trust began working with Appalachian Voices and many partners, such as the University of Tennessee, to apply for millions of dollars to build community-owned utility-scale solar. This would have provided the Land Trust a permanent source of electricity for low-income residents and a source of income for the institution. TNACE groups also worked to build coalitions to put solar on vital community infrastructure, mitigate flood risks associated with climate change, and start worker training programs that would feed into union apprenticeship programs, to secure good high-paying jobs for local people.

Conclusion: Finding New Pathways

As with the resounding effects of the War on Poverty in Appalachia and across the United States, the Biden agenda had potential for long-lasting effect. The recognitional politics of Justice40 and the language around community benefits provided invited spaces in which community groups could take part. These spaces created a building action, enabling groups to see their ability to make change and pushing them to further detail and develop a grassroots vision for a just transition and deepen their demands on state actors. Though the compounding forces of power in the first, second, and third dimensions made this moment of transition politically cramped, at the same time being able to access even small pieces of the Biden investments provided an opportunity for groups to continue to develop "power for," authoring narratives and visions for the Valley.

As Fox and colleagues report from other cases, we also find that "*sometimes* invited spaces created from above can be claimed and transformed from below."[41] As we have detailed, those spaces that brought resources from the Biden investments to grassroots actors, notably around incentives for funded projects to use organized labor and less restricted micro-grants for capacity building of small organizations, bolstered further collective organizing for social change on the ground. In areas where resources did not reach the grassroots, such as in the mandates for community benefits plans that do not require local input or involvement, the ability to use the current policies for social transformation was more limited.

Biden policies illustrated the contradictions and political constraints of the moment. As the largest public investments in US history since the War on Poverty, a set of fundamentally "green" Keynesian-style reforms, the Biden policy agenda came as both an expansion of an activist state seeking to rectify longstanding inequities, but also was tied up, and actively politically held back by antipublic, private sector-led strategies for economic development. As a compromise, the Biden agenda appeared to contend that a transition to clean energy would be publicly funded but privately implemented. Indeed, while the War on Poverty mandated for a brief period the "maximum feasible participation" of the poor in the development of antipoverty programs, many of these more recent initiatives limited community engagement to the discussion of downstream "community benefits" from programs led by private actors.

This policy landscape, however, was fragile. With the reelection of Donald Trump, and the ideological and political support to return to the old order, many of these openings were rapidly closed. In 2024, Trump pledged to "terminate the Green New Deal," and among his first executive orders was freezing all allocation of IRA funding.[42] In the first few months of the administration, Trump's regime quickly stalled or defunded projects that received federal money aimed at supporting environmental justice, disadvantaged communities, clean energy, decarbonization, and climate change mitigation.[43] Yet, where funding was already allocated, numerous projects remain underway. For these, however, the requirement to use community benefits plans or to allocate resources to disadvantaged communities no longer exist, and much uncertainty exists around the ability to access promised tax credits for clean energy and community and union participation. Seemingly overnight, the Biden agenda has been undone and the limited openings that came with it erased. In the interregnum between a coal-based and post-coal economy, the struggles for a new hegemony are raging.

CONCLUSION

An Interregnum between Past and Future?

> The crisis consists precisely in the fact that the old is dying and the new cannot be born; in this interregnum a great variety of morbid symptoms appear.
>
> —Antonio Gramsci, *Selections from the Prison Notebooks*

This book is about power, energy transitions, and how the two interact. In particular, it is about the contemporary challenge of how to make the transition away from fossil fuels to new forms of energy a just and inclusive one. By transition, we mean not simply the technical process of how to shift from one energy source to another (such as from coal to solar) but more fundamentally how we challenge and transform the forms of social, economic, political, and ideological power upon which the fossil fuel industry is built, and to which it is has deeply contributed. For communities whose histories have been shaped by extractive economies for over a century, such transitions are particularly profound.

Taking an in-depth grounded view, we have focused on how the dynamics of power have changed in one place at the front lines of this transition—a rural former mining valley spanning parts of Kentucky and Tennessee in the heart of the US Central Appalachian Region, which was historically the country's largest source of coal. We have explored several key questions: What happens to power relations when the extractive fossil fuel economy on which they are historically based declines? How do previously dominant actors struggle to hold on or adapt? What new actors emerge, and with what sorts of power? Does the decline of one order and the emergence of another create new spaces for previously suppressed and marginalized groups to gain more voice and control over their futures?

In this concluding chapter, we synthesize and elaborate further on what we have learned. While arguing that these questions must be grounded in the context of a single place, where we can see more concretely how multiple competing forces intersect, we also suggest that from this study of place we can draw broader lessons about the nature of power itself, and how it affects the possibilities of a just transition to a post–fossil fuel world.

Power and transition, we have argued, are mutually constitutive—each affects the other. Power relations condition the possibilities and shape of a just transition, affecting who benefits, who participates, and whose voices matter. But simultaneously the shift away from fossil-fuel–based economies changes the nature of power, moving it from a political economy based on extraction of natural resources that required local control of land and labor, to new forms of creating value, based more on the financialization of nature, and often centered in more distant financial markets. Without attention to power, a transition may occur from one set of elites to another, or from one political economic arrangement to another, without a more fundamental transformation of the underlying social and political order.

We have also argued that energy transitions, and the new landscapes of power that emerge within them, can be a period of what Gramsci and neo-Gramscian scholars call an "interregnum," the time *between* settled hegemonies that offers new possibilities and strategies for political action. We have drawn further upon the work of Gramsci to consider how political coalitions and hegemony—the arrangement of power—shift as economic, political, and social forces link up in new ways—that is, in what we have called novel *conjunctures*. The current conjuncture is one of interregnum between settled hegemonies. In Central Appalachia, the former hegemonic order was based around the political economy of coal extraction. Lines of contestation were clear, as were the arrangements of power. Now, as the old hegemonic order gives way, new actors and new contestations about the vision of a new future may emerge.

In such a period, when the new contours of power may not yet be entirely clear, the contours of previously more hidden and invisible forms of power become more exposed, potentially opening new pathways for action. Even as technologies and economies shift, changes in power relations do not immediately or automatically follow. Incumbent powers in the old regime struggle to hold on; new actors inherit or repurpose previous patterns of domination; internalized powerlessness among those long dominated by the old order also lingers, unless and until it gradually erodes as the limits of action are tested and confidence and capacities for collective action are rekindled and restored. When this begins to happen, especially when new openings from above and new mobilizations from below begin to align, significant change may happen quickly.

In the following pages, we elaborate on these points further. First, we revisit the Clearfork Valley and discuss how the broader political economies shaping it have changed over the decades. Then we reflect further on what we have learned about power, particularly in reference to our questions about how incumbent power holders cling on, how new forms of power emerge with new actors, and within these changes what new forms of mobilizations for empowerment have occurred. We revisit the consequences of these for just transition. And finally, we conclude by suggesting that we need to understand these changes on a larger canvas of a shift between conjunctures, which will have profound implications for sustainability and justice in this Valley as well as in other places at the front lines of transition around the world.

The Importance of Place

How transition occurs, what it looks like, and how power plays out in the process depends very much on both local context and how it is shaped by broader political economic structures. Who will participate, and in what spaces, will look different in communities with greater equality or histories of civic participation than in those places where the transition to a new future starts on an uneven playing field, based on the legacies of inequality, environmental damage, and asymmetric power relations left behind by an old order.

The Clearfork Valley falls in the latter category. Here, as we discussed in chapter 1, the closure of the mining industry has left in its wake enormous poverty and joblessness, as well as damaged land and streams from over fifty years of destructive mining practices. The process of disinvestment has hollowed out communities, with few new jobs, a declining tax base, weakening infrastructures, and a loss of public space. Such communities became fertile ground for other corporate predators, including, in this case, pharmaceutical companies, which have foisted opioid and drug dependency upon the residents as solutions to their pain, and as another way to extract corporate profit.

Such changes are highly racialized and gendered, with the relatively few historic Black communities in the coalfields being among the first to lose their jobs and homes in the process of change. While mining jobs were largely held by men, the new jobs that are emerging, in the lower-wage service or healthcare sector, are largely held by women. The miners' union, once a source of countervailing power to corporate control, is severely weakened, the result of a deliberate corporate campaign to do so.

As in other deindustrialized communities across the United States, these changes have also created fertile ground for the rise of authoritarian forms of politics, which play upon economic resentment, as well as racial and gendered identities, to deepen polarization and fear.[1]

The changes in the Valley are situated within a broader political economy, which has shifted dramatically over time. As we discussed in chapter 2, the period of coal's domination was ushered in through an "agrarian transition" in the late nineteenth century, where industrial elites fought agrarian elites for control of legal, political, and economic systems, to shift an agrarian economy into a site of industrial extraction. The subsequent century saw hegemonic control by the coal industry of Central Appalachian politics, economy, and culture, with much of the economic life of the Valley defined by the global political economy of coal for electricity.

Mechanization and strip mining required dramatically fewer miners than hand loading, and the number of miners dramatically fell in Appalachia from the 1950s onward. As the demand for Appalachian "steam" coal steadily declined after the 2000s, the result of depleting accessible stocks, Clean Air Act regulation that favored coal mining in western states, and Obama-era clean powerplant rules, jobs and investments left the region. The political economic landscape in Appalachia had also shifted from worker-heavy industries, such as resource extraction, to financialized rentier economies, such as land and resource speculation. While speculation was certainly not new, novel formats for financial speculation on minerals, fossil fuels, land, timber, biodiversity, and forest carbon emerged from the 2000s to the 2020s. As the coal industry continued to collapse, we witnessed the beginning of a new period of transition, one that is marked by an interregnum between the hegemonic order of the coal industry and whatever comes next.

Changing Power Relationships

Broader political economies also shape the nature of power. In examining power relations, we have returned to the frame of three dimensions of power first developed by Steven Lukes[2] and then elaborated by Gaventa in his earlier book on the Clearfork Valley (see chapter 3). As a reminder of this framework, the first dimension of power (also called "visible" power) focuses on who prevails on public issues that do arise and involves examining who participates and who wins in the public arena. The second dimension ("hidden" power) focuses on how issues and voices are kept off the agenda in the first place, through the use of symbols, procedures, and a generalized "mobilization of bias." The third dimension is about more "invisible" forms of power that affect whether and how people perceive an issue or grievance in the first place, and focuses on dominant narratives, ideologies, and beliefs and how they are instilled. Over time, these forms of power reinforce each other, yet when one form begins to crack, other forms may step in to maintain hegemony. In earlier chapters, all three forms of power have been seen as older fossil fuel actors seek to protect the status quo, as new power holders emerge, and as new mobilizations from below occur.

Entrenched Power Holders Cling On

A key lesson from this work is that existing power holders—the coal industry and associated elites—do not simply fade away even as their industry declines. As we examined in chapter 4, as the material base of their power lessens, they use multiple ways to cling on to their power. Initially, as in the first dimension of power, the industry poured huge amounts of funding into support for their allies in the state and federal governments, and then relied upon this network to continue to protect their interests and to discourage the development of alternative forms of energy. At the congressional levels, this also involved mobilizing historically built alliances with influential figures, including the Senators Mitch McConnell of Kentucky and Joe Manchin of West Virginia, both of whom had longstanding links to the coal industry. Even as space opened up under the Obama and Biden administrations for funding to support energy transitions, fossil fuel industry power was used to ensure that much of it still benefitted their fossil fuel allies, going into projects such as natural gas-to-hydrogen (so-called blue hydrogen) and carbon capture technology on fossil fuel production, in effect technical solutions to prolong the life of fossil fuels; and related industries, such as chemical complexes in Appalachia. They also helped to overlay spaces for participation by affected communities with sets of rules and procedures that led to more "cramped spaces" of engagement, rather than possibly more transformative ones, as we saw in chapter 8.

While shoring up political support, the industry also did what it could to keep issues of climate change or transition off the public agenda in the first place, and to preempt challenges to its even waning power, as in the second dimension of power. As chapter 4 described, a key strategy was the systematic destruction of the United Mine Workers of America, once the major countervailing force to challenge the industry and hold it accountable. Companies also used bankruptcies and various forms of corporate restructuring to hide their accountability behind a maze of legal processes and corporate shields. Even as it was declining in the face of market forces, the industry also sought to blame and discredit others who challenged it, labeling environmental activists as "outsiders," "tree huggers," "un-American," or threatening them with violence.

Each of these forms of power was shored up by another resource involving control of knowledge and discourse, as in the third dimension of power. In the first instance, the industry narrative sought to deny the realities of climate change, or the role of coal emissions within it, and therefore to preempt the need for public discussion about a post-coal future. As challenges to this denial emerged, the coal industry mobilized an intense PR campaign, using media, donations, and wielding of popular symbols to create a highly influential Friends of Coal movement, followed by the War on Coal campaign, which focused on attacking those who challenged coal hegemony. In so doing, the industry effectively shifted the discourse from one in which the interests of workers and community were often seen in tension with those of the corporate land and mine owners, to one in which they were ideological allies who need to work together to protect against attacks from outside others.

In addition, second and third dimensions of power worked to limit the narratives about the possibilities of alternative futures for the region. A sense that there was no possible economy other than fossil fuel extraction remained pervasive, a narrative foreclosure that development agencies, such as the Appalachian Regional Commission and others, worked to reinforce by the highly limited scope of what they would fund as economic development.

The efforts by the declining coal industry to desperately cling on to power were deeply intertwined by another ideological force: the growing support of right-wing, climate change–denying, often religious conservatism, which found a champion in Donald Trump and the promise to Make Coal Great Again, and more broadly to Make America Great Again (as seen in chapter 5). The rising movement was heavily funded by the fossil fuel industry, which poured millions into supporting conservative Republican deflection and denial of climate change. They simultaneously deftly deployed racialized and gendered tropes to shape attitudes and beliefs, appealing to images of masculinity, invoking a nostalgic image of a (largely white) past, blaming decline on often racialized others (e.g., immigrants), and using rhetoric of resource nationalism and Christianity to link the protection of coal to the love of God and country.[3]

Such third-dimensional efforts to maintain coal industry hegemony worked for a while, but gradually, despite the efforts to cling on, cracks and fissures began to emerge. Part of this was due to the gap between the rhetoric being deployed and the realities workers and communities faced on the ground as mines continued to close, and the environmental tolls of destructive mining practices became more visible. Also, beneath the politics and rhetoric of the industry, the ownership structure of the land was also changing, as the coal industry gradually disinvested and new owners began to appear.

Changing Ownership and the Rise of New Actors

As we discussed in chapter 6, as part of this trend, which began as early as the 1980s, natural resources increasingly became fragmented, with surface rights, mineral rights, oil and gas rights, even reclamation bonds, all being separated from one another and bought and sold in various speculative markets. This form of ownership, we argue, represents a new form of financialization of resources, "a pattern of accumulation in which profits accrue primarily through financial channels, rather than through trade and commodity production"[4] and of "rentierism," an accumulation strategy that relies on increasing rents, or the income derived from the control of access to a scarce resource or asset, rather than using labor to produce commodities for sale.[5]

An example of the new ownership structures is The Nature Conservancy's Cumberland Forest Project, the land deal comprising most of the former mining lands in the Valley (as seen in chapter 6). The project aims to generate sizable revenues for financial investors, illustrating both rentierism and financialization. TNC aims to sell carbon credits, promote tourism, lease land for sustainable timbering, secure conservation easements on the land, and lease former mines to solar developers, all to produce returns on these investments through conservation rather than extraction of natural resources. The size and scope of the project makes it one of the largest and most ambitious of such private equity investments for conservation purposes in the country.

With the new forms of ownership and strategies of accumulation also came new forms and dynamics of power. While the coal industry had historically built much of its power locally through the development and control of "coal camps," in which their workers resided, this new model had less need for labor, and indeed for the community infrastructure that supported laborers in the past. Increasingly, sites of power and decision-making were more distant, in relatively unknown and obscure carbon and financial markets, or through intermediaries, such as the state agencies to which land rights were now sold to manage recreation areas. Rather than TNC, the state now would collect the rents from tourists and natural amenity users (in the form of permits for hunting and riding trails). As is the case in many nature reserves around the world, residents perceived that their access to the forest was now more guarded and gated than in the past. With financialization and fragmentation of various resources and income streams, power also became more fragmented, and those to be held accountable more diffuse.

Delving further, though, we also can see the three dimensions of power at work here. First, on the third-dimensional "invisible" end of the spectrum, this new model of land ownership and accumulation brings with it a new ideological discourse, which focuses on the protection of nature, rather than the conquering of nature through extraction of its resources. Often promoted under the banner of "nature-based solutions," the new ideology seeks to marry the possibilities of climate goals with making profits, part of what is often termed "green capitalism." TNC has been an early proponent of this market-driven approach and has participated in various national and international venues to drive this vision forward. Presenting itself as "green," protecting biodiversity, supporting climate change, the vision is assumed to be a "good thing," much as the transformation of ownership in the last century, where agrarian communities' lands were taken over for extraction, was justified as necessary for "progress" and "development" of a so-called "backward" area.

In the second dimension, which has to do with how power shapes issues and concerns that do arise through what we term "hidden power," TNC prides itself at being transparent and open. Indeed, in doing research for this book we found TNC staff very willing to meet, share information, and when encouraged to do so, to meet with members of the community. And yet, even openness also has its limits, which serves to keep certain issues and voices more hidden. For instance, information about the investors in the Cumberland Forest Project or the income streams gained in this new model is still obscure. When asked, TNC and NatureVest simply said that it is customary to maintain confidentiality of the partners in an investment structure such as this, and that TNC is required to maintain such confidentiality. Complex and diffuse forms of ownership carry with them complex, diffuse, and often opaque lines of transparency and accountability.

Power is also manifest in whose voices and views TNC chooses to seek out, and to whom they choose to listen. Although TNC was proactive in holding initial consultation meetings about the project, these were often with more elite groups of elected officials, or mainstream environmental groups, with little effort (to our knowledge) to involve the more marginalized groups most directly affected by the previous mining practices on these lands. In drawing up plans for the site, technical expert knowledge was used, with little consultation with grassroots groups who had deep local knowledge of the land and biodiversity within it. As questions did begin to emerge from grassroots communities affected by the Cumberland Forest Project, to their credit representatives of TNC and NatureVest met to hear their concerns. Yet while TNC maintains openness to engage with broad members of the public, when disagreements emerge, certain boundaries or limits to this openness may emerge. When critical questions did begin to be raised by various community groups about the Cumberland Forest Project, we witnessed efforts to put boundaries around the dialogue, for instance, by TNC requesting that certain groups or individuals be excluded.

Finally, in the first dimension of power, we see TNC using its advocacy and resources to mobilize political influence over rules and policies that support and protect its approach to development. On its board sit influential politicians and policymakers, and TNC has connections with some of the most powerful corporations in the world as well. Throughout the year, its staff and members visit Congress advocating for legal frameworks and policies around biodiversity, clean energy, and conservation, and are one of the highest spenders on advocacy efforts among the large international environmental NGOs. Unlike the increasingly partisan positions taken by the coal industry, TNC promotes its approach as "Science-based. Practical. Nonpartisan." Yet, as we have seen, whose knowledge and voices shape these policy recommendations can itself be a power-laden process.

Mobilization from Below

As we have seen, with the decline of King Coal, not only do power holders in the waning regime work to cling on to power, but new actors also begin to enter the scene, bringing different ownership structures and different styles of power. In this period of change, as fissures in the previous order widen, new spaces and opportunities emerge for previously marginalized groups to act and think in new ways. However, the opening up of new spaces and opportunities does not mean that they will automatically be filled by new voices. Just as legacies of domination do not quickly fade away when the material base changes, neither do legacies of internalized powerlessness, which have arisen from over a century of domination.

Overcoming such power involves several steps (as outlined in figure 3.1). Previously suppressed groups first must deal with the lingering effects of powerlessness, including challenging the internalized acceptance of the status quo and the sense of powerlessness within it. They then must mobilize to build the networks and capacities for action to get previously suppressed issues and voices on the agenda, and then be able to advocate effectively in decision-making arenas. In focusing on this process, we shift our approach from domination, or forms of "power over," to understanding how previously quiescent groups build the "power within," to gain the "power to" act for themselves. Here, just as the dimensions of dominating power are accumulative and reinforcing, so too is this process of empowerment, such that success in one dimension of power creates the possibilities for change in the others. Once change begins to emerge, a snowballing effect can cause change to occur rather quickly.

In this book, especially in chapters 7 and 8, we have looked at how this process of gaining power—of empowerment—occurs. On the one hand, some of this has taken the form of "oppositional" politics where forms of community organizing and spontaneous community protest increasingly battle to hold the coal industry to account for its mining practices, often in the face of bankruptcies and abandonment of derelict land. On the other hand, different local groups have focused on creating economic and social alternatives, including a land trust, a community development corporation, a community center, and others, prefiguring, as well as visioning what a new post-coal future might look like.

These processes of building collective power from below illustrate our earlier theory of power and empowerment. First, small actions, focusing on building local capacities, helped to overcome internalized legacies of powerlessness. Direct action and media campaigns helped to build awareness of coalfield injustices more broadly (as in the third dimension of power), giving rise to growing public opposition and new demands for accountability. To overcome the effective ideological domination wielded by efforts such as the Friends of Coal campaign, however, a new kind of organizing was also needed to counter this discourse. This organizing provides a vision of the possibilities of a post-coal future, requiring what has been termed the "power for." Increasingly, as oppositional politics to demand restorative justice from the industry was growing, so too were new methods of listening and visioning used to develop and present a new transformative narrative for just transition, such that "propositional" politics from below became equally important to shape beliefs in what futures might be possible.

To counter the second dimension of power—that is, to get issues and voices into the public arena once the ideological control began to weaken—we have also seen a variety of approaches used: from organizing to visioning at the local level; from challenging inequities left by bankruptcies and abandoned mine lands; to thinking creatively and collectively about alternative forms of land use and ownership; and from civil disobedience to lobbying and advocacy in legislatures and policy arenas. While often these "oppositional" and more "propositional" forms of action sit in tension with one another, in the Valley, we gradually saw them come together through common networks and overlapping coalitions. Through well-connected cross-regional organizing, mass actions as well as direct lobbying and advocacy led to some successful policy victories (the first dimension of power), including on regulation of strip mining, changing unequal taxation of natural resources, and reclamation of mining lands.

In this process, it was not just the actions of any single group, nor any single strategy, but their interactions that have helped give rise to power. Using a variety of tactics, interlocking groups of actors worked across levels, from local, to state, to regional, to national. They created their own spaces for action, while also supporting legislation and rules for more "invited" forms of engagement, and then mobilized to take advantage of these, testifying at hearings, filing legal actions, lobbying public officials. Throughout this they also demanded transparency, to open closed spaces, to make the practices of the companies more visible to others. Of particular note are strategies of citizen knowledge, either through recovering a sense of their own assets and capacities; using their local knowledge of the land, water, and fauna as a basis for organizing; citizen monitoring to hold the industry and regulatory agencies to account from below; or citizen visioning, drawing upon local values and voices to develop discourses of what a just transition to a new post-coal order might look like. The roles of women and queer youth as key leaders, knowledge bearers, and activists also stand out strongly, in sharp contrast to the strong culture of masculinity associated with the mining industry.[6]

Following the model of the powercube (see chapter 3), we have argued that for transformative change to happen, struggles to shift power must also align across levels, from the local to the national or even the global. Looking historically, while grassroots struggles from below have long been emerging, it has been at certain key moments when these bottom-up efforts coincided with more top-down interventions that breakthroughs might emerge. Thus, it was following an intense period of organizing for the regulation of strip mining in the 1970s, followed by the election of the Carter administration, which was open to environmental regulation, that the Surface Mining Control and Reclamation Act (SMCRA) was passed in 1977. The precipitous decline of coal around the period 2008–2016 coincided with the climate-friendly initiatives of the Obama regime, allowing grassroots demands for reclaiming abandoned mine lands and for investing in a just transition to intersect with national policies, before being ignored again by the pro-coal, anti–climate change regime of Trump.

The election of the Biden administration in 2020 again brought new policy initiatives in economic and environmental justice, leading to the promise of investments in the region at a scale not known since the War on Poverty, and also opening possibilities for the energy and networks, which were now present at a more grassroots level, to gain voice. Yet, as chapter 8 explored, although the opportunity for bottom-up struggles for just transition to meet top-down reforms seem potentially transformative, these new spaces were also heavily bounded and shaped by pro-coal, pro–fossil fuel forces, and by competing discourses of what just transition should look like, leading to what we have called "cramped spaces" for citizen engagement. They were also fragile spaces, which once in power the Trump administration moved rapidly to close.

The Multiple Types of Just Transition

In all these struggles, what one means by a just transition and whose version of justice prevails become highly contested. As we saw in the introduction, literature on environmental justice often distinguishes between several types of justice—distributional, procedural, recognitional, and restorative—each of which we argue is inevitably tied to questions of power. We have seen examples of these diverse and often competing claims to justice throughout the volume. However, we also argue that just as power relations shape these forms of justice, so too a just transition will necessarily be one in which power inequities are themselves addressed, overcoming past inequalities and injustices, and creating the possibilities for more democratic and inclusive and equitable forms of control by previously disenfranchised groups.

Distributional justice is about who wins and who loses in the transition—age-old questions of power. We have seen many examples. Some revolve around who benefits and who pays for the costs of coal's decline. Exiting corporations often try and hide behind the shield of bankruptcy, so communities and some state authorities struggle to ensure that they pay for cleanup of their abandoned mines. Other distributional questions revolve around who will benefit from the transition to a new economy. The hidden investors in the Cumberland Forest Project, led by NatureVest and The Nature Conservancy, make millions from carbon credit schemes, simply by shifting logging practices to store more carbon, while local communities gain little. The allocation of massive amounts of federal funds under the

Biden administration for clean energy development also creates new sites for contention, as new corporate actors position themselves (and past mining actors reinvent themselves) to capture the benefits, even as communities struggle to gain access to these funds to support their local priorities.

Procedural justice is about who participates in the decision-making processes that surround a just transition. Yet, as we know from other settings, questions of participation in decision-making spaces are also power laden.[7] Here in Appalachia we see the continuation of many closed spaces—where decisions about corporate investment and disinvestment are still made behind closed doors without any pretense of public involvement, and with huge impacts on affected communities. At the same time, the Biden-era federal funds for clean energy development came with mandates from the administration that grassroots communities and workers should benefit from their distribution. As we have seen, however, forms of procedural power often make it difficult for marginalized communities to compete with more powerful actors to influence how the funds are distributed or how benefits are determined in this space.

Recognitional justice is about whose voices are listened to, and whose knowledge, values, and identities hold sway. Here too we have seen contests between those who see transition in more technical terms, to be guided by a narrow version of scientific expertise, and those whose knowledge derives more from their experiential knowledge of living on and close to the land. For many rural communities, as we saw in the Clearfork Valley, maintaining a relationship to the land and having access to and protecting nature are high values that should guide future developments. Yet, we see few spaces in which experiential knowledge, grounded in more cultural understandings of nature, are considered as important as more technical and market-led understandings.

Finally, the concepts of *restorative* or *reparatory* justice are about responsibilities for correcting previous abuses to land, people, and community brought on by decades of fossil fuel extraction. As in many fossil-fuel–affected communities around the world, to move to a new energy order without compensating or correcting for the loss of jobs, livelihoods, and environmental damage caused by previous energy-related mining would itself represent an injustice. Here we have seen (especially in chapters 7 and 8) struggles to ensure that abandoned mines are reclaimed and that polluted lands and streams are restored, through such initiatives as the RECLAIM coalition, or that miners living with black lung or other occupational injuries are adequately compensated, and damaged infrastructures, like roads, are repaired. The task of restoration also creates an economy of its own, what some have called the "reparative" economy, which carries with it other justice questions as well, in terms of who benefits and gains in this process.[8]

Thus, in the case of a single valley, we see examples of contestation over each of these forms of justice. Power relations may shape whose justice will prevail. But while conceptually distinct, ultimately, we argue when viewed from the perspective of a single place these multiple justices are deeply interconnected. Who participates affects whose knowledge and values are recognized, in turn affecting the notions of fair distribution of costs and benefits. In such a context, what is needed is a more intersectional notion of just transition, one that addresses the multiple forms of justice together. Without taking this into account, the promise of just transition may ring hollow to affected communities and receive little buy-in or support.

Transition or Transformation? The Current Conjuncture

We have also argued that we must place these processes of shifting power and transition on a larger canvas to understand how and when more systemic and transformational change occurs. As we reviewed in chapter 3, transition theorists have argued this process involves change across the scales of landscapes, regimes, and niches. As the landscape changes—as energy systems shift to meet public demands to reduce dependence on climate-damaging fossil fuels—the regimes of power associated with such landscapes may also shift. Meanwhile as existing regimes weaken, innovations that have been occurring in niches may also begin to grow and expand into the vacuum left behind. At one level, then, we can understand the struggles for a post-coal future in terms of how those groups and voices formerly in the niches are now finding greater voice and visibility in the cracks of an old regime.

We have additionally suggested that the theory of landscapes, regimes, and niches fits within a Gramscian theory of conjuncture, crisis, and hegemony. The conjuncture is the way that the constellations of social forces collide and articulate in one place in time—how political coalitions align and how ideologies, narratives, and ideas emerge within political economic landscapes. Conjunctures shift as hegemonic blocs, or ruling coalitions, contend with crises. If the crises are what Gramsci termed "organic," or fundamental to how hegemonies rule, an "interregnum" between epochs of settled hegemony will unroll: a period marked by unsettled alliances, upheaval, and political possibility. As Janice Peck observes, "In the period between the epochs, what Gramsci calls the 'interregnum,' contestations over competing interests and visions emerge most clearly, hegemonies shift, and strategic alliances realign."[9] The old forces of a previously settled hegemony may re-form coalitions, but they do so on new and unstable terrains, or landscapes, and emerging alliances of power are not potent enough to forge a new hegemony. As such, these are moments of tumult, but also of possibilities for social change and upheaval.

We have used conjunctural analysis to understand how power shifts in the history of the Appalachian coalfields and in the Clearfork Valley. Conjunctures appear at various scales, be it the national or regional, although they are always situated within global political economies and geopolitics, as neo-Gramscian geographers, such as Gillian Hart and Clyde Woods, have adeptly illustrated.[10] In the Appalachian Region, as we outlined in chapter 2, it was when outside capital driven by the appetite for fossil fuels encountered the region over a century ago that a system of power based on extraction, concentrated absentee land ownership, and direct control of labor and communities first emerged. At various moments in history, as that hegemony contended with various crises and weakened, we saw counterhegemonic forms of power emerge. For instance, we saw new spaces for action from below created during the Depression in the 1930s, when a weakening economy contributed to rising labor protests from below, and strong policy interventions from above in the form of the New Deal and strong labor law. During the War on Poverty, federally mandated programs opened opportunities for direct citizen participation in governing welfare funds. Yet, these realignments of political forces were all variations upon similar contestations between workers, poor communities, and the coal industry, struggles that occurred within a settled and clear hegemony.[11] Now, with the coal industry a ghost of its former self, those clear lines of struggle and alliance have been upended.

In this interregnum, new ideologies and new constellations of actors compete for hegemony. For instance, we have seen in the previous chapter contestations among several coalitions, each with their own narratives about the future. On the one hand, coal interests, linked to larger fossil fuel forces, continue to promote "discourses of climate delay,"[12] seeking to minimize the urgency of climate change, or to suggest that fossil fuels are part of the solution. On the other hand, new actors, such as NatureVest and TNC, as well as other corporate actors, offer an array of investments within a "green" capitalist paradigm, arguing that profit is to be made through preservation of nature, no longer through extracting resources from it, and that new alternative renewable technologies should be developed. There is no guarantee that these will be antagonistic actors, with green corporations and fossil fuel corporations benefiting from heavily deregulated financialized capitalism, but as of yet we have not seen this political coalition form. At the same time, bottom-up grassroots groups are arguing that simply shifting from one technology to another is not enough, but a more wholistic vision of transition must incorporate elements of justice, which will help to remedy the inequities of the past, while not replicating or reenforcing them for the future.[13]

Political theorists and historians, such as William Davies and Nicholas Gane, among others, diagnose the contemporary moment to be a "post-neoliberal" conjuncture, an interregnum where neoliberal hegemony wanes and a new hegemony has yet to replace it.[14] As the largest public infrastructure investments in US history since the War on Poverty, which were themselves a set of fundamentally pre-neoliberal reforms, the Biden policy agenda came as both an expansion of an activist state seeking to rectify longstanding inequities, but was also tied up, and actively politically held back by antipublic, private sector–led strategies for economic development. Caught in this tension, unable to shed neoliberal policies but also invoking a kind of "climate Keynesianism,"[15] the Biden agenda was forced to use an indirect approach, mandating that private companies that receive federal funds produce "community benefits" and use federal labor guidelines that empower labor unions to make federal resources address environmental justice and just transition concerns.

This analysis of hegemony raises questions about whether the current moment is one of transition from old power brokers to new ones, or of broader social transformation, which also reorganizes the underlying political economic drivers of inequality. On the whole, the coalitions that were emerging to make use of the limited Biden-era provisions for environmental justice in 2024 have not yet been able to build what David Ciplet has termed "transformative transition coalitions,"[16] which can mobilize for strategic power over the structures that sustain hegemony. While organizing efforts such as those in TNACE in the Valley, or the efforts of Appalachian Voices and the Alliance for Appalachia, built coalitions between union partners and environmental justice community organizations, the limited reach of their coalitions and the cramped spaces provided by Biden-era policies for grassroots involvement have not yet allowed them to build sufficient power for broader change. Although the interregnum remains laden with possibility, the prospect of social transformation seems for now to remain out of reach.

Gramsci wrote that in an interregnum, "a great variety of morbid symptoms appear."[17] The reelection of Donald Trump in 2024 as US president was one such symptom. Trump's return was in large part an indictment of the ideology that the neoliberal hegemony had relied upon. While Joe

Biden's clean energy agenda in many ways broke with neoliberal policy, much of the rest of his administration still trumpeted neoliberal ideas. However, while Trump's second term extends the control of a conservative Republican coalition—one still characterized by neoconservatives advocating for deregulated markets and the right-wing Christian movement—fundamental aspects of the neoliberal coalition are gone: namely, a consensus on globalization, multiculturalism, and free trade. In this new moment of nationalist, authoritarian, and dog-whistle racial politics, whether a right-wing movement can forge alliances to create a new period of hegemonic rule remains unclear. Trump's inability to present a clear ideology with which to make sense of the future suggests his rule may continue an incoherent and unstable period of interregnum. It may take decades for the new order to emerge from the old.

What is clear, however, is that with his campaign receiving massive financial support from the coal, oil, and gas lobbies, a Trump administration is assured to uplift fossil fuels, roll back commitments to addressing climate change and environmental justice, and attempt to end environmental regulation as it has been known. Perhaps signaling this, one of his first Cabinet nominations, for secretary of energy, Chris Wright, is a former oil and gas executive, who is on record as saying, "There is no climate crisis, and we're not in the midst of an energy transition either."[18] In April 2025, Trump held a press conference announcing the signing of a series of executive orders aimed at reviving coal's future. Surrounded by a crowd of miners at the White House and using language reminiscent of his 2016 campaign to Make Coal Great Again, he said, "I call it beautiful, clean coal . . . I tell my people never use the word coal, unless you put 'beautiful, clean' before it."[19]

The Trump administration has begun to rescind climate and fossil fuel regulations, but for activists in the Valley and across Appalachia, there is no going back. While social transformation may not be immediately to hand, the top-down policy reforms from the Biden agenda opened new sets of possibilities for future organizing. In this interregnum, people have come to articulate diverse and hopeful visions of a future beyond fossil fuel extraction and have built capacities to organize around these visions. New coalitions and alliances have formed. Once opened, these lines of imagined possibilities are not easily closed, as these narratives become increasingly visible in the regional political landscape and a national and global conversation. Unlike a pre-Trump moment, the question of a just transition is now firmly in the public discourse, and demands for a social transformation, not just transition, remain on the agenda.

The Valley Writ Large

In the previous pages we have tried to understand how contestations amid transition play out at a micro level, and how power relations change in the process. We conclude by simply suggesting that what this small Valley is experiencing is not unique—in fact it reflects the changing power dynamics in the process of transition writ large.

As we suggested in the introduction, around the world the development model based on natural resource extraction, and the systems of power that have supported it, have produced thousands of places that resemble the Valley and the inequalities that intersect there. In many parts of Africa, Asia, and Latin America, such communities have often been linked to and supported by systems of colonial power,[20] while extractive zones in the United States and other richer nations have also been referred to as "internal colonies," and internal peripheries.[21] Dismantling historical systems of power built on extraction also means confronting and challenging the legacies of colonial power as well.

In many of these same places, the race for new minerals to fuel an energy transition—cobalt, lithium, and others—which will power solar panels, wind turbines, batteries, electric vehicles, or other new technologies—deploy similar models of power based on extraction. As such, the so-called clean energy transition risks simply the replication of old forms of power, not its transformation, and the possible escalation of forms of violence, conflicts, and abuse of human rights.[22]

We also see new actors emerging, like NatureVest and TNC, which bring new ideologies of protecting and preserving nature, yet often within existing paradigms of market-led reform, leading to new forms of "green grabbing" and privately held resource control, which still may leave frontline communities relatively voiceless and with few benefits flowing to them.[23] Even more broadly, the dominant model of growth and progress we face itself depends on the availability of these mineral sources to fuel an economic system based on global supply changes, mass consumption, and cheap forms of energy, transport, and food and agriculture—all of which are subsidized by the abuse of planetary boundaries and protected by power elites, in ways that are often linked to rising forms of authoritarianism as well.[24]

At the same time, amid energy transition, around the world we also see new forms of contestation emerging, as social movements demand climate justice, communities and workers seek new forms of energy production and control, and development theorists seek alternatives to growth approaches. The demands for energy democracy and for just transition are growing,[25] from the grassroots to more global policy levels. But in this period of contestation and reshaping of hegemonies, the questions still remain: Whose justice will predominate in this transition? Who will be the winners and losers, whose voices will be heard, whose knowledge will be counted, and whose histories and futures will prevail?

Struggling toward a just transition in the twenty-first century means addressing these age-old questions in a way that not only recasts our dependency on fossil fuels, but also confronts and reshapes power inequities as well. Through this study we have found that power relations are in a period of interregnum, in between the old order and a new arrangement of power that is to come. But we do not yet know whose interests and voices will prevail. Nevertheless, witnessing and participating in the struggles for a post-coal future in places like the Clearfork Valley give us pause—but also cautious hope for the future.

Notes

Introduction

1. John Gaventa, *Power and Powerlessness: Quiescence and Rebellion in an Appalachian Valley* (Urbana: University of Illinois Press, 1982), https://www.press.uillinois.edu/books/?id=p009853.

2. Interview with community development practitioner in the Clearfork Valley, 18 October 2022.

3. Gaventa, *Power and Powerlessness*; Gabe Schwartzman, "After Coal: Power, Development, and Post-Coal Politics in Appalachia" (PhD diss., University of Minnesota, 2023), https://www.proquest.com/docview/2840970518?pq-origsite=gscholar&fromopenview=true.

4. Climate Analytics, "Coal Phase Out," Global Climate Science and Policy Institute, December 2015, https://climateanalytics.org/briefings/coal-phase-out/.

5. The Paris Agreement was an international treaty on meeting greenhouse gas reduction goals, the result of the Twenty-first Conference of the Parties (COP) to the United Nations Framework Convention on Climate Change, the annual meeting of that body where climate change negotiations are held.

6. United Nations Framework Convention on Climate Change (UNFCCC), "End of Coal in Sight at COP26," press release, 4 October 2021, https://unfccc.int/news/end-of-coal-in-sight-at-cop26.

7. Mine Safety and Health Administration, "Mine Employment and Coal Production," n.d., https://www.msha.gov/data-and-reports/statistics/mine-employment-and-coal-production.

8. Eric Bowen, John Deskins, Christiadi, and Brian Lego, "Coal Production and Employment in Appalachia, 2023" (Bureau of Business and Economic Research, West Virginia University, 31 August 2023), https://www.arc.gov/report/coal-production-and-employment-in-appalachia-2023/.

9. Eric Bowen, Christiadi, John Deskins, and Brian Lego, "Appalachian Regional Commission: An Overview of Coal and the Economy in Appalachia: Fourth Quarter 2020 Update" (Appalachian Regional Commission, 2020), https://www.arc.gov/wp-content/uploads/2021/04/Coal-and-the-Economy-in-Appalachia_Q4_2020-Update.pdf.

10. Andrew Curley, "A Failed Green Future: Navajo Green Jobs and Energy 'Transition' in the Navajo Nation," *Geoforum* 88 (1 January 2018): 57–65, https://doi.org/10.1016/j.geoforum.2017.11.012.

11. Kelli F. Roemer and Julia H. Haggerty, "Coal Communities and the U.S. Energy Transition: A Policy Corridors Assessment," *Energy Policy* 151 (2021): 112112, https://doi.org/10.1016/j.enpol.2020.112112.

12. Brian F. Snyder, "Vulnerability to Decarbonization in Hydrocarbon-Intensive Counties in the United States: A Just Transition to Avoid Post-Industrial Decay," *Energy Research & Social Science* 42 (1 August 2018): 36, https://doi.org/10.1016/j.erss.2018.03.004.

13. Rajat Shrestha, Sujata Rajpurohit, and Devashree Saha, "Redefining America's 'Energy Communities' Can Boost Clean Energy Investments Where It's Needed Most" (World Resource Institute, 31 July 2023), https://www.wri.org/insights/redefining-americas-energy-communities.

14. Michael C. Stanley, John Edwin, Rachel Bernice Perks, Helen Ba Tanh Nguyen, Wendy Cunningham, Achim Daniel Schmillen, and Michael Stephen McCormick, "Managing Coal Mine Closure: Achieving a Just Transition for All" (World Bank Group, 1 August 2018), 9, https://documents.worldbank.org/en/publication/documents-reports/documentdetail/484541544643269894/managing-coal-mine-closure-achieving-a-just-transition-for-all.

15. Judson Abraham, "Just Transitions for the Miners: Labor Environmentalism in the Ruhr and Appalachian Coalfields," *New Political Science* 39, no. 2 (4 March 2017): 218–40, https://doi.org/10.1080/07393148.2017.1301313; Andrea Furnaro, "Geographies of Devaluation: Spatialities of the German Coal Exit," *Environment and Planning A: Economy and Space* 55, no. 6 (2023): 1355–71, https://doi.org/10.1177/0308518X221148731; Andrea Furnaro, "The Last Subsidy: Regulating Devaluation in the German Coal Phase-Out," *New Political Economy* 28, no. 2 (4 March 2023): 190–205, https://doi.org/10.1080/13563467.2022.2084523.

16. Darryn Snell, "'Just Transition?' Conceptual Challenges Meet Stark Reality in a "Transitioning" Coal Region in Australia," *Globalizations* 15, no. 4 (7 June 2018): 550–64, https://doi.org/10.1080/14747731.2018.1454679; Furnaro, "Geographies of Devaluation: Spatialities of the German Coal Exit."

17. Global Energy Monitor, "100 Miners a Day Face Job Cuts as Industry Winds Down Coal," press release, 9 October 2023, https://globalenergymonitor.org/press-release/100-miners-a-day-face-job-cuts-as-industry-winds-down-coal/.

18. Michael Jakob and Jan C. Steckel, *The Political Economy of Coal: Obstacles to Clean Energy Transitions* (London: Routledge, 2022).

19. Stanley et al., "Managing Coal Mine Closure."

20. Crandall A. Shifflett, *Coal Towns: Life Work and Culture in Company Towns of Southern Appalachia, 1880–1960* (Knoxville: University of Tennessee Press, 1995), xiii, https://utpress.org/title/coal-towns/.

21. Barbara Freese, "How Coal Disrupted the World: A Short History of Black Gold, and Its Power over Us," *Politico*, 26 May 2015, sec. The Agenda: Future of Power, https://www.politico.com/agenda/story/2015/05/how-coal-disrupted-the-world-000004.

22. International Labour Organization (ILO), "ILO Welcomes COP26 Just Transition Declaration," press release, International Labour Organization, 5 November 2021, https://www.ilo.org/resource/news/ilo-welcomes-cop26-just-transition-declaration. "COP28: The Irresistible Rise of the Just Transition," Grantham Research Institute on Climate Change and the Environment, accessed 20 March 2024, https://www.lse.ac.uk/granthaminstitute/news/cop28-the-irresistible-rise-of-the-just-transition/.

23. Tony Mazzochi, "A Superfund for Workers," *Earth Island Journal* 9, no. 1 (1993): 40.

24. Mazzochi, "Superfund for Workers," 41.

25. Robert D. Bullard, *Dumping in Dixie: Race, Class, and Environmental Quality*, 2nd ed. (Boulder, CO: Westview Press, 1994).

26. Quoted in Michele Morrone and Geoffrey L. Buckley, *Mountains of Injustice: Social and Environmental Justice in Appalachia*, 1st ed. (Athens: Ohio University Press, 2011), https://muse.jhu.edu/book/12495.

27. David N. Pellow, "Toward a Critical Environmental Justice Studies: Black Lives Matter as an Environmental Justice Challenge," *Du Bois Review: Social Science Research on Race* 13, no. 2 (2016): 222, https://doi.org/10.1017/S1742058X1600014X.

28. Elizabeth Cripps, *What Climate Justice Means and Why We Should Care* (New York: Bloomsbury Publishing, 2022).

29. Snyder, "Vulnerability to Decarbonization in Hydrocarbon-Intensive Counties in the United States."

30. Darren McCauley and Raphael Heffron, "Just Transition: Integrating Climate, Energy, and Environmental Justice," *Energy Policy* 119 (1 August 2018): 1, https://doi.org/10.1016/j.enpol.2018.04.014; Xinxin Wang and Kevin Lo, "Just Transition: A Conceptual Review," *Energy Research & Social Science* 82 (December 2021): 102291, https://doi.org/10.1016/j.erss.2021.102291.

31. Just Transition Alliance, "Just Transition Principles," 2024, https://jtalliance.org/what-is-just-transition/.

32. Climate Justice Alliance, "Just Transition Principles," accessed 26 January 2024, https://climatejusticealliance.org/wp-content/uploads/2019/11/CJA_JustTransition_highres.pdf.

33. International Labour Organization (ILO), "ILO Welcomes COP26 Just Transition Declaration," press release, 5 November 2021, https://www.ilo.org/resource/news/ilo-welcomes-cop26-just-transition-declaration' and remove the existing one.

34. Amanda N. Ullman and Noah Kittner, "Are Global Efforts Coordinated

for a Just Transition? A Review of Civil Society, Financial, Government, and Academic Just Transition Frameworks," *Energy Research & Social Science* 108 (1 February 2024): 103371, https://doi.org/10.1016/j.erss.2023.103371.

35. Labor Network for Sustainability and Strategic Practice: Grassroots Policy Project, "'Just Transition'—Just What Is It? An Analysis of Language, Strategies, and Projects" (Labor Network for Sustainability), accessed 29 January 2024, https://www.labor4sustainability.org/uncategorized/just-transition-just-what-is-it/.

36. UMWA, "Preserving Coal Country: Keeping America's Coal Miners, Families, and Communities Whole in an Era of Global Energy Transition" (2021), https://umwa.org/wp-content/uploads/2021/04/UMWA-Preserving-Coal-Country-2021.pdf.

37. International Brotherhood of Teamsters, "ESG: What It Is and Why It Matters for the Future of Labor," *Teamster Magazine*, 2023, https://teamster.org/wp-content/uploads/2024/01/1924FINALMagTeamsterWINTER2023.pdf.

38. J. Mijin Cha, Manuel Pastor, Madeline Wander, James Sadd, and Rachel Morello-Frosch, "A Roadmap for an Equitable Low-Carbon Future: Four Pillars for a Just Transition," Climate Equity Network, April 2019, 30, https://justtransitionfund.org/wp-content/uploads/2022/08/A-Roadmap-To-An-Equitable-Low-Carbon-Future_Four-Pillars-For-A-Just-Transition.pdf; see also J. Mijin Cha, *A Just Transition for All: Workers and Communities for a Carbon-Free Future* (Cambridge, MA: MIT Press, 2024).

39. Christine Gyovai and Sierra Gladfelter, "Beyond Transition: Appalachia's Pathway to Justice and Transformation," Third Party Strategic Assessment (Highlander Center, 18 March 2021), https://highlandercenter.org/wp-content/uploads/2021/06/Final-Highlander-Center-Report_3_18_21_smaller_res-2.pdf.

40. David Ciplet, "Transition Coalitions: Toward a Theory of Transformative Just Transitions," *Environmental Sociology* 8, no. 3 (3 July 2022): 315–30, https://doi.org/10.1080/23251042.2022.2031512.

41. Dimitris Stevis, *Just Transitions: Promise and Contestation*, 1st ed. (Cambridge: Cambridge University Press, 2023), 55, https://doi.org/10.1017/9781108936569.

42. Stevis, *Just Transitions.*

43. Stephen Williams and Andréanne Doyon, "Justice in Energy Transitions," *Environmental Innovation and Societal Transitions* 31 (June 2019): 144–53, https://doi.org/10.1016/j.eist.2018.12.001; Noel Healy and John Barry, "Politicizing Energy Justice and Energy System Transitions: Fossil Fuel Divestment and a 'Just Transition,'" *Energy Policy* 108, no. September (2017): 451–59.

44. Stevis, *Just Transitions*, 1.

45. Movement Generation Justice and Ecology Project, "From Banks and Tanks to Cooperation and Caring: A Strategic Framework for a Just Transition" (Womanist Working Collective, 23 September 2021), 3, https://www.womanistworkingcollective.org/post/just-transitions-by-movement-generation.

46. Benjamin K. Sovacool, Shannon Elizabeth Bell, Cara Daggett, Christine Labuski, Myles Lennon, Lindsay Naylor, Julie Klinger, Kelsey Leonard, and Jeremy Firestone, "Pluralizing Energy Justice: Incorporating Feminist, Anti-Racist, Indigenous, and Postcolonial Perspectives," *Energy Research & Social Science* 97 (March 2023), https://doi.org/10.1016/j.erss.2023.102996; Göran Collste, *Global Rectificatory Justice* (London: Palgrave Macmillan UK, 2015), https://doi.org/10.1057/9781137466129.

47. David Ciplet and Jill Lindsey Harrison, "Transition Tensions: Mapping Conflicts in Movements for a Just and Sustainable Transition," *Environmental Politics* 29, no. 3 (15 April 2020): 435–56, https://doi.org/10.1080/09644016.2019.1595883.

48. Stevis, *Just Transitions*, 44.

49. Stevis, *Just Transitions*, 47.

50. Ian Scoones, Melissa Leach, and Peter Newell, eds., *The Politics of Green Transformations: Pathways to Sustainability* (London; New York: Routledge, 2015).

51. Throughout the book, we use the term "citizen" in an inclusive way to refer to people with universal rights, whether or not they have been recognized by the state. See, for instance, Naila Kabeer, ed., *Inclusive Citizenship: Meanings and Expressions*, Claiming Citizenship, vol. 1 (London; New York: Zed, 2005).

52. Scoones, Leach, and Newell, *The Politics of Green Transformations*, 6.

53. Sovacool et al., "Pluralizing Energy Justice."

54. Stevis, *Just Transitions*.

55. Andrew Curley, *Carbon Sovereignty: Coal, Development, and Energy Transition in the Navajo Nation* (Tucson: University of Arizona Press, 2023), https://uapress.arizona.edu/book/carbon-sovereignty.

56. Huw Beynon and Ray Hudson, *The Shadow of the Mine: Coal and the End of Industrial Britain* (London; New York: Verso, 2021), https://doi.org/10.1080/2325548X.2022.2144691.

57. Tom Hansell, *After Coal: Stories of Survival in Appalachia and Wales*, Illustrated edition (Morgantown: West Virginia University Press, 2018), https://wvupressonline.com/node/748.

58. Robert S. Lynd and Helen M. Lynd, *Middletown: A Study in Contemporary American Culture* (Oxford: Harcourt, Brace, 1929), https://archive.org/details/in.ernet.dli.2015.156473/page/n3/mode/2up; Robert S. Lynd and Helen M. Lynd, *Middletown in Transition: A Study in Cultural Conflicts* (Oxford: Harcourt, Brace, 1937), https://archive.org/details/in.ernet.dli.2015.166212.

59. Floyd Hunter, *Community Power Structure: A Study of Decision Makers* (Chapel Hill: University of North Carolina Press, 1953), http://archive.org/details/communitypowerst00hunt.

60. Floyd Hunter, *Community Power Succession: Atlanta's Policy Makers Revisited* (Chapel Hill: University of North Carolina Press, 1980).

61. Cynthia M. Duncan, *Worlds Apart: Poverty and Politics in Rural America*, 2nd ed. (New Haven, CT: Yale University Press, 2015).

62. Michael Burawoy, "Revisits: An Outline of a Theory of Reflexive Ethnography," *American Sociological Review* 68, no. 5 (October 2003): 645, https://doi.org/10.2307/1519757.

63. Amber Huff and Andrea Brock, "Introduction: Accumulation by Restoration and Political Ecologies of Repair," *Environment and Planning E: Nature and Space* 6, no. 4 (25 April 2023): 2113–33, https://doi.org/10.1177/25148486231168393.

Chapter 1. Intersecting Inequalities and the Failed Promises of Development

1. Michael Harrington, *The Other America* (New York: Simon and Schuster, 1997).

2. Interview with Clearfork Valley resident, 14 February 2022.

3. Interview with Clearfork Valley resident, 13 January 2022.

4. See map, Poverty Solutions at the University of Michigan and Princeton University, "Index of Deep Disadvantage," 2022, https://poverty.umich.edu/research-funding-opportunities/data-tools/understanding-communities-of-deep-disadvantage/.

5. Kathryn J. Edin, H. Luke Shaefer, and Timothy J. Nelson, *The Injustice of Place: Uncovering the Legacy of Poverty in America* (New York: Mariner Books, 2023), 8, https://www.harpercollins.com/products/the-injustice-of-place-kathryn-j-edinh-luke-shaefertimothy-j-nelson?variant=41069483556898.

6. Out of the 3,618 counties and cities studied by Edin, Shaefer, and Nelson, *The Injustice of Place*, Bell County ranks 58th, Whitley County 167th, Claiborne County 394th, and Campbell County 414th on their Index of Deep Disadvantage. The sub-county portions of the Valley would rank much higher than the county as a whole, due to uneven development within the counties themselves. Where possible we have compiled sub-county statistics into a data set on the Valley itself. To do so, Census County Divisions (CCDs) were chosen in Kentucky and Census Tracts in Tennessee, as they most relate to the unincorporated communities within the geographic boundaries of the Clearfork Valley. These included: Clairfield Census Tract 9704, Claiborne County, Tennessee; Habersham Census Tract 9501, Campbell County, Tennessee; Pearl CCD, Whitley County, Kentucky; Pruden-Fonde CCD, Bell County, Kentucky.

7. Interview with Clearfork resident, Clairfield, TN, 9 September 2021.

8. As Peter Hille, executive director of the Mountain Association, said on a webinar. Economic Transition Webinar, Reimagine Appalachia, June 10, 2021.

9. Interview with coal community resident, Clairfield, TN, 9 September 2021.

10. East TN Local Workforce Development Board, "East Regional Plan: Economic and Workforce Analysis" (East Tennessee Human Resource Agency, 12 May 2020), https://www.ethra.org/lib/file/manager/Workforce_Files/Regional_Plans/Draft_East_Region_Plan_Revised_vs2.pdf.

11. Sylvia Ryerson and Judah Schept, "Opinion: Eastern Kentucky Needs

Flood Relief, Not Another Federal Prison," *New York Times*, 29 March 2023, sec. Opinion, https://www.nytimes.com/2023/03/29/opinion/kentucky-prison-flood.html; Judah Schept and Sylvia Ryerson, "Building Prisons in Appalachia," *Boston Review*, 27 April 2018, http://bostonreview.net/law-justice/sylvia-ryerson-judah-schept-building-prisons-appalachia; "Coal, Cages, Crisis," *NYU Press* (blog), accessed 27 December 2021, https://nyupress.org/9781479858972/coal-cages-crisis.

12. Gabrielle Vincent, "Hidden in East Tennessee: Crypto Capitalists Lead Modern Day Rush for Electricity to Power Their Virtual Mining Operations," *Knoxville News Sentinel*, accessed 1 June 2023, https://web.archive.org/web/20220601021809/https://eu.knoxnews.com/in-depth/news/2022/06/01/tennessee-cryptocurrency-miners-lead-modern-day-electricity-rush/6795561001/.

13. Jordan Brooks, "Steel Manufacturer Breaks Ground on New Middlesboro Plant," *Claiborne Progress*, 25 October 2022, https://www.claiborneprogress.net/2022/10/25/steel-manufacturer-breaks-ground-on-new-middlesboro-plant/.

14. The Nature Conservancy, "The Conservancy Announces 17 New Clean Energy Projects on Former Appalachian Coal Mines with ENGIE and Sun Tribe Development," 11 February 2025, https://www.nature.org/en-us/newsroom/cumberland-clean-energy-former-mines/.

15. Interview with Valley resident, 14 February 2022.

16. Matthew N. Murray and Charles Sims, "Coal Mining and Tourism: Engines of Economic Development" (Tennessee Department of Environment and Conservation, 1 September 2015), https://bakercenter.utk.edu/wp-content/uploads/2022/08/Coal.Mining.And_.Tourism.pdf.

17. U.S. Census Bureau, "DP03: Selected Economic Characteristics," American Community Survey 5-Year Estimates (data.census.gov, 2021 2017), https://data.census.gov/table/ACSDP5Y2021.DP03?t=Employment%20and%20Labor%20Force%20Status&g=060XX00US2101392864,2123592712_1400000US47013950100,47025970400; U.S. Census Bureau, "S1810: Disability Characteristics," American Community Survey 5-Year Estimates (data.census.gov, 2021 2017), https://data.census.gov/table/ACSST5Y2021.S1810?t=Disability&g=060XX00US2101392864,2123592712_1400000US47013950100,47025970400.

18. Marc Edelman, "Hollowed Out Heartland, USA: How Capital Sacrificed Communities and Paved the Way for Authoritarian Populism," *Journal of Rural Studies* 82 (February 2021): 505, https://doi.org/10.1016/j.jrurstud.2019.10.045.

19. Evan Osnos, "When Wall Street Came to Coal Country: How a Big-Money Gamble Scarred Appalachia," *The Guardian*, 14 September 2021, sec. Environment, https://www.theguardian.com/environment/2021/sep/14/wall-street-coal-country-hedge-funds-coal-mining-appalachia-west-virginia.

20. "Coal's Decline Is Choking Appalachia Towns," *Bloomberg.Com*, 10 September 2015, https://www.bloomberg.com/news/articles/2015-09-10/coal-s-decline-is-choking-appalachia-towns.

21. Gaventa, *Power and Powerlessness*, 232.

22. U.S. Energy Information Administration, "Annual Coal Report 2020," Minerals Yearbook, October 2021, https://www.eia.gov/coal/annual/archive/0584_2020.pdf.

23. Edelman, "Hollowed Out Heartland, USA."

24. "Clearfork Utility District: Financial Statement 2021," End of Year Financial Report (Clairfield, TN: Clearfork Utility, 31 December 2021), https://comptroller.tn.gov/content/dam/cot/la/advanced-search/2021/utilities/2908-2021-u-clrud-rpt-cpa517-9-13-23.pdf.

25. Interview with coalfield resident, Eagan, 9 February 2022.

26. Shannon Elizabeth Bell, "'There Ain't No Bond in Town Like There Used to Be': The Destruction of Social Capital in the West Virginia Coalfields," *Sociological Forum* 24, no. 3 (2009): 631.

27. Matthew Desmond, *Poverty, by America* (New York: Penguin Books, 2023), https://www.penguin.co.uk/books/444975/poverty-by-america-by-desmond-matthew/9780141998800.

28. Economic Research Service, "Rural Poverty & Well-Being," U.S. Department of Agriculture, 15 November 2023, https://www.ers.usda.gov/topics/rural-economy-population/rural-poverty-well-being/.

29. Center for Regional Economic Competitiveness and West Virginia University, "Appalachia Then and Now: Examining Changes to the Appalachian Region since 1965," Executive Summary (Appalachian Regional Commission, February 2015), https://www.arc.gov/wp-content/uploads/2020/06/AppalachiaThenAndNowCompiledReports.pdf.

30. Appalachian Regional Commission, "County Economic Status and Distressed Areas in Appalachia 2024," Appalachian Regional Commission, 2024, https://www.arc.gov/classifying-economic-distress-in-appalachian-counties/.

31. U.S. Census Bureau, "S1701: Poverty Status in the Past 12 Months," American Community Survey 5-Year Estimates (data.census.gov, 2021 2017), https://data.census.gov/table/ACSST5Y2021.S1701?t=Poverty&g=050XX00US21013,21235,47013,47025_060XX00US2101392864,2123592712_1400000US47013950100,47025970400; U.S. Census Bureau, "1970 Census: Population by Poverty Status in 1969," n.d., https://www.census.gov/data/tables/time-series/dec/census-poverty.html.

32. Patrick Kesler, "Distressed Communities Index," 2022, https://eig.org/distressed-communities/2022-dci-interactive-map/. This index is based on seven components: no high school diploma, housing vacancy, adults not working, median income ratio, change in employment, and change in business establishments.

33. Kesler, "Distressed Communities Index."

34. Carter C. Price and Kathryn A. Edwards, "Trends in Income from 1975 to 2018" (RAND Corporation, 14 September 2020), https://www.rand.org/pubs/working_papers/WRA516-1.html.

35. Economic Innovation Group, "The Spaces between Us: The Evolution of American Communities in the New Century" (Economic Innovation Group, October 2020), https://eig.org/wp-content/uploads/2020/10/EIG-2020-DCI-Report.pdf.

36. Michael Meit, Megan Heffernan, Erin Tanenbaum, Maggie Cherney and Victoria Hallman, "Appalachian Diseases of Despair," Final Report (University of Chicago NORC, October 2020), https://www.arc.gov/wp-content/uploads/2023/08/Appalachian-Diseases-of-Despair-Update-July-2023.pdf.

37. CDC Injury Center, "United States Dispensing Rate Maps," 12 December 2023, https://www.cdc.gov/overdose-prevention/data-research/facts-stats/us-dispensing-rate-maps.html?CDC_AAref_Val=https://www.cdc.gov/drugoverdose/rxrate-maps/index.html#cdc_data_surveillance_section_2-dispensing-rate-maps.

38. Calculated from NORC, "Interactive Map: Drug Overdose Deaths in Appalachia," accessed 9 February 2024, http://overdosemappingtool.norc.org/.

39. Austin Frakt, "Reagan, Deregulation, and America's Exceptional Rise in Health Care Costs," *New York Times*, 4 June 2018, sec. The Upshot, https://www.nytimes.com/2018/06/04/upshot/reagan-deregulation-and-americas-exceptional-rise-in-health-care-costs.html.

40. Art Van Zee, "The Promotion and Marketing of OxyContin: Commercial Triumph, Public Health Tragedy," *American Journal of Public Health* 99, no. 2 (February 2009): 221, https://doi.org/10.2105/AJPH.2007.131714.

41. Appalachian Regional Commission and National Association of Counties, "Opioids in Appalachia: The Role of Counties in Reversing a Regional Epidemic" (Appalachian Regional Commission, May 2019), 6, https://www.naco.org/sites/default/files/documents/Opioids-Full.pdf.

42. Beth Macy, *Dopesick: Dealers, Doctors, and the Drug Company That Addicted America* (London: Head of Zeus, 2018), 18.

43. Wayne Coombs, "Analysis: The Pharmaceutical Colonization of Appalachia," *Daily Yonder*, 7 February 2018, http://dailyyonder.com/analysis-pharmaceutical-colonization-appalachia/2018/02/07/.

44. Anne Case and Angus Deaton, *Deaths of Despair and the Future of Capitalism*, Illustrated edition (Princeton, NJ: Princeton University Press, 2020).

45. Compared to 65 percent of adults in the United States. U.S. Census Bureau, "S1501: Educational Attainment," American Community Survey 5-Year Estimates (data.census.gov, 2021 2017), https://data.census.gov/table/ACSST5Y2021.S1501?t=Educational%20Attainment&g=050XX00US21013,21235,47013,47025_060XX00US2101392864,2123592712_1400000US47013950100,47025970400.

46. Willie Dodson, "Massive Mountaintop Removal Mine Threatens Clearfork Valley," *Appalachian Voices* (blog), 14 September 2017, https://appvoices.org/2017/09/14/massive_mtr_mine_threatens_clearfork_valley/.

47. Interview with Clearfork Valley resident, Roses Creek, TN, 1 June 2021.

48. Washington Post, "Child's Death by Mine Boulder Sets Off Avalanche of Rage," *Chicago Tribune*, 9 January 2005, https://www.chicagotribune.com/2005/01/09/childs-death-by-mine-boulder-sets-off-avalanche-of-rage/.

49. Laura Esch and Michael Hendryx, "Chronic Cardiovascular Disease Mortality in Mountaintop Mining Areas of Central Appalachian States," *Journal of Rural Health* 27, no. 4 (2 November 2011): 350–57, https://doi.org/10.1111/j.1748-0361.2011.00361.x; Michael Hendryx, "Personal and Family Health in Rural Areas of Kentucky With and Without Mountaintop Coal Mining," *Journal of Rural Health* 29, no. s1 (3 December 2013): s79–88, https://doi.org/10.1111/jrh.12016.

50. Maureen Halsema, "Prenter Hollow Sues Coal Companies Over Contaminated Water," *Appalachian Voice* (blog), 3 January 2009, https://appvoices.org/2009/01/03/prenter-hollow-sues-coal-companies-over-contaminated-water/; Paul J. Nyden, "Mediation in Rawl Water Pollution Cases Breaks Down," *Charleston Gazette-Mail*, 18 November 2010, https://www.wvgazettemail.com/news/special_reports/mediation-in-rawl-water-pollution-cases-breaks-down/article_58970455-3303-5697-93a1-a79ab207236d.html; "Sludge Safety | Your Guide to Sludge," accessed 2 December 2018, https://web.archive.org/web/20061021033815/http://www.sludgesafety.org/.

51. See further summary of effects of MTR here: Appalachian Voices, "Community Impacts of Mountaintop Removal," accessed 14 February 2024, https://appvoices.org/end-mountaintop-removal/community/.

52. Interview with Clearfork Valley resident, 13 January 2022.

53. Erin Savage, "Repairing the Damage: The Costs of Delaying Reclamation at Modern-Era Mines" (Appalachian Voices, 12 July 2021), https://appvoices.org/coal-impacts/repairing-the-damage/; Katelyn Weisbrod, "The Decline of Kentucky's Coal Industry Has Produced Hundreds of Safety and Environmental Violations at Strip Mines," *Inside Climate News* (blog), 18 April 2022, https://insideclimatenews.org/news/18042022/kentucky-coal-mining-violations/; Caroline Eggers, "Two-Thirds of Tennessee Coal Mine Permits Are in Bond Forfeiture," *WPLN News*, 9 January 2024, https://wpln.org/post/two-thirds-of-tennessee-coal-mine-permits-are-in-bond-forfeiture/.

54. Eggers, "Two-Thirds of Tennessee Coal Mine Permits Are in Bond Forfeiture."

55. Council on Environmental Quality, "Climate and Economic Justice Screening Tool," accessed 1 April 2022, https://web.archive.org/web/20230720182436/https://screeningtool.geoplatform.gov/en/#5.78/42.055/-93.333.

56. Interview with ginseng digger, 21 February 2022.

57. Interview with Clearfork Valley resident, 9 September 2021.

58. Interview with Clearfork Valley resident, 5 November 2021.

59. U.S. Census Bureau, "Table 33, General Characteristics for County Subdivisions: 1970," Archived Census Statistics (census.gov: 1970 Census of Population: Characteristics of the Population, 1970), 57, https://www2.census.gov/library/publications/decennial/1970/population-volume-1/00496492v1p44ch03.pdf; U.S. Census Bureau, "S0101: Age and Sex," American Community Survey 5-Year

Estimates, 2019 2016, https://data.census.gov/table/ACSST5Y2020.S0101?g=1400000US47013950100,47025970400&y=2020.

60. Interview with Clearfork Valley resident, 1 June 2021.

61. Interview with Clearfork Valley resident, Clairfield, TN, 1 December 2021.

62. For more details on community involvement and top-down approaches to development at ARC, see David E. Whisnant, *Modernizing the Mountaineer: People, Power, and Planning in Appalachia* (Knoxville: University of Tennessee Press, 1994).

63. Tara J. Melish, "Maximum Feasible Participation of the Poor: New Governance, New Accountability, and a 21st Century War on the Sources of Poverty," *Yale Human Rights and Development Law Journal* 13, no. 1 (1 January 2010): 1–134; Justin Randolph, "The Making of Appalachian Mississippi," *Southern Cultures* 4, no. 26 (2020), https://www.southerncultures.org/article/the-making-of-appalachian-mississippi/.

64. Whisnant, *Modernizing the Mountaineer*.

65. "Appalachia: A Report by the President's Appalachian Regional Commission, 1964" (Appalachian Regional Commission, 1964), https://www.govinfo.gov/content/pkg/GOVPUB-Y3_AP4_2-PURL-LPS99948/pdf/GOVPUB-Y3_AP4_2-PURL-LPS99948.pdf.

66. Randolph, "The Making of Appalachian Mississippi."

67. Albert P. Smith, Appalachia: Appalachian Regional Commission Oral History Project, interview by Barbara Griffith, 5 January 1982, https://kentuckyoralhistory.org/ark:/16417/xt71khmxswtvg.

68. Whisnant, *Modernizing the Mountaineer*.

69. Smith, Appalachia: Appalachian Regional Commission Oral History Project; Edward T. "Ned" Breathitt Jr., Appalachia: Appalachian Regional Commission Oral History Project, interview by Scott Ellsworth, 1 October 1983, Louie B. Nunn Center for Oral History, University of Kentucky Libraries, https://kentuckyoralhistory.org/ark:/16417/xt7pnv998t8d.

70. Ronald Eller, *Uneven Ground: Appalachia since 1945* (Lexington: University Press of Kentucky, 2008), https://www.kentuckypress.com/9780813142463/uneven-ground/.

71. Jamie Peck and Nick Theodore, "Still Neoliberalism?," *South Atlantic Quarterly* 118, no. 2 (2019): 245–65, https://doi.org/10.1215/00382876-7381122.

72. Jamie Peck, Neil Brenner, and Nik Theodore, "Actually Existing Neoliberalism," in *The Sage Handbook of Neoliberalism*, ed. Damien Cahill, Melinda Cooper, Martin Konings, and David Primrose (London: Sage, 2018), 3–15.

73. Center for Regional Economic Competitiveness and West Virginia University, "Appalachia Then and Now."

74. Gabe Schwartzman, "POWER and the Future of Appalachia: Discursive Framings of an Economic Transition," *Southeastern Geographer* 61, no. 4 (2021): 343–56, https://doi.org/10.1353/sgo.2021.0024; Michael H. Cecire, "The POWER Initiative: Energy Transition as Economic Development," Congressional Research Service report R46015, 20 November 2019.

Chapter 2. Setting the Context

1. Steven Stoll, *Ramp Hollow: The Ordeal of Appalachia* (New York: Hill and Wang, 2018), https://search.worldcat.org/title/1019935232.

2. Gregory D. Smithers, *The Cherokee Diaspora: An Indigenous History of Migration, Resettlement, and Identity* (New Haven: Yale University Press, 2015).

3. Stoll, *Ramp Hollow*.

4. Mary Beth Pudup, "Land before Coal: Class and Regional Development in Southeast Kentucky" (PhD diss., University of California at Berkeley, 1987), https://www.proquest.com/openview/7f203ed4f63e71bf29c3c71ac8d16fe0/1?pq-origsite=gscholar&cbl=18750&diss=y; Mary Beth Pudup, "The Boundaries of Class in Preindustrial Appalachia," *Journal of Historical Geography* 15, no. 2 (1 April 1989): 139–62, https://doi.org/10.1016/S0305-7488(89)80019-2.

5. Wilma A. Dunaway, *The First American Frontier: Transition to Capitalism in Southern Appalachia, 1700–1860* (Chapel Hill: University of North Carolina Press, 1996), https://uncpress.org/book/9780807845400/the-first-american-frontier/.

6. Richard Branford, "A Brief Introduction to Hazy" (Coal River Folklife Collection, 1999), AFC 1999/008: ms0009, Library of Congress, https://www.loc.gov/item/cmns000020/; Stoll, *Ramp Hollow*.

7. Altina L. Waller, *Feud: Hatfields, McCoys, and Social Change in Appalachia, 1860–1900* (Chapel Hill: University of North Carolina Press, 1988).

8. Stoll, *Ramp Hollow*.

9. These companies were far from the originators of such ideas about progress, key concepts in western Enlightenment narratives. For a recent discussion of the politics of concepts, see David Graeber and David Wengrow, *The Dawn of Everything: A New History of Humanity* (New York: Farrar, Straus and Giroux, 2021).

10. Gaventa, *Power and Powerlessness*, 61.

11. Ronald L. Lewis, *Transforming the Appalachian Countryside: Railroads, Deforestation, and Social Change in West Virginia, 1880–1920* (Chapel Hill: University of North Carolina Press, 1988).

12. Shannon Elizabeth Bell, *Fighting King Coal: The Challenges to Micromobilization in Central Appalachia*, Urban and Industrial Environments (Cambridge, MA: MIT Press, 2016), 39, https://mitpress.mit.edu/9780262528801/fighting-king-coal/.

13. We find it important to note that while conditions in Appalachia may resemble colonialism, the region is not a colony. Scholars have critiqued an "internal colony model" of Appalachian development for erasing actual colonization of Indigenous lands, distracting from any analysis of the region's place in capitalist social relations, and reproducing myths about Appalachia's homogeneity and whiteness. See Stephen Pearson, "'The Last Bastion of Colonialism': Appalachian Settler Colonialism and Self-Indigenization," *American*

Indian Culture and Research Journal 37, no. 2 (1 January 2013): 165–84, https://escholarship.org/uc/item/0wd9z381; Steve Fisher and Barbara Ellen Smith, "Internal Colony—Are You Sure? Defining, Theorizing, Organizing Appalachia," *Journal of Appalachian Studies* 22, no. 1 (2016): 45–50, https://doi.org/10.5406/jappastud.22.1.0045.

14. Appalachian Land Ownership Task Force, *Who Owns Appalachia? Landownership and Its Impact* (Lexington: University Press of Kentucky, 1983), https://www.jstor.org/stable/j.ctt130j5d6; Shaunna Scott, "The Appalachian Land Ownership Study Revisited," *Appalachian Journal* 35, no. 3 (2008): 236–52.

15. Appalachian Land Ownership Task Force, *Who Owns Appalachia?*, 14.

16. Appalachian Land Ownership Task Force, *Who Owns Appalachia?*, 15.

17. Beth Spence, Cathy Kunkel, Elias Schewel, Ted Boettner, and Lou Martin, "Who Owns West Virginia?," (Charleston: West Virginia Center on Budget and Policy, 2013), https://wvpolicy.org/wp-content/uploads/2018/5/land-study-paper-final3.pdf.

18. Appalachian Land Study, "About," accessed 7 February 2024, https://www.appalachianlandstudy.org/about.

19. Lindsay Shade and Levi Van Sant, "Geographies of Land Ownership Change in the Rural United States: Challenges, Methods, and Possibilities," *Professional Geographer* 75, no. 5 (27 April 2023): 844–54, https://doi.org/10.1080/00330124.2023.2194367.

20. Barbara Ellen Smith and Stephen Fisher stress this point in a special issue of the *Journal of Appalachian Studies* on the internal colony model. Fisher and Smith, "Internal Colony."

21. H. Floyd Fansler, *History of Tucker County, West Virginia* (Parsons, WV: McClain Printing Co., 1962), https://catalog.hathitrust.org/Record/102005441; Lou Martin, *Smokestacks in the Hills: Rural-Industrial Workers in West Virginia* (Urbana: University of Illinois Press, 2015), https://www.jstor.org/stable/10.5406/j.ctt17t75tt.

22. Shifflett, *Coal Towns*, 34.

23. Michael Kline, "Esau in the Coal Fields: Owing Our Souls to the Company Store," *Appalachian Heritage* 39, no. 3 (2011): 69–84; Wess Harris, ed., *Dead Ringers: Why Miners March: Buried Truth from the Mountains* (Gay, WV: Appalachian Community Services, 2012), https://search.worldcat.org/it/title/dead-ringers-why-miners-march-buried-truth-from-the-mountains/oclc/801402105.

24. Margaret M. Mulrooney, "A Legacy of Coal: The Coal Company Towns of Southwestern Pennsylvania," *Vernacular Architecture Forum* 4 (1991): 130–37, https://doi.org/10.2307/3514228; Shifflett, *Coal Towns*.

25. Edris H. Miller, interview by Rita Wicks-Nelson and Ancella Radford Bickley, 1998, transcript, 0064: Marshall University Oral History Collection, Marshall University Special Collections, https://mds.marshall.edu/oral_history/583.

26. Stoll, *Ramp Hollow*.

27. Cicero Fain, "Into the Crucible: The Chesapeake and Ohio Railroad and the Black Industrial Worker in Southern West Virginia, 1870–1900," *Journal of Appalachian Studies* 17, no. 1/2 (2011): 42–65; Cicero M. Fain, *Black Huntington: An Appalachian Story* (Urbana: University of Illinois Press, 2019), https://doi.org/10.5406/j.ctvgs0cbj.

28. Scott Reynolds Nelson, *Steel Drivin' Man: John Henry, The Untold Story of an American Legend* (Oxford: Oxford University Press, 2008), https://global.oup.com/academic/product/steel-drivin-man-9780195341195?cc=us&lang=en&; Fain, "Into the Crucible."

29. Paul Nyden, "Black Coal Miners in the United States," *American Institute for Marxist Studies*, Occasional Papers, 15 (1974); Ronald L. Lewis, *Black Coal Miners in America: Race, Class, and Community Conflict, 1780–1980* (Lexington: University Press of Kentucky, 2009).

30. Robert Armstead, *Black Days, Black Dust: The Memories of an African American Coal Miner* (Knoxville: University of Tennessee Press, 2002), https://utpress.org/title/black-days-black-dust-2/; Gabe Schwartzman, "Anti-Blackness, Black Geographies, and Racialized Depopulation in Coalfield Appalachia from 1940 to 2000," *Journal of Appalachian Studies* 28, no. 2 (1 October 2022): 125–43, https://doi.org/10.5406/23288612.28.2.02.

31. Interview with Clearfork Valley resident, Eagan, TN, 23 October 2021.

32. Ronald L. Lewis, "From Peasant to Proletarian: The Migration of Southern Blacks to the Central Appalachian Coalfields," *Journal of Southern History* 55, no. 1 (1989): 77–102, https://doi.org/10.2307/2209720; Lewis, *Black Coal Miners in America*.

33. Joe William Trotter, *Coal, Class, and Color: Blacks in Southern West Virginia, 1915–32*, Blacks in the New World (Urbana: University of Illinois Press, 1990), https://searchworks.stanford.edu/view/576642; Joe W. Trotter, *African American Workers and the Appalachian Coal Industry* (Morgantown: West Virginia University Press, 2022), https://wvupressonline.com/african-american-workers-and-the-appalachian-coal-industry.

34. Plain Talk History, "Map of White Supremacy's History of Lynchings: A Racial Order in the US Enforced by Communal Murder, 1848–2020," accessed 18 April 2024, https://plaintalkhistory.com/monroeandflorencework/explore/. Thanks to the organization Black in Appalachia for pointing us to this data.

35. Ann Dudley Matheny, *The Magic City: Footnotes to the History of Middlesborough, Kentucky, and the Yellow Creek Valley* (Middlesboro, KY: Bell County Historical Society, 2003), 127–31, https://search.worldcat.org/title/magic-city-footnotes-to-the-history-of-middlesborough-kentucky-and-the-yellow-creek-valley/oclc/53159260.

36. E.g., see Armstead, *Black Days, Black Dust*.

37. Karida L. Brown, *Gone Home: Race and Roots through Appalachia* (Chapel Hill: University of North Carolina Press, 2018), https://uncpress.org/

book/9781469647036/gone-home/; William H. Turner, *The Harlan Renaissance: Stories of Black Life in Appalachian Coal Towns* (Morgantown: West Virginia University Press, 2021), http://www.wvupressonline.com/node/887.

38. Thomas E. Wagner and Phillip J. Obermiller, *African American Miners and Migrants: The Eastern Kentucky Social Club* (Urbana: University of Illinois Press, 2004).

39. Matheny, *Magic City*, 130.

40. Matheny, *Magic City*.

41. Suzanne E. Tallichet, *Daughters of the Mountain: Women Coal Miners in Central Appalachia* (University Park: Pennsylvania State University Press, 2006), https://www.psupress.org/books/titles/0-271-02903-X.html.

42. Katharyne Mitchell, Sally A. Marston, and Cindi Katz, *Life's Work: Geographies of Social Reproduction*, Antipode Book Series (Hoboken, NJ: Wiley-Blackwell, 2004), https://books.google.it/books?id=LwPsiK4ZUjMC.

43. Jessica Wilkerson, *To Live Here, You Have to Fight: How Women Led Appalachian Movements for Social Justice* (Urbana: University of Illinois Press, 2018).

44. Mary K. Anglin, *Women, Power, and Dissent in the Hills of Carolina* (Urbana: University of Illinois Press, 2002).

45. Interview with Clearfork Valley resident, 6 May 2021.

46. David R. Roediger and Elizabeth D. Esch, *The Production of Difference: Race and the Management of Labor in U.S. History* (Oxford: Oxford University Press, 2012), https://global.oup.com/academic/product/the-production-of-difference-9780199739752?cc=gb&lang=en&; Linda McDowell, "Class, Gender, and Space: Scale and the Production of Difference and Inequality," in *Citizenship and Its Others*, ed. Bridget Anderson and Vanessa Hughes (London: Palgrave Macmillan UK, 2015), 184–90, https://doi.org/10.1057/9781137435088_18.

47. While we illustrate the rich histories of resistance here, we explore more contemporary struggles in chapters 7 and 8.

48. James Green, *The Devil Is Here in These Hills: West Virginia's Coal Miners and Their Battle for Freedom* (New York: Atlantic Monthly Press, 2015).

49. Karin A. Shapiro, *A New South Rebellion: The Battle against Convict Labor in the Tennessee Coalfields, 1871–1896* (Chapel Hill: University of North Carolina Press, 2017), https://uncpress.org/book/9780807847336/a-new-south-rebellion/.

50. David Corbin, *Life, Work, and Rebellion in the Coal Fields: The Southern West Virginia Miners, 1880–1922* (Urbana: University of Illinois Press, 1989).

51. Ginny Savage Ayers, Lon Kelly Savage, and Lou Martin, *Never Justice, Never Peace: Mother Jones and the Miner Rebellion at Paint and Cabin Creeks* (Morgantown: West Virginia University Press, 2018), https://wvupressonline.com/node/750.

52. W.E.B. DuBois, *Black Reconstruction in America, 1860–1880* (New York: Free Press, 1998).

53. John W. Hevener and Robert Gipe, *Which Side Are You On? The Harlan County Coal Miners, 1931–39*, reprint ed. (Urbana: University of Illinois Press, 2002); Alessandro Portelli, *They Say in Harlan County: An Oral History*, Oxford Oral History (New York: Oxford University Press, 2012), https://global.oup.com/academic/product/they-say-in-harlan-county-9780199934850?cc=us&lang=en&; Paul F. Taylor, *Bloody Harlan* (Lynchburg, OH: Commonwealth Book Company, 2020); Gaventa, *Power and Powerlessness*, 96–104.

54. Brandon Nida, "Demystifying the Hidden Hand: Capital and the State at Blair Mountain," *Historical Archaeology* 47, no. 3 (1 September 2013): 52–68, https://doi.org/10.1007/BF03376908.

55. Eller, *Uneven Ground*.

56. "The Promise of 1946," *UMWA* (blog), accessed 27 August 2023, https://umwa.org/news-media/journal/the-promise-of-1946/.

57. "The Promise of 1946," *United Mine Workers of America* (blog), accessed 10 April 2024, https://umwa.org/news-media/journal/the-promise-of-1946/.

58. John R. Bowman, "When Workers Organize Capitalists: The Case of the Bituminous Coal Industry," *Politics & Society* 14, no. 3 (1 September 1985): 289–327, https://doi.org/10.1177/003232928501400302.

59. Richard P. Mulcahy, *Social Contract for Coal Fields: United Mine Workers Welfare and Retirement Funds* (Knoxville: University Tennessee Press, 2001), https://utpress.org/title/a-social-contract-for-the-coal-fields/.

60. Barbara Ellen Smith, *Digging Our Own Graves: Coal Miners and the Struggle over Black Lung Disease* (Philadelphia: Temple University Press, 1987), https://wellcomecollection.org/works/jsbvm6tf.

61. Paul F. Clark, *The Miners' Fight for Democracy: Arnold Miller and the Reform of the United Mine Workers* (Ithaca, NY: ILR Press, 1981).

62. Shaunna L. Scott, *Two Sides to Everything: The Cultural Construction of Class Consciousness in Harlan County, Kentucky*, SUNY Series in Oral and Public History (Albany: State University of New York Press, 1995), https://sunypress.edu/Books/T/Two-Sides-to-Everything; Portelli, *They Say in Harlan County*.

63. Warren Brown, "Reagan Nominees Lean toward Management," *Washington Post*, 6 September 1981, https://www.washingtonpost.com/archive/politics/1981/09/07/reagan-nominees-lean-toward-management/948cf5c4-c17b-4df8-bfdc-d3b2e2ffda63/.

64. *Mine War on Blackberry Creek*, Vimeo Video, 2018, https://vimeo.com/226773637; Richard A. Brisbin, *A Strike Like No Other Strike: Law and Resistance during the Pittston Coal Strike of 1989–1990* (Morgantown: West Virginia University Press, 2010), https://wvupressonline.com/node/84; Peter A. Galuszka, *Thunder on the Mountain: Death at Massey and the Dirty Secrets behind Big Coal* (New York: St. Martin's Press, 2012), https://catalog.lib.msu.edu/Record/folio.in00005073159.

65. Brisbin, *A Strike Like No Other Strike*.

66. Thomas Kiffmeyer, *Reformers to Radicals: The Appalachian Volunteers*

and the War on Poverty (Lexington: University Press of Kentucky, 2008), https://www.kentuckypress.com/9780813125091/reformers-to-radicals/; Annelise Orleck and Lisa Gayle Hazirjian, eds., *The War on Poverty: A New Grassroots History, 1964–1980*, Illustrated edition (Athens: University of Georgia Press, 2011), https://ugapress.org/book/9780820339498/the-war-on-poverty/.

67. Huey Perry and Jeff Biggers, *They'll Cut Off Your Project: A Mingo County Chronicle* (Morgantown: West Virginia University Press, 2011), https://wvupressonline.com/node/91.

68. Chad Montrie, *To Save the Land and People: A History of Opposition to Surface Coal Mining in Appalachia* (Chapel Hill: University of North Carolina Press, 2003), https://uncpress.org/book/9780807854358/to-save-the-land-and-people/; Chad Montrie, "'To Have, Hold, Develop, and Defend': Natural Rights and the Movement to Abolish Strip Mining in Eastern Kentucky," *Journal of Appalachian Studies* 11, no. 1/2 (2005): 64–82.

69. Montrie, *To Save the Land and People.*

70. Stephen L. Fisher, ed., *Fighting Back in Appalachia: Traditions of Resistance and Change* (Philadelphia: Temple University Press, 1993).

71. Jillean McCommons, "'Not Just Whites in Appalachia': The Black Appalachian Commission, Regional Black Power Politics, and the War on Poverty, 1965–1975" (PhD diss. University of Kentucky, 2022), https://uknowledge.uky.edu/history_etds/73.

72. Walter Davis and June Roston, "The Southern Empowerment Project: Homegrown Organizing Gone Too Soon," in *Transforming Places: Lessons from Appalachia*, ed. Stephen L. Fisher and Barbara Ellen Smith (Urbana: University of Illinois Press, 2012), 122–32, https://www.jstor.org/stable/10.5406/j.cttlxcjnd.

73. *Morristown: In the Air and Sun Trailer*, Vimeo Video, 2017, https://vimeo.com/226763842; John Gaventa, Barbara Ellen Smith, and Alex Willingham, eds., *Communities in Economic Crisis: Appalachia and the South* (Philadelphia: Temple University Press, 1990).

74. *Mine War on Blackberry Creek.*

75. Hansell, *After Coal.*

76. Wilkerson, *To Live Here, You Have to Fight.*

77. "Gathering Wild Greens: Foodways Lessons from Appalachia's Past," in *Appalachia in Regional Context: Place Matters*, ed. Dwight B. Billings and Ann E. Kingsolver (Lexington: University Press of Kentucky, 2018), 133–52, https://doi.org/10.2307/j.cttlz27j0k; Elizabeth S. D. Engelhardt, *The Tangled Roots of Feminism, Environmentalism, and Appalachian Literature* (Athens: Ohio University Press, 2003), https://search.worldcat.org/en/title/52047422.

78. Karen Beckwith, "Gender Frames and Collective Action: Configurations of Masculinity in the Pittston Coal Strike," *Politics & Society* 29, no. 2 (1 June 2001): 297–330, https://doi.org/10.1177/0032329201029002006.

79. Shannon Elizabeth Bell, *Our Roots Run Deep as Ironweed: Appalachian Women and the Fight for Environmental Justice* (Urbana: University of Illinois

Press, 2013), https://www.press.uillinois.edu/books/?id=p079467; Shannon Elizabeth Bell and Yvonne A. Braun, "Coal, Identity, and the Gendering of Environmental Justice Activism in Central Appalachia," *Gender & Society* 24, no. 6 (December 2010): 794–813, https://doi.org/10.1177/0891243210387277; Barbara Ellen Smith, "Another Place Is Possible? Labor Geography, Spatial Dispossession, and Gendered Resistance in Central Appalachia," *Annals of the Association of American Geographers* 105, no. 3 (2015): 567–82.

80. Ronald L. Lewis, "Race and the United Mine Workers' Union in Tennessee: Selected Letters of William R. Riley, 1892–1895," *Tennessee Historical Quarterly* 36, no. 4 (1977): 524–36.

81. Martin Mendez, interview by Gabe Schwartzman, 20 July 2012, Louie B. Nunn Center for Oral History, University of Kentucky Libraries, https://www.kentuckyoralhistory.org/ark:/16417/xt7m639k6g2g.

82. Smith, *Digging Our Own Graves*.

83. Ramana Ramaswamy and Robert Rowthorn, "Economic Issues 10: Deindustrialization: Its Causes and Implications," Economic Issues (Washington, DC: International Monetary Fund, 1997), https://www.imf.org/external/pubs/ft/issues10/index.htm.

84. Mine Safety and Health Administration (MSHA), "Coal Fatalities for 1900 through 2022," Table (Arlington: United States Department of Labor, 2022), https://arlweb.msha.gov/stats/centurystats/coalstats.asp.

85. Montrie, *To Save the Land and People*.

86. U.S. Energy Information Administration, "Annual Coal Report 2021," Minerals Yearbook, October 2022, https://www.eia.gov/coal/annual/archive/0584_2021.pdf.

87. Michael Hendryx and Benjamin Holland, "Unintended Consequences of the Clean Air Act: Mortality Rates in Appalachian Coal Mining Communities," *Environmental Science & Policy* 63 (1 September 2016): 1–6, https://doi.org/10.1016/j.envsci.2016.04.021.

88. Eric Bowen, Christiadi, John Deskins, and Brian Lego, "An Overview of the Coal Economy in Appalachia," *Appalachian Regional Commission Report*, 2018, 6.

89. Eric Bowen, John Deskins, and Brian Lego, "An Overview of Coal and the Economy in Appalachia," Appalachian Regional Commission, Fourth Quarter 2020 Update (Morgantown: West Virginia University, 2020), 6, https://www.arc.gov/wp-content/uploads/2021/04/Coal-and-the-Economy-in-Appalachia_Q4_2020-Update.pdf.

90. Bowen, Deskins, and Lego, "An Overview of Coal and the Economy in Appalachia," 4.

91. Brown, *Gone Home*, 6.

92. Schwartzman, "Anti-Blackness, Black Geographies, and Racialized Depopulation in Coalfield Appalachia from 1940 to 2000"; Trotter, *African American Workers and the Appalachian Coal Industry*; Ronald L. Lewis, "From Peasant to Proletarian: The Migration of Southern Blacks to the Central Appa-

lachian Coalfields," *Journal of Southern History* 55, no. 1 (1989): 77–102, https://doi.org/10.2307/2209720; Trotter, *Coal, Class, and Color*.

93. Jillean McCommons, "Appalachian Hillsides as Black Ecologies: Housing, Memory, and the Sanctified Hill Disaster of 1972," *AAIHS* (blog), 16 June 2020, https://www.aaihs.org/appalachian-hillsides-as-black-ecologies-housing-memory-and-the-sanctified-hill-disaster-of-1972/.

94. Armstead, *Black Days, Black Dust*.

95. Brown, *Gone Home*.

96. US Census Bureau, "DP05: ACS Demographic and Housing Estimates," accessed 17 March 2025, https://data.census.gov/table/ACSDP5Y2023.DP05?q=black+population+McDowell+County,+West+Virginia; West Virginia State Archives, "A Brief History of African Americans in West Virginia," *Archives* (blog), 2021, https://archive.wvculture.org/hiStory/archives/blacks/blachist.html.

97. US Census Bureau, "Census Bureau Data," accessed 18 April 2024, https://data.census.gov/advanced; Robert P. Stuckert, "Black Populations of Southern Appalachian Counties: 1850–1980" (Black in Appalachia: Community History Digital Archive, 1987), https://blackinappalachia.omeka.net/items/show/1615.

98. Interview with coal community resident, Clairfield, TN, 19 September 2021.

99. Tallichet, *Daughters of the Mountain*.

100. Gaventa, Smith, and Willingham, *Communities in Economic Crisis*.

101. Linda McDowell, "Life without Father and Ford: The New Gender Order of Post-Fordism," *Transactions of the Institute of British Geographers* 16, no. 4 (1991): 400–419, https://doi.org/10.2307/623027; Linda McDowell, "Gender, Work, Employment, and Society: Feminist Reflections on Continuity and Change," *Work, Employment, and Society* 28, no. 5 (1 October 2014): 825–37, https://doi.org/10.1177/0950017014543301.

102. *Fast Food Women*, dir. Anne Lewis, POV documentary, 1992.

103. Ann M. Oberhauser, "Towards a Gendered Regional Geography: Women and Work in Rural Appalachia," *Growth and Change* 26, no. 2 (April 1995): 217–44, https://doi.org/10.1111/j.1468-2257.1995.tb00169.x; Ann M. Oberhauser, "Industrial Restructuring and Women's Homework in Appalachia: Lessons from West Virginia," *Southeastern Geographer* 33, no. 1 (1993): 23–43; Ann M. Oberhauser, "Gender and Household Economic Strategies in Rural Appalachia," *Gender, Place & Culture* 2, no. 1 (1 March 1995): 51–70, https://doi.org/10.1080/09663699550022080.

Chapter 3. Power and Transitions

1. Alexander Cooley and Daniel H. Nexon, "How Hegemony Ends," *Foreign Affairs* 99 (2020): 143; Paul K. MacDonald and Joseph M. Parent, "Graceful Decline? The Surprising Success of Great Power Retrenchment," *International Security* 35, no. 4 (1 April 2011): 7–44, https://doi.org/10.1162/ISEC_a_00034.

2. Peter Newell, *Power Shift: The Global Politics of Energy Transitions* (Cambridge: Cambridge University Press, 2021), 37, https://doi.org/10.1017/9781108966184.

3. Newell, *Power Shift*, 37.

4. Frank W. Geels, "Regime Resistance against Low-Carbon Transitions: Introducing Politics and Power into the Multi-Level Perspective," *Theory, Culture & Society* 31, no. 5 (1 September 2014): 21–40, https://doi.org/10.1177/0263276414531627; Marie Claire Brisbois, "Powershifts: A Framework for Assessing the Growing Impact of Decentralized Ownership of Energy Transitions on Political Decision-Making," *Energy Research & Social Science* 50 (April 2019): 151–61, https://doi.org/10.1016/j.erss.2018.12.003; Newell, *Power Shift*.

5. Geels, "Regime Resistance against Low-Carbon Transitions," 28.

6. Ian Scoones, Melissa Leach, and Peter Newell, eds., *The Politics of Green Transformations*, Pathways to Sustainability (London; New York: Routledge, 2015), 8.

7. Scoones, Leach, and Newell, *Politics of Green Transformations*.

8. By "material basis of power," we mean the political and economic organization of production and consumption within which contestations over power take place. Unlike some orthodox Marxist approaches, we have no assumption that power is inherently determined by material relations, but instead, as Stuart Hall writes, are a "determination in the first instance" (Hall, *Marxism without Guarantees*, 43). Material or economic relations are not a final determination of how power will play out but the terrain on which political struggle takes place.

9. Newell, *Power Shift*, 76.

10. Adrian Ford and Peter Newell, "Regime Resistance and Accommodation: Toward a Neo-Gramscian Perspective on Energy Transitions," *Energy Research & Social Science* 79 (1 September 2021): 102163, https://doi.org/10.1016/j.erss.2021.102163.

11. Tobias Haas, "Struggles in European Union Energy Politics: A Gramscian Perspective on Power in Energy Transitions," *Energy Research & Social Science* 48 (1 February 2019): 68–69, https://doi.org/10.1016/j.erss.2018.09.011.

12. Benjamin K. Sovacool and Marie-Claire Brisbois, "Elite Power in Low-Carbon Transitions: A Critical and Interdisciplinary Review," *Energy Research & Social Science* 57 (1 November 2019): 1, https://doi.org/10.1016/j.erss.2019.101242.

13. Newell, *Power Shift*, 120.

14. James Fairhead, Melissa Leach, and Ian Scoones, "Green Grabbing: A New Appropriation of Nature?," *Journal of Peasant Studies* 39, no. 2 (1 April 2012): 237, https://doi.org/10.1080/03066150.2012.671770.

15. Sovacool and Brisbois, "Elite Power in Low-Carbon Transitions," 1.

16. Newell, *Power Shift*, 213–19.

17. Flor Avelino and Julia M. Wittmayer, "Shifting Power Relations in Sus-

tainability Transitions: A Multi-Actor Perspective," *Journal of Environmental Policy & Planning* 18, no. 5 (19 October 2016): 628–49, https://doi.org/10.1080/1523908X.2015.1112259.

18. Avelino and Wittmayer, "Shifting Power Relations in Sustainability Transitions," 629.

19. Avelino and Wittmayer, "Shifting Power Relations in Sustainability Transitions," 642.

20. Stevis, *Just Transitions*, 6.

21. Geels, "Regime Resistance against Low-Carbon Transitions."

22. See for instance, Ford and Newell, "Regime Resistance and Accommodation"; Avelino and Wittmayer, "Shifting Power Relations in Sustainability Transitions."

23. Newell, *Power Shift*, 37.

24. Avelino and Rotmans, "Power in Transition," 545. While niches initially in the more socio-technical sense referred to niche technologies such as alternative forms of energy, here they are used more broadly as alternative ideas, innovations, and practices. Avelino defines them as "configurations in which non-conformism and innovation can develop" (545).

25. Frank W. Geels, "Ontologies, Socio-Technical Transitions (to Sustainability), and the Multi-Level Perspective," *Research Policy*, Special Section on Innovation and Sustainability Transitions, 39, no. 4 (1 May 2010): 495, https://doi.org/10.1016/j.respol.2010.01.022; Ford and Newell, "Regime Resistance and Accommodation," 30.

26. Avelino and Rotmans, "Power in Transition," 545.

27. Avelino and Rotmans, "Power in Transition," 560.

28. Harald Winkler, "Towards a Theory of Just Transition: A Neo-Gramscian Understanding of How to Shift Development Pathways to Zero Poverty and Zero Carbon," *Energy Research & Social Science* 70 (1 December 2020): 101789, https://doi.org/10.1016/j.erss.2020.101789.

29. Peter Newell, "Trasformismo or Transformation? The Global Political Economy of Energy Transitions," *Review of International Political Economy* 26, no. 1 (2 January 2019): 28, https://doi.org/10.1080/09692290.2018.1511448.

30. Clyde Woods, *Development Arrested: The Blues and Plantation Power in the Mississippi Delta*, 2nd ed. (London; New York: Verso, 2017); Clyde Woods, *Development Drowned and Reborn: The Blues and Bourbon Restorations in Post-Katrina New Orleans*, ed. Laura Pulido and Jordan T. Camp (Athens: University of Georgia Press, 2017); Stuart Hall, Doreen Massey, and Michael Rustin, eds., *After Neoliberalism? The Kilburn Manifesto* (London: Lawrence & Wishart, 2015).

31. Here we build on the work of numerous scholars whose work on conjunctural analysis informs our understanding of periodization and transformation of power and hegemony, including Hart, "Why Did It Take So Long?" We find the conjuncture to be a useful conceptual and methodological tool for considering power in transition because it offers a lens to consider site-specific

contingencies of power struggles, while also recognizing that, as Tania Li argues, "a conjuncture is dynamic but it is not random. There is path dependence." Jamie Peck, *Constructions of Neoliberal Reason*, reprint ed. (Oxford: Oxford University Press, 2013); Peck and Theodore, "Still Neoliberalism?"; Tania Murray Li, *Land's End* (Durham, NC: Duke University Press, 2014), http://www.jstor.org/stable/j.ctv1131b52.

32. Stuart Hall, *The Hard Road to Renewal: Thatcherism and the Crisis of the Left* (London: Verso, 1988), https://www.versobooks.com/en-gb/products/1252-the-hard-road-to-renewal.

33. Stuart Hall, "The Great Moving Right Show," *Marxism Today* 23, no. 1 (January 1979): 14, https://mrc-catalogue.warwick.ac.uk/records/EJH/4/5/1/25.

34. Hall, *The Hard Road to Renewal*, 96; Ruth Wilson Gilmore, *Abolition Geography: Essays towards Liberation* (London: Verso Books, 2022), 64, https://www.versobooks.com/en-gb/products/2615-abolition-geography.

35. Hall, *The Hard Road to Renewal*; Gillian Hart, *Rethinking the South African Crisis: Nationalism, Populism, Hegemony* (Athens: University of Georgia Press, 2014), https://ugapress.org/book/9780820347172/rethinking-the-south-african-crisis; Gilmore, *Abolition Geography*.

36. Gilmore, *Abolition Geography*; Stuart Hall, "The State and Society, 1890–1930," in *The State and Society, 1890–1930*, ed. Bill Schwarz and Mary Langan (London: Hutchinson Educational, n.d.), 288.

37. Antonio Gramsci, *Selections from the Prison Notebooks*, ed. Quintin Hoare and Geoffrey Nowell Smith (1971; rpt., New York: International Publishers Co., 1989), 276.

38. Steven Lukes, *Power: A Radical View*, 3rd ed. (London: Bloomsbury Publishing, 2021), https://www.bloomsbury.com/uk/power-9781352012347/.

39. Robert A. Dahl, *Who Governs? Democracy and Power in the American City*, 2nd ed. (New Haven: Yale University Press, 2005), https://yalebooks.yale.edu/9780300103922/who-governs; Nelson W. Polsby, *Community Power and Political Theory* (New Haven: Yale University Press, 1974).

40. Peter Bachrach and Morton S. Baratz, "Two Faces of Power," *American Political Science Review* 56, no. 4 (December 1962): 947–52, https://doi.org/10.2307/1952796.

41. Lisa VeneKlasen and Valerie Miller, *A New Weave of Power, People, and Politics: The Action Guide for Advocacy and Citizen Participation* (Oklahoma City: World Neighbors, 2002), https://doi.org/10.3362/9781780444208; John Gaventa, "Finding the Spaces for Change: A Power Analysis," *Institute of Development Studies Bulletin* 37, no. 6 (November 2006): 23–33, https://doi.org/10.1111/j.1759-5436.2006.tb00320.x.

42. E. E. Schattschneider, *The Semisovereign People: A Realist's View of Democracy in America* (New York: Holt, Rinehart and Winston, 1960).

43. "Theme 2: Multiple Forms and Arenas of Power," *Making Sense of Power—Just Power*, chap. 3 (pressbooks.pub).

44. Clarissa Rile Hayward, "De-Facing Power," *Polity* 31, no. 1 (1998): 1, https://doi.org/10.2307/3235365. For an excellent discussion of the relationship of agency, structure, and power see also Clarissa Hayward and Steven Lukes, "Nobody to Shoot? Power, Structure, and Agency: A Dialogue," *Journal of Power* 1, no. 1 (1 April 2008): 5–20, https://doi.org/10.1080/17540290801943364. While a Foucauldian approach argues that "power is everywhere," Lukes insisted that it was held by actors, who in turn could be held accountable for their actions.

45. Lukes, *Power*, 1.

46. Lukes, *Power*, 157.

47. Lukes, *Power*, 17.

48. Lukes, *Power*, 187.

49. Gaventa, *Power and Powerlessness*, 256.

50. Gaventa, *Power and Powerlessness*, 23.

51. Gaventa, *Power and Powerlessness*, 256–57.

52. Gaventa, *Power and Powerlessness*, 24–25; Lukes, *Power*, 187.

53. Gaventa, "Finding the Spaces for Change"; John Gaventa, "Linking the Prepositions: Using Power Analysis to Inform Strategies for Social Action," *Journal of Political Power* 14, no. 1 (10 February 2021): 190–30, https://doi.org/10.1080/2158379X.2021.1878409.

54. Lisa VeneKlasen, Molly Reilly, and Cindy Clark, "Making Change Happen: Power," short series, Concepts for Revisioning Power for Justice, Equality, and Peace (Just Associates, 2006), https://justassociates.org/wp-content/uploads/2020/08/mch3_2011_final_0.pdf.

55. Naila Kabeer, *Reversed Realities: Gender Hierarchies in Development Thought* (London; New York: Verso, 1994); Srilatha Batliwala, "All About Power: Understanding Social Power and Power Structures" (New Delhi: CREA, 2019), https://reconference.creaworld.org/wp-content/uploads/2019/05/All-About-Power-Srilatha-Batliwala.pdf.

56. John Gaventa, "Linking the Prepositions: Using Power Analysis to Inform Strategies for Social Action," *Journal of Political Power* 14, no. 1 (2 January 2021): 5, https://doi.org/10.1080/2158379X.2021.1878409.

Chapter 4. Old Powerholders Cling On

1. Freese, "How Coal Disrupted the World."

2. Robinson Meyer, "The Secret Political Power of Fossil Fuels," *The Atlantic*, 27 October 2020, Weekly Planet edition, sec. Newsletters, https://www.theatlantic.com/newsletters/archive/2020/10/the-secret-political-power-of-fossil-fuels/616869/.

3. James M. Van Nostrand, *The Coal Trap: How West Virginia Was Left Behind in the Clean Energy Revolution* (Cambridge: Cambridge University Press, 2022), https://doi.org/10.1017/9781108902403.

4. See earlier discussion, chapter 3, pp. 59–60.

5. Freese, "How Coal Disrupted the World."

6. Eric Bowen, Christiadi, John Deskins, and Brian Lego, "An Overview of Coal and the Economy in Appalachia: Fourth Quarter 2020 Update," https://www.arc.gov/wp-content/uploads/2021/04/Coal-and-the-Economy-in-Appalachia_Q4_2020-Update.pdf.

7. Karin Kirk, "Fossil Fuel Political Giving Outdistances Renewables 13 to One," *Yale Climate Connections*, 6 January 2020, sec. Policy and Politics, http://yaleclimateconnections.org/2020/01/fossil-fuel-political-giving-outdistances-renewables-13-to-one/.

8. OpenSecrets, "Coal Mining Lobbying: Annual Lobbying Totals, 1998–2023," accessed 5 February 2024, https://www.opensecrets.org/industries/lobbying?cycle=2012&ind=E1210.

9. Ken Ward Jr., "The Presidential Race's 'Coal Conundrum,'" *Coal Tattoo* (blog), 15 August 2012, https://web.archive.org/web/20160508103200/http://blogs.wvgazettemail.com/coaltattoo/2012/08/15/the-presidential-races-coal-conundrum/.

10. Taylor Kuykendall, "Appalachian Coal Groups Line Up behind a Pro-Coal Romney," *WV News*, 13 August 2012, https://www.wvnews.com/statejournal/news/appalachian-coal-groups-line-up-behind-a-pro-coal-romney/article_db94170f-7490-5c9a-bdd2-0b38889ad8a1.html.

11. James Bruggers, "McConnell's Record on Coal Has Become a Hot Topic in His Senate Campaign," *Inside Climate News*, 24 September 2019, https://insideclimatenews.org/news/24092019/mitch-mcconnell-coal-miners-pensions-fund-appalachia-senate-campaign/.

12. Bruggers, "McConnell's Record on Coal."

13. Taylor Giorno and Jimmy Cloutier, "Joe Manchin Vows to Block 'Radical Climate Agenda,' Rakes in Oil and Gas Industry Contributions," *OpenSecrets News*, 12 May 2023, sec. News and Analysis, https://www.opensecrets.org/news/2023/05/manchins-vows-to-block-radical-climate-agenda/.

14. Giorno and Cloutier, "Joe Manchin Vows to Block 'Radical Climate Agenda.'"

15. OpenSecrets, "Oil & Gas Recipients: Top 20 Member Recipients of Money from Oil & Gas, 2021–2022," accessed 5 February 2024, https://www.opensecrets.org/industries/summary?cycle=2022&ind=E01&recipdetail=M&sortorder=U.

16. Scott Waldman, "Lawyers for Jim Justice Say His Coal Companies 'Chronically Scarce' on Cash," *Politico*, 1 June 2023, https://www.politico.com/news/2023/06/01/stretched-to-the-limit-jim-justices-shrinking-coal-empire-pelted-by-legal-attacks-00099575.

17. Interview, 28 April 2023.

18. Interview, 16 March 2023.

19. Sam Stockard, "Tennessee to Retake Coal Mining Regulation with Industry at Rock Bottom," *Timesfreepress.Com*, 31 May 2021, sec. Local Regional, https://www.timesfreepress.com/news/local/story/2021/may/31/state-retake-coal-mining-regulatiindustry-roc/547902/.

20. Isabelle Chapman, Ella Nilsen, and Casey Tolan, "Republican Lawmakers Are Making It Harder for Power Companies to Pivot Away from Coal. Their Constituents May Be Paying the Price," *CNN*, 6 June 2023, sec. Investigates, https://www.cnn.com/2023/06/06/us/coal-plants-republican-lawmakers-energy-transition-invs/index.html; Van Nostrand, *Coal Trap*; James Van Nostrand, "How Coal Maintains Its Political Hold on West Virginia," audio, Energy Policy Now, accessed 15 June 2023, https://kleinmanenergy.upenn.edu/podcast/how-coal-maintains-its-political-hold-on-west-virginia/.

21. Interview, 24 April 2023.

22. "Truth about Unions," accessed 15 October 2024, https://www.truthaboutunions.org/2018/11/27/charts-on-the-decline-of-union-membership/.

23. Abraham, "Just Transitions for the Miners," 235.

24. Donna Sockell and John Thomas Delany, "Union Organizing and the Reagan NLRB," *Contemporary Economic Policy* 5, no. 4 (October 1987): 28–45, https://doi.org/10.1111/j.1465-7287.1987.tb00270.x.

25. Abraham, "Just Transitions for the Miners," 236.

26. Smith, *Digging Our Own Graves*, 12.

27. Beckwith, "Gender Frames and Collective Action"; Brisbin, *A Strike Like No Other Strike*.

28. Smith, *Digging Our Own Graves*, 234.

29. Smith, *Digging Our Own Graves*, 16.

30. Taylor Sisk, "Black Lung Resurgence Drives Push to Protect Coal Miners against Silica Dust," *Daily Yonder*, 13 March 2023, http://dailyyonder.com/black-lung-resurgence-drives-push-to-protect-coal-miners-against-silica-dust/2023/03/13/.

31. Abraham, "Just Transitions for the Miners," 240. While this was the case for the union as an organization, some retired members became very active in both the anti-mountaintop-removal efforts, and the efforts for just transition, examined in chapters 7 and 8.

32. Gabriel Winant, *The Next Shift: The Fall of Industry and the Rise of Health Care in Rust Belt America* (Cambridge, MA: Harvard University Press, 2021), https://www.hup.harvard.edu/books/9780674292192.

33. UMWA, "Preserving Coal Country: Keeping America's Coal Miners, Families, and Communities Whole in an Era of Global Energy Transition," https://umwa.org/wp-content/uploads/2021/04/UMWA-Preserving-Coal-Country-2021.pdf; Noam Scheiber, "A Coal Miners Union Indicates It Will Accept a Switch to Renewable Energy in Exchange for Jobs," *New York Times*, 19 April 2021, sec. Business, https://www.nytimes.com/live/2021/04/19/business/stock-market-today.

34. Shirley Stewart Burns, *Bringing Down the Mountains: The Impact of Mountaintop Removal on Southern West Virginia Communities* (Morgantown: West Virginia University Press, 2007), http://wvupressonline.com/node/70; Shirley Stewart Burns, Mari-Lynn Evans, and Silas House, eds., *Coal Country: Rising Up against Mountaintop Removal Mining* (Berkeley, CA: Sierra Club Books, 2009), https://search.worldcat.org/title/

Coal-country-:-rising-up-against-mountaintop-removal-mining/oclc/320804167.

35. Sylvia Ryerson, "Precarious Politics: Friends of Coal, the UMWA, and the Affective Terrain of Energy Identification," *American Quarterly* 72, no. 3 (2020): 731.

36. Lukes, *Power*.

37. Shannon Elizabeth Bell and Richard York, "Community Economic Identity: The Coal Industry and Ideology Construction in West Virginia," *Rural Sociology* 75, no. 1 (2010): 126–27, https://doi.org/10.1111/j.1549-0831.2009.00004.x (quoting Friends of Coal document of 2007).

38. Van Nostrand, *Coal Trap*.

39. "Count on Coal," accessed 5 March 2025, https://www.countoncoal.org/; Global Energy Monitor Wiki, "American Coal Foundation," *Wikipedia*, GEM Wiki, 14 July 2021, https://www.gem.wiki/American_Coal_Foundation.

40. Friends of Coal, "Friends of Coal: Ladies Auxiliary," accessed 15 February 2024, https://www.friendsofcoalladies.com/about.

41. Bell and York, "Community Economic Identity," 134–35.

42. Bell and York, "Community Economic Identity," 135.

43. Facebook, "Friends of Coal Tennessee," accessed 15 February 2024, https://www.facebook.com/FriendsofCoalTN.

44. Rebecca R. Scott, *Removing Mountains: Extracting Nature and Identity in the Appalachian Coalfields* (Minneapolis: University of Minnesota Press, 2010).

45. Bell and York, "Community Economic Identity," 130.

46. Ryerson, "Precarious Politics," 729.

47. Interview, 24 April 2023.

48. Bell and York, "Community Economic Identity."

49. Van Nostrand, *Coal Trap*, 111.

50. Philip G. Lewin, "'Coal Is Not Just a Job, It's a Way of Life': The Cultural Politics of Coal Production in Central Appalachia," *Social Problems* 66, no. 1 (19 October 2017): 13, https://doi.org/10.1093/socpro/spx030; John Cheves, Bill Estep, and Linda B. Blackfoot, *Fifty Years of Night* (Lexington, KY: Lexington Herald-Leader, 2014), 160, https://leanpub.com/night.

51. *Dead Aim: Joe Manchin for West Virginia TV Ad* (Youtube, 2010), https://www.youtube.com/watch?v=xIJORBRpOPM.

52. Ryerson, "Precarious Politics," 731.

53. Ryerson, "Precarious Politics," 733.

54. Interview, 24 April 2023.

55. Ryerson, "Precarious Politics," 731.

56. Rich Kirby, "Speak Your Piece: Wars and Rumors of Wars," *Daily Yonder*, 27 June 2013, sec. Environment, Rural Economy, https://dailyyonder.com/speak-your-piece-coals-enemy/2013/06/27/.

57. Kirby, "Speak Your Piece."

58. Shelly Annette Biesel, "When Disinformation Makes Sense: Contextualizing the War on Coal in Appalachian Kentucky," *Economic Anthropology* 8, no. 1 (2021): 7–21, https://doi.org/10.1002/sea2.12194.

59. Gabe Schwartzman, "Where Appalachia Went Right: White Masculinities, Nature, and Pro-Coal Politics in an Era of Climate Change," Center for Right-Wing Studies, Department of Geography, University of California at Berkeley, 15 May 2014, 71, https://www.academia.edu/53702598/Where_Appalachia_Went_Right_White_Masculinities_Nature_and_Pro_Coal_Politics_in_an_Era_of_Climate_Change.

60. Interview, September 28, 2022.

61. Aysha Bodenhamer, "King Coal: A Study of Mountaintop Removal, Public Discourse, and Power in Appalachia," *Society & Natural Resources* 29, no. 10 (2016): 1151, https://doi.org/10.1080/08941920.2016.1138561.

62. Bell and York, "Community Economic Identity," 111.

63. Bell and York, "Community Economic Identity," 139.

64. Sylvia Ryerson, "Precarious Politics: Friends of Coal, the UMWA, and the Affective Terrain of Energy Identification," *American Quarterly* 72, no. 3 (2020): 731, https://dx.doi.org/10.1353/aq.2020.0042.

65. Interview, 21 October 2022.

66. Florian Egli, Nicolas Schmid, and Tobias Schmidt, "Electoral Response to the Decline of Coal Mining in the United States," SSRN Scholarly Paper (Rochester, NY, 12 October 2020), https://doi.org/10.2139/ssrn.3710589.

67. Van Nostrand, *Coal Trap*, 114.

68. "Biden Has Waged War on Affordable Energy and It Will Hurt Kentucky," News, *Louisville Courier Journal* (blog), 6 June 2023, https://www.courier-journal.com/story/opinion/2023/06/06/mcconnell-president-bidens-war-on-affordable-energy-hurts-kentucky/70289360007/.

69. Adam Mayer, "More than Just Jobs: Understanding What Drives Support for a Declining Coal Industry," *Extractive Industries and Society* 9 (March 2022): 3, https://doi.org/10.1016/j.exis.2021.101038.

70. Benjamin Brown and Samuel J. Spiegel, "Coal, Climate Justice, and the Cultural Politics of Energy Transition," *Global Environmental Politics* 19, no. 2 (1 May 2019): 149, https://doi.org/10.1162/glep_a_00501.

Chapter 5. Protecting the Hegemony of Coal

1. James David Vance, *Hillbilly Elegy: A Memoir of a Family and Culture in Crisis* (London: William Collins, 2016).

2. *Hillbilly Elegy* has been strongly critiqued by many Appalachian scholars for its simplistic generalizations and misrepresentations of the region. See, for instance, Anthony Harkins and Meredith McCarroll, eds., *Appalachian Reckoning: A Region Responds to Hillbilly Elegy* (Morgantown: West Virginia University Press, 2019), https://wvupressonline.com/node/774.

3. Eric Lipton, "'The Coal Industry Is Back,' Trump Proclaimed. It Wasn't," *New York Times*, October 5, 2020, https://www.nytimes.com/2020/10/05/us/politics/trump-coal-industry.html?searchResultPosition=1.

4. The research for this chapter was done prior to the reelection of the Donald Trump in the 2024 elections. Although we have updated the chapter slightly, the interviews and most of the analysis refers to the earlier period, especially the 2016 elections in which Trump was first elected.

5. Valerie Volcovici, "Trump Seeks to Ax Appalachia Economic Programs, Causing Worry in Coal Country," *Reuters*, 17 March 2017, sec. Business, https://www.reuters.com/article/us-usa-trump-budget-appalachia-idUSKBN16N2VF.

6. Elizabeth Catte, "Passive, Poor, and White? What People Keep Getting Wrong about Appalachia," *The Guardian*, 6 February 2018, sec. US news, https://www.theguardian.com/us-news/2018/feb/06/what-youre-getting-wrong-about-appalachia.

7. Dan Balz, "Rural America Lifted Trump to the Presidency. Support Is Strong, but Not Monolithic," *Washington Post*, 8 April 2023, https://www.washingtonpost.com/politics/rural-america-lifted-trump-to-the-presidency-support-is-strong-but-not-monolithic/2017/06/16/df4f9156-4ac9-11e7-9669-250d0b15f83b_story.html.

8. Shannon M. Monnat and David L. Brown, "More than a Rural Revolt: Landscapes of Despair and the 2016 Presidential Election," *Journal of Rural Studies* 55 (October 2017): 231, https://doi.org/10.1016/j.jrurstud.2017.08.010.

9. Monnat and Brown, "More than a Rural Revolt," 229, quoted in Shannon M. Monnat, "Deaths of Despair and Support for Trump in the 2016 Presidential Election" (Pennsylvania State University, 4 December 2016), https://doi.org/10.13140/RG.2.2.27976.62728.

10. Edelman, "Hollowed Out Heartland, USA," 505.

11. "The Geography of Voting—and Not Voting," *Washington Post*, accessed 9 February 2024, https://www.washingtonpost.com/graphics/2018/politics/voter-turnout/.

12. Daniel Faber, Jennie Stephens, Victor Wallis, Roger Gottlieb, Charles Levenstein, Patrick CoatarPeter, and Boston Editorial Group of CNS, "Trump's Electoral Triumph: Class, Race, Gender, and the Hegemony of the Polluter-Industrial Complex," *Capital Nature Socialism* 28, no. 1 (2017): 1–15, https://doi.org/10.1080/10455752.2017.1279867, drawing from Konstantin Kilibarda and Daria Roithmayr, "The Myth of the Rust Belt Revolt," *Slate*, 1 December 2016, sec. Politics, https://slate.com/news-and-politics/2016/12/the-myth-of-the-rust-belt-revolt.html.

13. Gaventa, *Power and Powerlessness*, 142.

14. Lawrence Grossback and Allan Hammock, "Overcoming One-Party Dominance: How Contextual Politics and West Virginia Helped Put George Bush in the White House," *Politics & Policy* 31, no. 3 (2003): 406–31, https://doi.org/10.1111/j.1747-1346.2003.tb00155.x.

15. Secretary of State, "Tennessee State Historical Election Results," accessed

26 February 2024, https://sos.tn.gov/elections/results. Represents precincts in White Oak, Habersham, and Clairfield. Complete data was not available for the two precincts on the Kentucky side, despite numerous searches. However, the numbers there are quite small. It was also not possible to obtain turnout data over time at the precinct level.

16. Egli, Schmid, and Schmidt, "Electoral Response to the Decline of Coal Mining in the United States."

17. Chip Berlet and Spencer Sunshine, "Rural Rage: The Roots of Right-Wing Populism in the United States," *Journal of Peasant Studies* 46, no. 3 (16 April 2019): 480–513, https://doi.org/10.1080/03066150.2019.1572603.

18. Mark Edelman, "Sacrifice Zones in Rural and Non-Metro USA: Fertile Soil for Authoritarian Populism," *openDemocracy*, 18 February 2018, https://www.opendemocracy.net/marc-edelman/sacrifice-zones-in-rural-and-non-metro-usa-fertile-soil-for-authoritarian-populism; Claudine M. Pied, "Ethnography and the Making of 'The People': Uncovering Conservative Populist Politics in the United States," *American Journal of Economics and Sociology* 78, no. 3 (20 May 2019): 761–86, https://doi.org/10.1111/ajes.12280; Faber et al., "Trump's Electoral Triumph."

19. Ian Scoones, Mark Edelman, Saturnino M. Borras Jr., Ruth Hall, Wendy Wolford, and Ben White, "Emancipatory Rural Politics: Confronting Authoritarian Populism," *Journal of Peasant Studies* 45, no. 1 (2 January 2018): 6, https://doi.org/10.1080/03066150.2017.1339693.

20. Pied, "Ethnography and the Making of 'The People,'" 778.

21. John Clarke and Janet Newman, "'People in This Country Have Had Enough of Experts': Brexit and the Paradoxes of Populism," *Critical Policy Studies* 11, no. 1 (2 January 2017): 101–16, https://doi.org/10.1080/19460171.2017.1282376; Mikko Lehtonen, "'What's Going On?' in Finland: Employing Stuart Hall for a Conjunctural Analysis," *International Journal of Cultural Studies* 19, no. 1 (1 January 2016): 71–84, https://doi.org/10.1177/1367877915599612, quoted in Pied, "Ethnography and the Making of 'The People,'" 778.

22. Pied, "Ethnography and the Making of 'The People,'" 779.

23. David Roberts, "Hillary Clinton's 'Coal Gaffe' Is a Microcosm of Her Twisted Treatment by the Media," *Vox*, 15 September 2017, https://www.vox.com/energy-and-environment/2017/9/15/16306158/hillary-clinton-hall-of-mirrors.

24. Ken Ward Jr., "'What Happened': Hillary Clinton on 'Country Roads,' the Coalfields, the Quote, and Don Blankenship," News, *Coal Tattoo* (blog), 12 September 2017, http://blogs.wvgazette.com/coaltattoo/2017/09/12/what-happened-hillary-clinton-on-country-roads-the-coalfields-the-quote-and-don-blankenship/.

25. Justin Worland, "Why Trump's Promise to Save the Coal Industry Does More Damage Than Good," *Time*, 12 August 2016, sec. U.S. Energy, https://time.com/4447586/trump-coal-industry-energy/.

26. Interview, 21 March 2023.

27. Katherine J. Cramer, *The Politics of Resentment: Rural Consciousness in Wisconsin and the Rise of Scott Walker* (Chicago: University of Chicago Press, 2016), https://press.uchicago.edu/ucp/books/book/chicago/P/bo22879533.html; Arlie Russell Hochschild, *Strangers in Their Own Land: Anger and Mourning on the American Right* (New York: New Press, 2016), https://thenewpress.com/books/strangers-their-own-land.

28. Arlie Russell Hochschild, *Stolen Pride: Loss, Shame, and the Rise of the Right* (New York: New Press, 2024).

29. Elizabeth Catte, "Who's to Blame for White Poverty?," *Boston Review*, 5 September 2024, https://www.bostonreview.net/articles/whos-to-blame-for-white-poverty/.

30. Interview, 23 March 2023.

31. Interview, 22 September 2022.

32. Interview, 20 April 2023.

33. Edelman, "Hollowed Out Heartland, USA," 507.

34. Interview, 28 September 2022.

35. Interview, 28 April 2023.

36. Interview, 7 May 2021.

37. Interview, 21 March 2023.

38. Miriam Jordan, "In Rare Victory, Immigrants Prevail in Suit Over Meat Plant Raid," *New York Times*, 27 February 2023, sec. U.S., https://www.nytimes.com/2023/02/27/us/meat-plant-raid-immigrants-tennessee.html.

39. Michael J. Coyle and Stephen T. Young, "The Fight for Black Lives to Matter: Appalachian Social Movement Intersections and the Capitalist Carceral State," in *No Justice, No Police? The Politics of Protest and Social Change*, edited by Matt Clement (Winchester, UK: Zer0 Books, 2023), 209–25, https://pure.royalholloway.ac.uk/ws/files/47997842/jhpnjnpfinalprrofs_1_.pdf#page=221; Erica Chenoweth, "The Floyd Protests Are the Broadest in U.S. History—and Are Spreading to White, Small-Town America," *Washington Post*, 6 June 2020, sec. Analysis, https://www.washingtonpost.com/politics/2020/06/06/floyd-protests-are-broadest-us-history-are-spreading-white-small-town-america/.

40. Mason Adams, "How #NoHateInMyHoller Became the War Cry for Appalachia," *Daily Yonder*, 30 August 2017, http://dailyyonder.com/nohateinmyholler-became-war-cry-appalachia/2017/08/30/.

41. "The Sunup Initiative," Coalition, accessed 16 February 2024, https://sunupcorbin.com; *The Corbin Expulsion of 1919* (YouTube: Black in Appalachia, 2020), https://www.youtube.com/watch?v=TNydvshLlgU.

42. "Black in Appalachia: Histories of the Mountain South," Black in Appalachia: Research, Education and Support, accessed 16 February 2024, https://www.blackinappalachia.org.

43. Interview, 24 March 2023.

44. Interview, 24 March 2023.

45. Gabe Schwartzman, "Anti-Blackness, Black Geographies, and Racialized Depopulation in Coalfield Appalachia from 1940 to 2000," *Journal*

of Appalachian Studies 28, no. 2 (1 October 2022): 125–43, https://doi.org/10.5406/23288612.28.2.02; Rebecca R. Scott, "Appalachia and the Construction of Whiteness in the United States," *Sociology Compass* 3, no. 5 (2009): 803–10, https://doi.org/10.1111/j.1751-9020.2009.00235.x; Barbara Ellen Smith, "De-Gradations of Whiteness: Appalachia and the Complexities of Race," *Journal of Appalachian Studies* 10, no. 1/2 (2004): 38–57.

46. Eduardo Bonilla-Silva, *Racism without Racists: Color-Blind Racism and the Persistence of Racial Inequality in America*, 6th ed. (Lanham, MD: Rowman & Littlefield, 2021).

47. Isabel Wilkerson, *Caste: The Origins of Our Discontents* (New York: Penguin Random House, 2023), 19, https://www.penguinrandomhouse.com/books/653196/caste-by-isabel-wilkerson/.

48. W.E.B. DuBois, *Black Reconstruction in America, 1860–1880* (New York: Free Press, 1998), 700; David R. Roediger, *The Wages of Whiteness: Race and the Making of the American Working Class*, New Ed. (London; New York: Verso, 2007).

49. Interview, 20 April 2023.

50. Edelman, "Hollowed Out Heartland, USA," 506.

51. Monnat and Brown, "More than a Rural Revolt," 233–34.

52. Berlet and Sunshine, "Rural Rage."

53. Gene Zubovich, "Christian Nationalism Is Surging. It Wasn't Inevitable," *Washington Post*, 6 May 2022, sec. Perspective, https://www.washingtonpost.com/outlook/2022/05/06/christian-nationalism-is-surging-it-wasnt-inevitable/.

54. Berlet and Sunshine, "Rural Rage."

55. Paul Matzko, *The Radio Right: How a Band of Broadcasters Took on the Federal Government and Built the Modern Conservative Movement* (Oxford: Oxford University Press, 2020).

56. Interview, 29 September 2022.

57. Interview, 23 March 2023.

58. Interview with Campbell County commissioner, 7 June 2021.

59. "Encore: In Appalachia, Sex Educators Suspend Their Work after Threats," *All Things Considered* (NPR, 21 January 2023), https://www.npr.org/2023/01/21/1150605302/encore-in-appalachia-sex-educators-suspend-their-work-after-threats.

60. Interview, 23 March 2023.

61. Jamie Lucke, "One Arts Gathering Flees, Another Cancels after Confrontation in Harlan County," *Kentucky Lantern*, 23 August 2023, https://kentuckylantern.com/2023/08/23/one-arts-gathering-flees-another-cancels-after-confrontation-in-harlan-county/.

62. Interview, 24 March 2023.

63. Faber et al., "Trump's Electoral Triumph," 9.

Chapter 6. Financialization and the Rise of Corporate Conservation

1. Katrina S. Rogers, "Soft Power, NGOs, and Climate Change: The Case of The Nature Conservancy," in *Climate Change and Environmental Ethics*, ed. Ved P. Nanda (New York: Routledge, 2011).

2. Adam Bloom, "The Cumberland Forest Project: 253,000 Acres of Preserved Land," Nature Conservancy, 14 July 2019, https://www.nature.org/en-us/what-we-do/our-priorities/protect-water-and-land/land-and-water-stories/cumberland-forest-project/.

3. Bloom, "The Cumberland Forest Project."

4. Andrew Gunnoe, Conner Bailey, and Lord Ameyaw, "Millions of Acres, Billions of Trees: Socioecological Impacts of Shifting Timberland Ownership," *Rural Sociology* 83, no. 4 (2018): 799–822, https://doi.org/10.1111/ruso.12210.

5. Fairhead, Leach, and Scoones, "Green Grabbing."

6. Gabe Schwartzman, "Climate Rentierism after Coal: Forests, Carbon Offsets, and Post-Coal Politics in the Appalachian Coalfields," *Journal of Peasant Studies* 49, no. 5 (29 July 2022): 924–44, https://doi.org/10.1080/03066150.2022.2078710.

7. Emrah Karakilic, "Rentierism and the Commons: A Critical Contribution to Brett Christophers' Rentier Capitalism," *Environment and Planning A: Economy and Space* 54, no. 2 (6 December 2021): 422–29, https://doi.org/10.1177/0308518X211062233.

8. Huff and Brock, "Introduction."

9. Gaventa, *Power and Powerlessness*, 237–49.

10. Gaventa, *Power and Powerlessness*, 78.

11. Greta R. Krippner, "The Financialization of the American Economy," *Socio-Economic Review* 3, no. 2 (1 May 2005): 174, https://doi.org/10.1093/SER/mwi008.

12. Appalachian Land Ownership Task Force, *Who Owns Appalachia?*, 30.

13. Appalachian Land Ownership Task Force, *Who Owns Appalachia?*

14. Kelly Kay, "Rural Rentierism and the Financial Enclosure of Maine's Open Lands Tradition," *Annals of the American Association of Geographers* 107, no. 6 (29 June 2017): 1–17, https://doi.org/10.1080/24694452.2017.1328305.

15. "RMK Timberland Group: Company Profile and News," News, *Bloomberg.com*, accessed 22 February 2024, https://www.bloomberg.com/profile/company/0096643D:US.

16. Molpus Woodlands Group, "Molpus Woodlands Group Acquires 192,000 Acres of Timberland in Louisiana: Acquisitions 11.09.15," 9 November 2015, https://www.molpus.com/2015/11/molpus-woodlands-group-acquires-192000-acres-of-timberland-in-louisiana/.

17. JW Randolph, "US Coal: Keeping the Lights On . . . in Chinese Boardrooms?," *Front Porch* (blog), 25 July 2012, https://web.archive.org/web/20121230171147/https://appvoices.org/2012/07/25/us-coal-keeping-the-lights-on-in-chinese-boardrooms/.

18. Although in many instances across the region, mineral and surface rights had been owned separately, in the case of the American Association, they were largely owned together.

19. "Natural Resource Partners L.P.," accessed 7 March 2024, https://nrplp.com/.

20. Kean Birch and Fabiana Muniesa, eds., *Assetization* (Cambridge, MA: MIT Press, 2020), https://mitpress.mit.edu/9780262539173/assetization/.

21. Shade and Van Sant, "Geographies of Land Ownership Change in the Rural United States"; Lindsay Shade, "Politics below the Surface: A Political Ecology of Mineral Rights and Land Tenure Struggles in Appalachia and the Andes," PDF (Lexington, University of Kentucky, 2017), https://doi.org/10.13023/ETD.2017.195.

22. Zoeann Murphy, "In Virginia, Abandoned Coal Mines Are Transformed into Solar Farms," *Washington Post*, 3 March 2022, sec. Climate Solutions, https://www.washingtonpost.com/climate-solutions/2022/03/03/coal-mines-solar-farms-climate-change-video/.

23. The Nature Conservancy, "Conserving the Appalachians: Hope in a Changing Climate," accessed 7 March 2024, https://www.nature.org/en-us/about-us/where-we-work/priority-landscapes/appalachians/.

24. In TNC's nonprofit tax disclosure form 990 for 2021, 140. TNC's share of income from this investment in 2021 amounted to $336,651, and share of assets was $5,744,701. "TNC Annual Reports, Financials, IRS Forms," The Nature Conservancy, accessed 7 May 2024, https://www.nature.org/en-us/about-us/who-we-are/accountability/annual-report/.

25. Bloom, "Cumberland Forest Project." "Ataya" refers to the same land, but is under different ownership from the Ataya referred to earlier.

26. "Impact Fund of the Year: The Nature Conservancy's Sustainable Forestry Fund," Environmental Finance, accessed 6 June 2023, https://www.environmental-finance.com/content/awards/sustainable-investment-awards-2020/winners/impact-fund-of-the-year-the-nature-conservancys-sustainable-forestry-fund.html.

27. Interview with TNC staff member, 22 March 2023.

28. Schwartzman, "Climate Rentierism after Coal," 924.

29. California Air Resources Board, "Compliance Offset Program," accessed 7 March 2024, https://ww2.arb.ca.gov/our-work/programs/compliance-offset-program.

30. According to the California Air Resources Board Issuance Table, the CF Ataya forest carbon project (5315) has received 4,230,122 ARB credits, defined as "the number of ARB offset credits in this issuance, including any credits for the Forest Buffer Account." This includes 710,399 of Forest Buffer Account credits, defined as "the number of ARB offset credits placed in the Forest Buffer Account for each Forest project" (see section 95983 of the Cap-and-Trade Regulation and Appendix D of the relevant Forest protocol). California Air Resources Board Issuance Table, April 2024, https://ww2.arb.ca.gov/resources/documents/arb-offset-credit-issuance-table.

31. We estimate the price of carbon forest offsets to be roughly $11 per metric ton, a recent price for voluntary market carbon forest offsets in 2023, although the actual prices are not disclosed, and have changed drastically since TNC began selling them in 2019. The current price for metric ton of carbon in the allowances in California and Quebec carbon markets are $41/mt, an all-time high in 2024. However, carbon forest offsets are meant to be cheaper alternatives to ease market pressure, and thus are assumed to be lower. Daniel Weeks, "California-Quebec Carbon Allowance Costs Hit Record High for Third Time in a Row," S&P Global, 22 February 2024, https://www.spglobal.com/commodityinsights/en/market-insights/latest-news/electric-power/022224-california-quebec-carbon-allowance-costs-hit-record-high-for-third-time-in-a-row.

32. Peter Kareiva, Craig Groves, and Michelle Marvier, "REVIEW: The Evolving Linkage between Conservation Science and Practice at The Nature Conservancy," *Journal of Applied Ecology* 51, no. 5 (19 May 2014): 1137–47, https://doi.org/10.1111/1365-2664.12259.

33. The Nature Conservancy, *From Mine Lands to Forests* (YouTube, 2023), https://www.youtube.com/watch?v=J7DIJA9Me_M.

34. Tennessee Wildlife Resource Agency, "The Nature Conservancy, TWRA Announce Conservation Easement to Benefit North Cumberland WMA's Ed Carter Unit," Tennessee State Government, January 10, 2022, https://www.tn.gov/twra/news/2022/1/10/the-nature-conservancy-twra-announce-conservation-easement-to-benefit-north-cumberland-wma-s-ed-carter-unit.html.

35. SBC Executive Subcommittee, "STATE BUILDING COMMISSION Executive Subcommittee Minutes October 31, 2019" (Tennessee State Government, 31 October 2019), 13, https://www.tn.gov/content/dam/tn/statearchitect/agenda-minutes/OctESC19.pdf.

36. "Senator Yager Praises Action by State Building Commission to Acquire Land at Tackett Creek Wildlife Management Area," *WLAF*, sec. Sports, accessed 15 March 2021, https://web.archive.org/web/20210228192214/https://1450wlaf.com/2021/02/22/senator-yager-praises-action-by-state-building-commission-to-acquire-land-at-tackett-creek-wildlife-management-area/; Tennessee Wildlife Resource Agency, "The Nature Conservancy, TWRA Announce Conservation Easement to Benefit North Cumberland WMA's Ed Carter Unit."

37. "Ed Carter Unit of the North Cumberland Wildlife Management Area Will Be Permanently Protected," *Sparta Live*, 10 January 2022, https://spartalive.com/stories/ed-carter-unit-of-the-north-cumberland-wildlife-management-area-will-be-permanently-protected,42134.

38. Dulles Regional Chamber of Commerce, "Commonwealth of Virginia and The Nature Conservancy Partner to Permanently Protect 22,856 Acres in Southwest Virginia," accessed 7 March 2024, https://www.dulleschamber.org/commonwealth-of-virginia-and-the-nature-conservancy-partner-to-permanently-protect-22856-acres-in-southwest-virginia.

39. The Nature Conservancy, "The Nature Conservancy Announces 17 New

Clean Energy Projects on Former Appalachian Coal Mines with ENGIE and Sun Tribe Development," 11 February 2025, https://www.nature.org/en-us/newsroom/cumberland-clean-energy-former-mines/.

40. Emma Marris, "In a Warming Climate, We Need to Radically Rethink How We Conserve Nature," *National Geographic*, 22 August 2022, https://www.nationalgeographic.com/magazine/article/in-a-warming-climate-we-need-to-rethink-how-we-conserve-nature-feature.

41. "Impact Fund of the Year: The Nature Conservancy's Sustainable Forestry Fund," *Sustainable Finance* (2020) accessed 19 March 2025, https://www.environmental-finance.com/content/awards/sustainable-investment-awards-2020/winners/impact-fund-of-the-year-the-nature-conservancys-sustainable-forestry-fund.html.

42. Cleary Gottlieb Steen and Hamilton LLP, "Cumberland Forest Project Wins Environmental Finance 'Impact Fund of the Year' Award," accessed 6 June 2023, https://www.clearygottlieb.com//news-and-insights/news-listing/cumberland-forest-project-wins-environmental-finance-impact-fund-of-the-year-award.

43. Grayson Badgley, Jeremy Freeman, Joseph J. Hamman, Barbara Haya, Anna T. Trugman, William R. L. Anderegg, and Danny Cullenward, "Systematic Over-crediting in California's Forest Carbon Offsets Program," *Global Change Biology* 28, no. 4 (20 October 2022): 1433–45, https://doi.org/10.1111/gcb.15943; Barbara K. Haya, Samuel Evans, Letty Brown, Jacob Bukoski, Van Butsic, Bodie Cabiyo, Rory Jacobson, Amber Kerr, Matthew Potts, and Daniel L. Sanchez, "Comprehensive Review of Carbon Quantification by Improved Forest Management Offset Protocols," *Frontiers in Forests and Global Change*, Forest Carbon Credits as a Nature-Based Solution to Climate Change?, 6 (21 March 2023), https://doi.org/10.3389/ffgc.2023.958879.

44. Nina Lakhani, "Corporations Invested in Carbon Offsets That Were 'Likely Junk,' Analysis Says," *The Guardian*, 30 May 2024, sec. Environment, https://www.theguardian.com/environment/article/2024/may/30/corporate-carbon-offsets-credits.

45. Evan Halper, "Burned Trees and Billions in Cash: How a California Climate Program Lets Companies Keep Polluting," *Los Angeles Times*, 8 September 2021, sec. Politics, https://www.latimes.com/politics/story/2021-09-08/what-is-the-california-climate-credit-does-it-cut-pollution.

46. Ben Elgin, "A Top U.S. Seller of Carbon Offsets Starts Investigating Its Own Projects," *Bloomberg.com*, 5 April 2021, sec. Green Finance, https://www.bloomberg.com/news/features/2021-04-05/a-top-u-s-seller-of-carbon-offsets-starts-investigating-its-own-projects.

47. Georgette Kilgore, "How The Nature Conservancy Sparked a Global Investigation into Carbon Offsets," *8 Billion Trees: Carbon Offset Projects & Ecological Footprint Calculators* (blog), 22 November 2023, https://8billiontrees.com/carbon-offsets-credits/best-programs-providers-companies-2021/nature-conservancy/.

48. Loka Ashwood, *For-Profit Democracy: Why the Government Is Losing the Trust of Rural America*, Yale Agrarian Studies Series (New Haven: Yale University Press, 2018), https://yalebooks.yale.edu/9780300215359/for-profit-democracy.

49. Interview with Clearfork resident, 21 March 2023.

50. Interview with Clearfork resident, 25 January 2022.

51. Schwartzman, "Climate Rentierism after Coal," 933.

52. The Nature Conservancy, "Cumberland Forest Community Fund," 15 August 2023, https://www.nature.org/en-us/about-us/where-we-work/priority-landscapes/appalachians/stories/cumberland-forest-community-fund/.

53. Gabe Schwartzman, "Carbon Offsets Bring New Investment to Appalachia's Coal Fields, but Most Appalachians Aren't Benefiting," *The Conversation*, 20 February 2024, http://theconversation.com/carbon-offsets-bring-new-investment-to-appalachias-coal-fields-but-most-appalachians-arent-benefiting-217430.

54. Interview with TNC staff member, 22 March 2023.

55. Gaventa, *Power and Powerlessness*, 152.

56. Fieldnotes, 10 April 2023.

57. Kareiva, Groves, and Marvier, "REVIEW."

58. Elizabeth Koehler, "Nature Conservancy," *ProPublica*, 4 March 2024, https://projects.propublica.org/nonprofits/organizations/530242652.

59. Nature Conservancy, "Who We Are," 4, accessed 1 March 2024, https://www.nature.org/en-us/about-us/who-we-are/.

60. Rogers, "Soft Power, NGOs, and Climate Change."

61. Joseph S. Nye, "Soft Power," *Foreign Policy*, no. 80 (1990): 153–71, https://doi.org/10.2307/1148580.

62. Gregory M. Thaler, "Ethnography of Environmental Governance: Towards an Organizational Approach," *Geoforum* 120 (1 March 2021): 123, https://doi.org/10.1016/j.geoforum.2021.01.026.

63. Naomi Klein, *This Changes Everything: Capitalism vs. the Climate* (New York: Simon and Schuster, 2015), 191, https://www.simonandschuster.com/books/This-Changes-Everything/Naomi-Klein/9781451697391.

64. Klein, *This Changes Everything*, 196.

65. Steven J. McCormick, "Balancing The Nature Conservancy Story," *Washington Post*, 12 May 2003, sec. Opinion, https://www.washingtonpost.com/archive/opinions/2003/05/13/balancing-the-nature-conservancy-story/9c6d57d4-b24c-4361-8e26-ee28dddfc411/; David B. Ottaway and Joe Stephens, "Nonprofit Land Bank Amasses Billions," *Washington Post*, 4 May 2003, Big Green: Inside The Nature Conservancy edition, https://www.washingtonpost.com/archive/politics/2003/05/04/nonprofit-land-bank-amasses-billions/10fdb070-d956-40e7-a508-b03483c21899/; Joe Stephens and David B. Ottaway, "Nature Conservancy Suspends Land Sales: Board of Nonprofit to Review Practices," *Washington Post*, 12 May 2003, sec.

Politics, https://www.washingtonpost.com/archive/politics/2003/05/13/nature-conservancy-suspends-land-sales/ccd75a02-7f0b-4f31-8209-85640b4b42eb/.

66. Ottaway and Stephens, "Nonprofit Land Bank Amasses Billions."

67. Dogwood Alliance, "The Nature Conspiracy" (March 2022), 8, https://johnmuirproject.org/wp-content/uploads/2022/04/The-Nature-Conspiracy-Magazine.pdf.

68. "The Nature Conservancy."

69. Gregory M. Thaler, "Ethnography of Environmental Governance: Towards an Organizational Approach," *Geoforum* 120 (1 March 2021): 122–31, https://doi.org/10.1016/j.geoforum.2021.01.026; Gregory M. Thaler, *Saving a Rainforest and Losing the World: Conservation and Displacement in the Global Tropics* (New Haven: Yale University Press, 2024).

70. Chris Lang, "Nature Conservancy Role in World Bank REDD Initiative Highlights Growing US NGO Isolation on Forests and Climate Policy," *REDD Monitor*, 27 October 2008, accessed April 8, 2025, https://reddmonitor.substack.com/p/nature-conservancy-role-in-world.

71. World Rainforest Movement, "'Nature-Based Solutions': Concealing a Massive Land Robbery," *Bulletin*, April 2021, https://www.wrm.org.uy/sites/default/files/bulletin-pdfs/Boletin-255_ENG.pdf.

72. Rogers, "Soft Power, NGOs, and Climate Change," 222.

73. Nature Conservancy, "Who We Are," https://www.nature.org/en-us/about-us/who-we-are/our-science/.

74. As science and technology scholars point out, scientific discourse is always a field of contested knowledges, and the question of whose scientific knowledge is given authority becomes paramount. Donna Haraway, "Situated Knowledges: The Science Question in Feminism and the Privilege of Partial Perspective," *Feminist Studies* 14, no. 3 (October 1988): 575–99, https://doi.org/10.2307/3178066.

75. Kathy Egland, "Logging Is Slashing US Forests' Ability to Absorb Carbon by Over One-Third," *Truthout*, 13 July 2022, np, https://truthout.org/articles/logging-is-slashing-us-forests-ability-to-absorb-carbon-by-over-one-third/.

76. Dogwood Alliance, "Open Letter to The Nature Conservancy: Stop Perpetuating Forest Destruction, Pollution, Carbon Emissions, and Environmental Injustice," 5 April 2022, 3, https://johnmuirproject.org/wp-content/uploads/2022/04/2022.04.05-Letter-to-Jennifer-Morris-of-TNC-from-158-orgs.pdf; Christopher Ketcham, "Latest Loathsome Antics of The Nature Conservancy, or, Why You Can't Trust Corporate Prostitutes to Be Environmentalists," *Denatured: The Writings of Christopher Ketcham* (blog), 27 July 2022, https://www.christopherketcham.com/?p=343.

77. Interview with Clearfork community leader, 21 March 2023.

78. Interview with longtime community organizer, 6 March 2023.

79. See, for instance, Chris Lang, "Community Voices on The Nature Conservancy's Guaraqueçaba Climate Action Project," *REDD Monitor*, 7 June 2012,

3, https://redd-monitor.org/2012/06/07/community-voices-on-the-nature-conservancys-guaraquecaba-climate-action-project-were-suffering-here-to-help-them-over-there/.

80. Fairhead, Leach, and Scoones, "Green Grabbing."

81. Schwartzman, "Climate Rentierism after Coal."

82. Brett Christophers, *Rentier Capitalism: Who Owns the Economy, and Who Pays for It?* (London: Verso, 2020), https://www.versobooks.com/en-gb/products/871-rentier-capitalism; Brett Christophers, *Our Lives in Their Portfolios: Why Asset Managers Own the World* (London: Verso, 2023).

83. Kay, "Rural Rentierism and the Financial Enclosure of Maine's Open Lands Tradition," June 29, 2017; see also Gunnoe, "The Political Economy of Institutional Landownership"; Gunnoe, Bailey, and Ameyaw, "Millions of Acres, Billions of Trees."

84. Romain Felli, "On Climate Rent," *Historical Materialism* 22, no. 3–4 (2 December 2014): 251–80, https://doi.org/10.1163/1569206X-12341368; Patrick Bigger and Wim Carton, "Finance and Climate Change," in *The Routledge Handbook of Financial Geography*, ed. Janelle Knox-Hayes and Dariusz Wójcik (London; New York: Routledge, 2020); Patrick Bigger and Nate Millington, "Getting Soaked? Climate Crisis, Adaptation Finance, and Racialized Austerity," *Environment and Planning E: Nature and Space* 3, no. 3 (1 September 2020): 601–23, https://doi.org/10.1177/2514848619876539.

85. Kelly Kay, "A Hostile Takeover of Nature? Placing Value in Conservation Finance," *Antipode* 50, no. 1 (January 2018): 164–83, https://doi.org/10.1111/anti.12335; Stefan Ouma, Leigh Johnson, and Patrick Bigger, "Rethinking the Financialization of 'Nature,'" *Environment and Planning A: Economy and Space* 50, no. 3 (1 May 2018): 500–511, https://doi.org/10.1177/0308518X18755748.

86. Schwartzman, "Climate Rentierism after Coal."

Chapter 7. Building Collective Power from Below

1. Gaventa, *Power and Powerlessness*, 251.

2. Interview, 21 March 2023.

3. Interview, 21 March 2023.

4. Focus group discussion, 26 September 2022.

5. Interview, 27 September 2022.

6. Focus group discussion, 21 March 2003.

7. Interview, 24 April 2023.

8. John Kretzmann and John L. McKnight, *Building Communities from Inside Out: A Path toward Finding and Mobilizing a Community's Assets* (Chicago: ACTA Publications, 1993).

9. Alison Mathie, Jenny Cameron, and Katherine Gibson, "Asset-Based and Citizen-Led Development: Using a Diffracted Power Lens to Analyze the Possibilities and Challenges," *Progress in Development Studies* 17, no. 1 (1 January 2017): 54–66, https://doi.org/10.1177/1464993416674302.

10. Named this by community residents as a response to the Model Cities program established by President Lyndon Johnson in 1966 as part of his War on Poverty and Great Society initiatives.

11. Gaventa, *Power and Powerlessness*, 212–17.

12. Later, this model was to change to one based on rentals.

13. Eliza Spellman, "Woodland Community Land Trust: An Antidote to Extraction in Rural Appalachia," *Agrarian Trust* (blog), 18 April 2019, https://agrariantrust.org/news/woodland-community-land-trust/.

14. Michael Corkery, "Will a Dollar General Ruin a Rural Crossroads?" *New York Times*, 5 June 2023, sec. Business, https://www.nytimes.com/2023/06/02/business/dollar-general-ebony-virginia.html.

15. For an account of decades of work see her 2000 Schumacher lecture: Marie Cirillo, "Stories from an Appalachian Community," *Schumacher Center for a New Economics* (blog), accessed 17 October 2024, https://centerforneweconomics.org/publications/stories-from-an-appalachian-community/. Cirillo died in 2024.

16. "Carol Judy: An Interview with Felix Bivens of Empyrean Research," Video, 26 March 2017, https://www.youtube.com/watch?v=204Kobj_HKw.

17. Michelle Mockbee, "Community-Led Action Research: An Intergenerational Process of Creating Spaces, Skills, and Voices for Change," Program Report (Eagan, TN: Clearfork Community Institute, 29 August 2012), 1.

18. "Clearfork Valley Community Asset Mapping Project" (mimeo, n.d.).

19. Focus group discussion, 21 March 2023.

20. Interview, 18 May 2023.

21. TNACE mission statement.

22. Focus group discussion, 26 September 2022.

23. Focus group discussion, 21 March 2023.

24. Aaron Schutz and Mike Miller, *People Power: The Community Organizing Tradition of Saul Alinsky* (Nashville: Vanderbilt University Press, 2015), https://www.vanderbiltuniversitypress.com/9780826520425/people-power/; Hahrie Han, Elizabeth McKenna, and Michelle Oyakawa, *Prisms of the People: Power & Organizing in Twenty-First-Century America* (Chicago: University of Chicago Press, 2021), https://press.uchicago.edu/ucp/books/book/chicago/P/bo68659118.html.

25. Interview, 28 September 1922.

26. Interview with SOCM organizer, 27 September 2018.

27. Connie White, "Fighting Back in Appalachia: Reports for the Front: Plenary Session—Appalachian Studies Conference," *Journal of the Appalachian Studies Association* 6 (1994): 7.

28. White, "Fighting Back in Appalachia," 10.

29. Interview, 24 April 2023.

30. Interview, 28 September 2022.

31. Email to author, 17 July 2023.

32. Focus group discussion, 26 September 2022.

33. Scott, *Removing Mountains*; Mark Baller and Leor Joseph Pantilat, "Defenders of Appalachia: The Campaign to Eliminate Mountaintop Removal Coal Mining and the Role of Public Justice," *Environmental Law* 37, no. 3 (2007): 629–63; Nicholas Stump, "Mountain Resistance: Appalachian Civil Disobedience in Critical Legal Research Modeled Law Reform," *Environs Environmental Law and Policy Journal* 41, no. 1 (1 May 2017): 69–131.

34. Tricia Shapiro, *Mountain Justice: Homegrown Resistance to Mountaintop Removal for the Future of Us All* (Oakland, CA: AK Press, 2010).

35. Stump, "Mountain Resistance," 110, quoted in Joseph D. Witt, *Religion and Resistance in Appalachia: Faith and the Fight against Mountaintop Removal Coal Mining*, Place Matters: New Directions in Appalachian Studies (Lexington: University Press of Kentucky, 2016), 37, https://doi.org/10.2307/j.ctt1gr7dhc.

36. Montrie, *To Save the Land and People*; Montrie, "To Have, Hold, Develop, and Defend."

37. Montrie, "To Have, Hold, Develop, and Defend," 78.

38. Montrie, *To Save the Land and People*; Robert Todd Perdue and Christopher McCarty, "Unearthing a Network of Resistance: Law and the Anti-Strip Mining Movement in Central Appalachia," *Studies in Law, Politics, and Society* 66 (January 2014): 41.

39. Alliance for Appalachia, "Our History," accessed 3 December 2024, https://thealliance for appalachia.org/history/.

40. Hansen and Hannah were arrested in a West Virginia mining protest. *The Guardian*, 24 June 2009, accessed December 3, 2024.

41. Dean Hill Rivkin, Chris Irwin, and Anne Passino, "Strip-Mining and Grassroots Resistance in Appalachia: Community Lawyering for Environmental Justice," *LA Journal of Public Interest Law* 1, no. 2 (26 September 2009): 13. In Tennessee the term "cross ridge mining" is used rather than "mountaintop removal."

42. Rivkin, Irwin, and Passino, "Strip-Mining and Grassroots Resistance in Appalachia."

43. Alliance for Appalachia, "Our History," accessed 27 February 2024, https://theallianceforappalachia.org/history/.

44. Bell, *Fighting King Coal*, 6.

45. Interview, 27 September 2022.

46. Alliance for Appalachia, "Our Mission," accessed 27 February 2024, https://theallianceforappalachia.org/mission-values/.

47. Perdue and McCarty, "Unearthing a Network of Resistance," 35.

48. Perdue and McCarty, "Unearthing a Network of Resistance," 52.

49. Philip Lewin, "'I Just Keep My Mouth Shut': The Demobilization of Environmental Protest in Central Appalachia," *Social Currents* 6, no. 6 (2019): 534–52, https://doi.org/10.1177/2329496519852947.

50. Bell, *Fighting King Coal*.

Chapter 8. Bottom Up Meets Top Down

1. Molly Moore, "ACE Conference Starts Needed Conversation," *Across Appalachia* (blog), 30 October 2008, https://appvoices.org/2008/10/30/ace-conference-starts-needed-conversation/.

2. "Kentuckians for the Commonwealth," accessed 28 February 2024, https://kftc.org.

3. Climate Justice Alliance, "History of the Climate Justice Alliance," accessed 28 February 2024, https://climatejusticealliance.org/cja-history/.

4. Lyndsay Tarus, Mary Hufford, and Betsy Taylor, "A Green New Deal for Appalachia: Economic Transition, Coal Reclamation Costs, Bottom-Up Policymaking (Part 2)," *Journal of Appalachian Studies* 23, no. 2 (1 October 2017): 13, https://doi.org/10.5406/jappastud.23.2.0151.

5. Tarus, Hufford, and Taylor, "A Green New Deal for Appalachia."

6. Erica Peterson and Sydney Boles, "SOAR at Six: Group's Lofty Goals for Coal Country Meet Challenges on the Ground," *Louisville Public Media*, 16 September 2019, sec. News, https://www.lpm.org/news/2019-09-16/soar-at-six-groups-lofty-goals-for-coal-country-meet-challenges-on-the-ground.

7. Highlander Research and Education Center, "Beyond Transition: Appalachia's Pathway to Justice and Transformation," 2021, 4, https://highlandercenter.org/wp-content/uploads/2021/06/Final-Highlander-Center-Report_3_18_21_smaller_res-2.pdf.

8. AV's Intern Team, "The STAY Project Celebrates 10 Years," *Appalachian Voices* (blog), 10 August 2018, https://appvoices.org/2018/08/09/the-stay-project-celebrates-10-years/.

9. Kevin Ridder, "A Just Transition for Coal Communities," *Appalachian Voice* (blog), 25 February 2020, https://appvoices.org/2020/02/25/a-just-transition-for-coal-communities/.

10. David J. Hess, Rachel G. McKane, and Kaelee Belletto, "Advocating a Just Transition in Appalachia: Civil Society and Industrial Change in a Carbon-Intensive Region," *El Sevier* 75, no. Energy Research & Social Science (1 May 2021): 102004, https://doi.org/10.1016/j.erss.2021.102004.

11. Hess, McKane, and Belletto, "Advocating a Just Transition in Appalachia."

12. Tarus, Hufford, and Taylor, "A Green New Deal for Appalachia," 10–11.

13. "2020 WV Primary Candidates: Governor," *Charleston Gazette-Mail*, 24 May 2020, https://www.wvgazettemail.com/2020-wv-primary-candidates-governor/article_c12263bb-9a83-5113-9a7b-d46ef258cac5.html.

14. Mitch McConnell vs. Amy McGrath Kentucky Senate Debate Transcript, 12 October 2020, https://www.rev.com/blog/transcripts/mitch-mcconnell-vs-amy-mcgrath-kentucky-senate-debate-transcript-october-12.

15. Schwartzman, "POWER and the Future of Appalachia."

16. Gyovai and Gladfelter, "Beyond Transition," 4.

17. Gyovai and Gladfelter, "Beyond Transition," 9.

18. Peter Newell, Freddie Daley, Olga Mikheeva, and Iva Peša, "Mind the Gap: The Global Governance of Just Transitions," *Global Policy* 14, no. 3 (25 June 2023): 425–37, https://doi.org/10.1111/1758-5899.13236.

19. Sovacool et al., "Pluralizing Energy Justice"; Collste, *Global Rectificatory Justice*.

20. Interview, 27 September 2022.

21. Eric L. Dixon and Kendall Bilbrey, "Abandoned Mine Land Program: A Policy Analysis for Central Appalachia and the Nation" (AML Policy Priorities Group, 8 July 2015), 17, https://aclc.org/wp-content/uploads/2020/08/aml-policy-paper.pdf.

22. Betsy Taylor, Mary Hufford, and Kendall Bilbrey, "A Green New Deal for Appalachia: Economic Transition, Coal Reclamation Costs, Bottom-Up Policymaking (Part 1)," *Journal of Appalachian Studies* 23, no. 1 (April 2017): 8–27, https://doi.org/10.5406/jappastud.23.1.0008.

23. Interview with community organizer, 21 October 2022.

24. These included selenium discharge levels from abandoned and current mine lands.

25. Savage, "Repairing the Damage"; Alliance for Appalachia, "Coal Mine Bonding, Bankruptcy, and Unreclaimed Post Law Mines," February 2021, https://theallianceforappalachia.org/coal-mine-bonding-bankruptcy-and-unreclaimed-post-law-mines/.

26. Alliance for Appalachia, "Coal Mine Bonding, Bankruptcy, and Unreclaimed Post Law Mines."

27. Interview with Bonnie Swinford, 27 September 2022.

28. The White House, "Executive Order on Tackling the Climate Crisis at Home and Abroad" (2021), https://bidenwhitehouse.archives.gov/briefing-room/presidential-actions/2021/01/27/executive-order-on-tackling-the-climate-crisis-at-home-and-abroad/.

29. The White House, "Tackling the Climate Crisis."

30. The White House, "FACT SHEET: Biden-Harris Administration Holds Justice40 Week of Action to Highlight Historic Investments in Overburdened and Underserved Communities," Press Release, The White House, 23 May 2022, https://bidenwhitehouse.archives.gov/briefing-room/statements-releases/2022/05/23/fact-sheet-biden-harris-administration-holds-justice40-week-of-action-to-highlight-historic-investments-in-overburdened-and-underserved-communities/.

31. The White House, "FACT SHEET: President Biden Sets 2030 Greenhouse Gas Pollution Reduction Target Aimed at Creating Good-Paying Union Jobs and Securing U.S. Leadership on Clean Energy Technologies," https://bidenwhitehouse.archives.gov/briefing-room/statements-releases/2021/04/22/fact-sheet-president-biden-sets-2030-greenhouse-gas-pollution-reduction-target-aimed-at-creating-good-paying-union-jobs-and-securing-u-s-leadership-on-clean-energy-technologies/

32. Interagency Working Group on Coal and Power Plant Communities and Economic Revitalization, "Initial Report to the President on Empower-

ing Workers through Revitalizing Energy Communities" (Washington, DC: US Department of Energy, April 2021), 2, https://energycommunities.gov/wp-content/uploads/2021/11/Initial-Report-on-Energy-Communities_Apr2021.pdf.

33. The White House, "FACT SHEET: Biden-Harris Administration Holds Justice40 Week of Action."

34. The White House, "Justice40: A Whole-of-Government Initiative," Press Release, The White House, 2022, https://bidenwhitehouse.archives.gov/environmentaljustice/justice40/.

35. Jonathan Fox, Rachel Sullivan Robinson, and Naomi Hossain, "Building State-Society Synergy through Sandwich Strategies" (Washington DC: American University, December 2022), https://accountabilityresearch.org/wp-content/uploads/2023/01/Sandwich-Strategy-Paper_2023_01_23.pdf.

36. Hande Gülen and Ceyda Sungur, "Cramped Spaces, W(r)Iggle Room, and Everyday Politics: An Introduction," in *At the Frontiers of Everyday Life: New Research in Cramped Spaces*, ed. Hande Gülen, Ceyda Sungur, and Adem Yeşilyurt, Urban Book Series (Cham: Springer Nature Switzerland, 2023), 1–15, https://doi.org/10.1007/978-3-031-46580-2_1; Gilles Deleuze, *Cinema II: The Time-Image*, trans. Hugh Tomlinson and Robert Galeta (London: Bloomsbury Publishing, 2013), 216; Lauren Berlant, *Cruel Optimism* (Durham, NC: Duke University Press, 2011), https://www.dukeupress.edu/cruel-optimism.

37. Giorno and Cloutier, "Joe Manchin Vows to Block 'Radical Climate Agenda,' Rakes in Oil and Gas Industry Contributions."

38. Christopher Flavelle, Julie Tate, and Erin Schaff, "How Joe Manchin Aided Coal, and Earned Millions," *New York Times*, 27 March 2022, sec. Climate, https://www.nytimes.com/2022/03/27/climate/manchin-coal-climate-conflicts.html.

39. Jill Lindsey Harrison, *From the Inside Out: The Fight for Environmental Justice within Government Agencies*, Urban and Industrial Environments (Cambridge, MA: MIT Press, 2019), https://mitpress.mit.edu/9780262537742/from-the-inside-out/.

40. Fieldnotes, Meeting with EPA EJ staff, December 2023.

41. Fox, Robinson, and Hossain, "Building State-Society Synergy through Sandwich Strategies."

42. Kelsey Tamborino, "Trump Vows to Pull Back Climate Law's Unspent Dollars," *Politico*, 5 September 2024. https://www.politico.com/news/2024/09/05/trump-inflation-reduction-act-00177493.

43. Julie, Strupp, "Trump Funding Free Leaves IIJA and IRA Projects in Limbo," Utility Dive, 28 January 2025, https://www.utilitydive.com/news/trump-funding-freeze-iija-ira-projects/738628/.

Conclusion

1. Edelman, "Hollowed Out Heartland, USA."
2. Lukes, *Power*.

3. Schwartzman, "Masculinities in the Decline of Coal: Queer Futures in the Appalachian Coalfields," in *Deviant Hollers: Queering Appalachian Ecologies for a Sustainable Future*, ed. Stephanie Foote, Rebecca Scott, and Zane McNeill (Lexington: University Press of Kentucky, 2024), 183–206, https://muse.jhu.edu/pub/185/edited_volume/chapter/3793341.

4. Krippner, "The Financialization of the American Economy," 174.

5. Schwartzman, "Climate Rentierism after Coal."

6. Smith, "Another Place Is Possible?"; Bell and Braun, "Coal, Identity, and the Gendering of Environmental Justice Activism in Central Appalachia"; Foote, Scott, and McNeill, *Deviant Hollers*.

7. Gaventa, "Finding the Spaces for Change."

8. Huff and Brock, "Introduction."

9. Janice Peck, "Itinerary of a Thought: Stuart Hall, Cultural Studies, and the Unresolved Problem of the Relation of Culture to 'Not Culture,'" *Cultural Critique* no. 48 (2001): 235.

10. Clyde Woods, *Development Arrested: The Blues and Plantation Power in the Mississippi Delta*, 2nd ed. (London; New York: Verso, 2017); Clyde Woods, *Development Drowned and Reborn: The Blues and Bourbon Restorations in Post-Katrina New Orleans*, ed. Laura Pulido and Jordan T. Camp (Athens: University of Georgia Press, 2017); Gillian Hart, *Rethinking the South African Crisis: Nationalism, Populism, Hegemony* (Athens: University of Georgia Press, 2014), https://ugapress.org/book/9780820347172/rethinking-the-south-african-crisis. For an analysis of hegemonic shifts in urban geography, see also Owen Toews, *Stolen City: Racial Capitalism and the Making of Winnipeg* (Winnipeg: Arbeiter Ring Publishing, 2018).

11. In Gramscian terms, these were "conjunctural crises," or crises that did not threaten the fundamental reproduction of hegemonic alliances and rule.

12. William F. Lamb, Giulio Mattioli, Sebastian Levi, J. Timmons Roberts, Stuart Capstick, Felix Creutzig, Jan C. Minx, Finn Müller-Hansen, Trevor Culhane, and Julia K. Steinberger, "Discourses of Climate Delay," *Global Sustainability* 3, no. e17 (2020): 1–5, https://doi.org/10.1017/sus.2020.13.

13. For more on such competing narratives, see Saturnino M. Borras Jr., Ian Scoones, Amita Baviskar, Marc Edelman, Nancy Lee Peluso, and Wendy Wolford, "Climate Change and Agrarian Struggles: An Invitation to Contribute to a JPS Forum," *Journal of Peasant Studies* 49, no. 1 (2022): 1–28, https://doi.org/10.1080/03066150.2021.1956473.

14. William Davies and Nicholas Gain, "Post-Neoliberalism? An Introduction," *Theory Culture, and Society* 38, no 6 (2021): 3–28. https://doi.org/10.1177/02632764211036722.

15. Our use of "climate Keynesianism" draws on similar conceptions articulated as "green" and "environmental" Keynesianism: "Green Keynesianism: Beyond Standard Growth Paradigms," Working or Discussion Paper, GDAE Working Papers Series, February 2013, Global Development and Environment Institute, Tufts University, https://doi.org/10.22004/ag.econ.179111; Bill Black-

water, "Two Cheers for Environmental Keynesianism," *Capitalism Nature Socialism*, Rethinking Green Economics, 23, no. 2 (1 May 2012): 51–74, https://doi.org/10.1080/10455752.2012.675232; Jeremy Green, "Greening Keynes? Productivist Lineages of the Green New Deal," *Anthropocene Review* 9, no. 3 (25 October 2022): 324–43, https://doi.org/10.1177/20530196221128369; Tomasz Legiedz, "The Ecological Boundaries of Green Keynesianism," *International Journal of Public Administration, Management and Economic Development* 8, no. 2 (31 December 2023): 90–255, https://doi.org/10.60026/ijpamed.v8i2.114.

16. Ciplet, "Transition Coalitions."

17. Gramsci, *Selections from the Prison Notebooks*, 276.

18. "Chris Wright: Trump Nominates Fracking Executive to Lead Energy Department," *BBC News*, 17 November 2024, https://www.bbc.com/news/articles/c93qjdjwnxko.

19. Molly Taft, "Donald Trump Wants to Save the Coal Industry. He's Too Late," *Wired*, 9 April 2025, https://www.wired.com/story/donald-trump-wants-to-save-the-coal-industry-hes-too-late/?bxid=5fa7b15f8f616f7bf274fbd5&cndid=62658284&hasha=f84e5ac04f021896598d9107641bfee0&hashc=9417d8b4b961919ffc1186b1875b2d245763fc71e609085edf732ffbc8b77586&esrc=MARTECH_ORDERFORM.

20. Antoine Acker, Elizabeth Chatterjee, Lukas Becker, Matthew Shutzer, and Nathalia Capellini, "Fossil Fuels from Extraction to Emissions," in *The Routledge Handbook of Environmental History*, ed. Emily O'Gorman, William San Martin, Mark Carey, and Sandra Swart (Abingdon: Routledge, 2024), 478.

21. Edin, Shaefer, and Nelson, *The Injustice of Place*.

22. Clare Church and Alec Crawford, "Minerals and the Metals for the Energy Transition: Exploring the Conflict Implications for Mineral-Rich, Fragile States," in *The Geopolitics of the Global Energy Transition*, ed. Manfred Hafner and Simone Tagliapietra (Cham: Springer International Publishing, 2020), 279–304, https://doi.org/10.1007/978-3-030-39066-2_12.

23. Fairhead, Leach, and Scoones, "Green Grabbing."

24. James McCarthy, "Authoritarianism, Populism, and the Environment: Comparative Experiences, Insights, and Perspectives," *Annals of the American Association of Geographers*, Environmental Governance in a Populist/Authoritarian Era, 109, no. 2 (4 March 2019): 301–13, https://doi.org/10.1080/24694452.2018.1554393.

25. Andrea M. Feldpausch-Parker, Danielle Endres, Tarla Rai Peterson, and Stephanie L. Gomez, eds., *Routledge Handbook of Energy Democracy* (Abingdon: Routledge, 2022), https://www.routledge.com/Routledge-Handbook-of-Energy-Democracy/Feldpausch-Parker-Endres-Peterson-Gomez/p/book/9781032130521; Peter Newell, Roz Price, and Freddie Daley, "Landscapes of (In)Justice: Reflecting on Voices, Spaces, and Alliances for Just Transition," IDS Working Paper (Brighton: Institute of Development Studies, 18 September 2023), https://doi.org/10.19088/IDS.2023.047; Newell, *Power Shift*.

Index

abandoned mine lands (AML), 144; fund, 146–47, 149, 151
abandonment, 93–100; economies, 27–28, 144–45
Abbott, Lisa, 133, 142–43
absenteeism, political, 90, 103
absentee land ownership, 40–43, 105–9, 116. *See also* The Nature Conservancy (TNC)
acid mine drainage, 33
activists, 6, 20, 70, 96, 128–29, 133–34; feeling discouraged, 74, 120, 125; global, 48; power and, 1, 61, 66, 130–31, 150–52; pro-coal, 81–83, 140; scholars as, 12; "tree huggers," 70, 80–83, 137, 162; youth, 70, 81–82, 136, 167. *See also* Statewide Organizing for Community eMpowerment (SOCM); Tennessee Appalachian Community Economics (TNACE); unions
addiction, 2, 10, 13, 15, 20, 25–27; nonparticipation and, 125–26, 128–29; opioid epidemic rise, 30–32
Advisory Business Council (TNC), 117
African American communities. *See* Black communities
After Coal (Hansell), 11
agency, 61, 66
agrarian transition, 40–41
Alinksy, Saul, 130
Alliance for Appalachia, 138, 143–49
American Association, 40–42, 105, 107, 209n18
American Coal Foundation, 79
American Federation of Labor and Congress of Industrial Organizations (AFL-CIO), 7
anger, 82, 88, 93–100
antiracism, 9, 97–98
anti-strip-mining movement. *See* civil disobedience; Statewide Organizing for Community eMpowerment (SOCM)
Appalachia, Virginia, 135
Appalachian Citizens Enforcement Project, 147
Appalachian Citizens Law Center, 122, 155
Appalachian Community Economics. *See* Tennessee Appalachian Community Economics (TNACE)
Appalachian Land Ownership Task Force (1979), 42, 107
Appalachian Regional Commission (ARC), 22, 29, 142; economic development spending, 35–37; Partnerships for Opportunity and Workforce and Economic Revitalization (POWER) Initiative, 37, 145, 152

Appalachian Regional Initiative for Stronger Economies (ARISE) program, 37
Appalachian Studies Association Conference, 132
Appalachian Sustainable Development (Virginia), 142
Appalachian Transition Fellowships (Highlander Center), 144–45
Appalachian Voices, 148, 155
Appalachian Volunteers and Community Action programs, 47
Appalachia Rising, 83, 137
Appalachia's Bright Future, 143
Appalshop, 82
Ashwood, Loka, 113–14
asset-based community development (ABCD), 126–30
assetization, 108
asset mapping, 35, 129, 145
Ataya Hardwoods, LLC, 107, 109–10
Atlantic (magazine), 70
A. T. Massey. *See* Massey Energy
Avelino, Flor, 57

Bachrach, Peter, 60
bankruptcy, 27, 33, 76, 147–48
Battle of Blair Mountain, 46
Bean Station, Tennessee, 97
Bell, Shannon Elizabeth, 28, 41, 79–80, 84, 137; *Fighting King Coal,* 140
Bell County, Kentucky, 22, 24–26, 28–30, 182n6
Benham, Kentucky, 44
Berlant, Lauren, 152
Beynon, Huw, 11
"Beyond Transition" (Highlander Center), 145–46
Biden, Joe, 16, 86
Biden administration, 77, 85; clean energy investments of, 26, 33–34, 112, 140–41, 148–56, 168–69; climate policies of, 15–16, 74, 172–73; Justice40 Initiative, 16, 148–49, 155
biodiversity conservation, 56, 108, 160, 164–65
Bipartisan Infrastructure Law (BIL), 16, 37, 148, 152–53, 155
Bituminous Coal Operators Agreement, 15, 46–47
Black Belt, 21, 29
Black coal miners, 44, 46, 49
Black communities, 5–6, 44, 50–51, 98, 132, 159
Black in Appalachia, 98, 102
Black Lives Matter, 97
black lung disease, 24, 77; Black Lung Movement, 47, 49
Black railroad workers, 43
Blair, West Virginia, 83
Blair Mountain, West Virginia, 46
Blankenship, Don, 42
Bloody Harlan, 46
Bloomberg News, 27; Bloomberg Green, 113
Blue Diamond Mining Company, 127
blue hydrogen, 153, 161
Bodenhamer, Aysha, 84
bonds, reclamation, 33, 74, 146–48
Bonilla-Silva, Eduardo, 98
bottom-up organizing, 9–10, 16, 36–37, 62, 148–52, 167–68, 172. *See also* grassroots organizing; top-down policies
Bowen, Eric, 50
Bradley, JW, 131
Brisbois, Marie-Claire, 56
Brookside Mine, 47
Brown, David, 89–90, 99
Brown, Karida, 50
Buffalo, Tennessee, 23
Build Back Better Challenge, 150
Bullard, Robert, 5–6
Burawoy, Michael, 11
Bush, George W., 71, 90–92

Cabin Creek, West Virginia, 46
California Air Resources Board (ARB), 111, 113, 209n30
California carbon market, 14, 111, 209n30, 210n31
campaigns, pro-coal, 70, 78–84, 143; Friends of Coal, 14–15, 79–84, 92, 94, 137

Campbell County, Tennessee, 22–31, 44, 86, 107, 136, 182n6; Chamber of Commerce, 115
Capacity Building for Repurposing Energy Assets award, 152
capitalism, 17, 40, 45, 61, 95; conservation and, 112–13, 117; "green," 14–16, 56, 164, 171–72; vulture, 76
carbon capture, utilization, and storage technology, 7, 77, 153, 161
carbon credits, 9, 14, 111, 163, 168. *See also* carbon markets
carbon emissions, 70–74, 109. *See also* greenhouse gas emissions reductions
carbon markets, 55–56, 118; California, 14, 111, 209n30, 210n31
carbon offsets, 2, 109, 120–21, 210n31
carbon sequestration, 56, 109, 111
Carbon Sovereignty (Curley), 11
Carter administration, 167
Caste (Wilkerson), 99
Catte, Elizabeth, 89, 95
Census County Divisions (CCDs), 182n6
Central Appalachian region, 2–3; agrarian transition, 40–41; historical transitions, 10–11; MTR in, 32; political economy of, 39–52; poverty in, 29–30. *See also* Clearfork Valley
CF Ataya, 109–11, 114, 209n30
CF Highlands, 109–10, 112
Cha, Mijin, 7
Charles Ryan Associates, 79
Charleston Gazette, 72
China, 4, 107
Christian conservative movement, 86–88, 93–94, 100–103
chronic obstructive pulmonary disease (COPD), 20
Ciplet, David, 172
Cirillo, Marie, 128–29
citizen-led pathway, 9
citizens, meaning of, 181n51
Citizens for Coal, 83
civil disobedience, 76–77, 123–24, 167; against MTR, 15, 48, 135–39
Claiborne County, Tennessee, 21–30, 44, 154, 182n6
claimed spaces, 64–65, 142
Clairfield, Tennessee, 21, 23–25, 29, 91, 127, 182n6
Clean Air Act (1970), 15, 50, 85, 160
Clean Energy on Mine Lands program, 150–51, 153–54
Clean Power Plan (2015), 87
Clean Water Act (1972), 147
Clearfork Community Institute (CCI), 23, 126–29, 150
Clearfork River, 21, 23
Clearfork Utility District, 28
Clearfork Valley, 1–3; communities of, 21–23; decline of coal in, 49–50; disadvantage in, 21–22, 182n6; economic context of, 13; employment in, 24–27; in global context, 174–75; Index of Deep Disadvantage, 182n6; land ownership in, 42, 105–8; map of, 21; migration to and from, 20, 34–35; physical place of, 21–23; population loss of, 35; poverty in, 2, 19–20, 29; racial demographics of, 51; resident commitment to, 34–35; TNC land ownership impact on, 113–14; voting in, 88–92, 205n15. *See also* Central Appalachian region; Cumberland Forest Limited Partnership; Kentucky; Tennessee; The Nature Conservancy (TNC); Virginia; West Virginia; Woodland Community Land Trust
climate, energy, and environmental justice, 6
Climate Action Plan (2008), 15
Climate and Economic Justice Screening Tool, 33–34
climate change, 34, 56, 117; denial, 72–74, 82–87, 103, 153, 161–62, 168, 171–73; mitigation, 2, 121, 155–56; United Nations Framework Convention on Climate Change (UNFCCC), 3, 87, 177n5; urgency of, 2–4, 6. *See also* Biden administration; greenhouse gas emissions reductions

Climate Investment Funds (World Bank), 55
Climate Justice Alliance (CJA), 6–7, 143
climate migration, 108
climate rentierism, 121
Clinch Coalition, 122
Clinchfield Coal, 109
Clinch-Powell Resource Conservation and Development organization (Tennessee), 114
Clinch River, 108
Clinton, Hillary, 89; *What Happened,* 94–95
closed spaces, 64–65
Coady International Institute, 126
coal ash, 134
coal camps. *See* company towns
coal companies, 4–5; American Association, 40–42, 105, 107, 209n18; bankruptcy of, 27, 33, 76, 147–148; Blue Diamond Mining Company, 127; Clinchfield Coal, 109; Consol Energy Company, 24; Davis Creek Energy, 134–35; decline of, 49–50, 63; domination of, 41–45, 62–63, 123–24; Enersystems, 74; Kopper Glo, 32–33, 108; Massey Energy, 42, 47, 76; National Coal Corporation, 136–37; Pittston Coal, 47, 109; political donations of, 71–75; power of, 1–2, 69–75, 116; reclamation bonds of, 33, 74, 146–48; resistance to, 45–49; taxation and, 27; UMWA agreements with, 15, 46–47. *See also* company towns; Friends of Coal movement; pollution; United Mine Workers of America (UMWA); "War on Coal"
Coal Creek War, 46
coal employment decrease, 3–4, 28, 49–50, 73; in Clearfork Valley, 15, 20–21, 24–25, 35; Republican voting and, 84–85, 92, 94
"Coal Exit" policy (EU), 4
Coalfield Development (West Virginia), 150
COALition Romney, 72
coal production decrease, 24, 49–50, 87
collective power, 70, 75–77, 123–40, 166–68
commodifying and marketizing nature, 9. *See also* financialization; nature-based solutions
communities of color, 5–6. *See also* Black communities
community cohesion, 28, 34–35; coal industry and, 80–81; drug addiction damaging, 125–26, 129
Community Development Initiatives map, 23
community-engaged research, 12
community facilities and services, 4–5, 15, 20–21
community meetings, 116–17
community organizing, power through, 130–35
community power studies, 11, 60–61
company towns, 4–5, 9, 18, 21–22, 114, 127; destruction and closure, 107, 121; power in, 42–43, 163; racial segregation in, 44, 51
Conference of the Parties (COP), 15; COP21 (Paris), 177n5; COP26 (Glasgow), 3, 5; COP28 (Dubai), 5
conjuncture, 64, 66–68, 93, 158–59, 170–73, 197n31; introduction to, 59–60
conservation, 2; capitalism and, 112–13, 117; easements, 104, 111–12, 121
conservative politics. *See* Republicanism
Consol Energy Company, 24
Cooper Ridge, 32–33
Corbin, Kentucky, 97–98
Corporate Accountability, 113
Corrigan TLP LLC, 107
Cotton Belt, 21
Council of Appalachian Governors, 36
Count on Coal, 79
court cases, 41, 51, 74, 131, 137
COVID-19, 126
crafts cooperative, 126
Cramer, Katherine, 95
crises of hegemony, 59–60, 170

cryptocurrency mining sites, 23, 26, 135
culture wars, 100–103
Cumberland Forest Community Fund, 114–15, 120
Cumberland Forest Limited Partnership, 2, 164–65; CF Ataya, 109–11, 114, 209n30; CF Highlands, 109–10, 112; corporate structure, 110; jobs from, 114; solar sites (proposed), 23, 26, 112; value of, 111, 210n31
Cumberland Forest Project (CFP), 14, 23, 104–6
Cumberland Gap, 22, 41
Curley, Andrew, 11

Dahl, Robert, 61
Dale, Jayme, 89
Davidson, Jeremy, 32, 135, 138
Davies, William, 172
Davis Creek Energy, 134–35
Dayton, Ohio, 20, 35
deaths of despair, 31
decarbonization, 6–7, 11, 37, 59, 156
Declaration on Just Transition, 5
deindustrialization, 49–52, 160
Deleuze, Gilles, 152
demobilization, 140
Democratic voting, 2, 14, 71; decrease of, 87, 90–92, 100–101
Department of Energy (DOE), 26, 173; Capacity Building for Repurposing Energy Assets, 152; Clean Energy on Mine Lands, 150–51, 153–54; OCED, 150–51; SolveIt Prize, 152
Department of Labor, 45
"Designated Survivor" (TV show), 101
Deskins, John, 50
Desmond, Matthew, 29
development, 28, 30; early twentieth century, 41; economics, 141; studies, 65; top-down approach to, 35–38
Dickenson County, Virginia, 115
direct action, 123–24, 135–39, 143, 166. *See also* civil disobedience; protests
disabilities, 26–27, 134–35
disadvantaged communities, 16; funding for, 33–34, 112, 148–49, 153–54, 156; Index of Deep Disadvantage, 21, 182n6. *See also* Justice40 Initiative
Distressed Communities Index, 29–30, 184n32
distributional justice, 8, 146, 152, 168–69
Dollar General Store, 127
Dopesick (Macy), 31
"Drill Baby Drill," 87
drug abuse. *See* addiction
DuBois, W.E.B., 99
Duff, Tennessee, 21, 23
Dumping in Dixie (Bullard), 5–6
Duncan, Cynthia, 11
dust, 32, 133–34

Eagan, Tennessee, 1, 21, 23, 127
EarthFirst!, 136
Earth Summit (1994), 15
East Kentucky Social Club, 44
East Tennessee Jobs with Justice, 150
ecological justice, 8
ecology of mobilizations, 56–57
economic development, top-down approach to, 35–38
Economic Development Areas map, 23
economic justice, 5–8, 132–33
Economic Research Service (ERS), 29
ecotourism, 104, 111–12
Edelman, Marc, 27
Edin, Kathryn J., 21, 182n6
elites, 67–68; agrarian, 40–41; industrial, 40–41; local, 42–43, 116; political, 36, 59–60; private, 55–56; *trasformismo* and, 59
Elk Valley, Tennessee, 137
emissions, 70–74, 109; reductions, 74, 81, 113, 148–49, 177n5; regulations, 50, 73, 81–82, 87, 173
employment. *See* jobs
empowerment, 14, 48, 56, 132, 159, 166; three dimensions of power and, 62–63, 66–67, 139
Energy and Natural Resources Committee, 73

energy communities, 16, 37, 141, 149, 152
energy justice, 8, 150–51, 155
energy transition, 53–58. *See also* just transition
Enersystems, 74
environmental, social, and governance (ESG), 109
environmental degradation, 5, 21, 28, 32–34, 77–78. *See also* pollution
Environmental Finance (magazine), 113
Environmental Protection Agency (EPA), 81, 138, 153–54; Recreational Economies for Rural Communities program, 151–52
Equal Opportunity Employment Act of 1972, 44
Europe, 4–5

Facebook, 80, 83
Fain, Cicero, 43
Fairhead, James, 120
Fast Food Women (film), 51–52
fear, 42, 114, 116; generational, 123–25, 139; politics and, 82–83, 88, 92–96, 102, 160
feminism, 9, 66
feminization of labor, 51–52
Fighting King Coal (Bell), 140
financialization, 121; assetization, 108; definition of, 105; of natural resources, 2, 15, 55–57, 105–112; nature-based solutions, 9, 14–15, 118
financiers, 55–57
flooding, 32–34, 135, 155
Floyd, George, 97
Fonde, Kentucky, 21, 23
Forest Carbon Partnership Facility (World Bank), 118
forestry, sustainable, 104–5, 111, 114, 119, 121
Forestry Stewardship Council (FSC), 111
Fork Ridge, Tennessee, 44
For-Profit Democracy (Ashwood), 113–14
fossil fuel industry, 53, 58; global complex, 55–56; political power of, 68–70, 73–75, 85–87, 161–162; TNC collaboration with, 117–18. *See also* coal companies; Manchin, Joe; McConnell, Mitch
Foucault, Michel, 61, 199n44
Fox, Jonathan, 149, 155–56
Fox News, 82, 100
Freedom of Information Act (FOIA), 33
"Friends of America" rally, 81–82
Friends of Coal movement, 14–15, 79–84, 92, 94, 137
Friends of the Earth, 55
Frist, Bill, 118
frustration, 95–96. *See also* anger

Gane, Nicholas, 172
Gaventa, John, 11–12, 64–66. See also *Power and Powerlessness* (Gaventa)
Geels, Frank W., 54
gendered labor, 44–45, 51–52
Germany, 4, 70, 77
ginseng, 34, 114
Gipe, Robert, 99
Global Energy Monitor, 4
global organizing connections, 48
Gore, Al, 71, 90–91
Gramsci, Antonio, 14, 53, 60, 66–67, 158; neo-Gramsci thinkers, 14, 58–59; *Selections from the Prison Notebooks,* 157
grants, 26, 37, 112, 114–15, 126–27, 149–56
grassroots organizing, 15–17, 36, 48, 59; twentieth century, 47–49; challenges to, 41–42, 69; citizen-led pathway, 9; funding and, 141–56, 169; NGOs and, 57, 116–19, 164–65. *See also* civil disobedience; Friends of Coal movement; Kentuckians for the Commonwealth (KFTC); protests; Statewide Organizing for Community eMpowerment (SOCM); Tennessee Appalachian Community Economics (TNACE); unions; Woodland Community Land Trust
"green" capitalism, 14–16, 56, 164, 171–72

green grabbing, 55–56, 120–21, 174
greenhouse gas emissions reductions, 74, 81, 113, 148–49, 177n5
Green New Deal, 156
Greenpeace, 55
The Guardian (newspaper), 113
Guizhou Guochuang Energy Holding Group, 107

Haas, Tobias, 55
Habersham, Tennessee, 91, 182n6
Hall, Stuart, 93, 196n8
Hannah, Daryl, 136, 216n40
Hannity, Sean, 82
Hansell, Tom, 11
Hansen, James, 136, 216n40
Harlan County, Kentucky, 44, 46, 102; Appalachia's Bright Future, 143; Brookside Mine, 47
Harrington, Michael, 19
Harrison, Jill, 153
Hart, Gillian, 171
Hatfield-McCoy feud, 40
Health and Retirement Fund (UMWA), 46
health clinics, 31–32, 37, 126–27
health conditions, 26–27; from coal mining, 24, 31, 77; from drug abuse, 30; nonparticipation and, 125–26; from pollution, 32–33
hegemony, 53, 66, 158; blocs, 59; counter-hegemonic ideology, 59, 67; crises of, 59–60, 170–72; green and grey projects, 55–56; introduction to, 58–60; masculine, 79
Henry, John, 43
Herald Leader (newspaper), 83
hidden power, 61–65, 160, 164
Highlander Center, 144; "Beyond Transition," 145–46
highway construction, 36–37
Hillbilly Elegy (Vance), 87, 89, 203n2
Hispanic communities, 21, 29, 97–98
Hochschild, Arlie, 95
homelessness, 34
hospitals, 25, 28, 46–47
Houston, Texas, 107–8
Huber Resource, 107
Hudson, Ray, 11
Hufford, Mary, 144
Hughes, Adam, 151
Hunter, Floyd, 11
hunting, 111–14
hydropower, 26

identity politics, 93–95
immigrants, 94–95, 97–99, 162
Improved Forestry Management (IFM), 111, 113
incumbent power, 55–56, 59, 63–64, 67, 69, 158–59
Index of Deep Disadvantage, 21, 182n6
indigenous communities, 4, 6, 9, 21, 29, 40, 98
inequalities, 8, 13, 19–20, 28–34
Inflation Reduction Act (IRA) (2022), 16, 37, 148, 152–53, 155–56
The Injustice of Place (Edin, Shaefer, and Nelson), 21, 29, 182n6
Inman, Virginia, 135
Institute of Development Studies, 65
instrumental power, 54
Interagency Working Group (IWG) on Coal and Power Plant Communities and Economic Revitalization, 149
International Labor Organization (ILO), 7
International Monetary Fund (IMF), 55
internet access, 126–27
interregnum, 59–60, 67, 157–58, 170–71
In the Shadow of the Mine (Beynon and Hudson), 11
investments, 27–28, 107, 109, 113, 121. *See also* Cumberland Forest Limited Partnership
investors, 18; green capitalism and, 14–15, 55–57; just transition and, 6–7; TNC and, 2, 104–5, 107–13, 115–16, 118–21
invisible power, 61–65, 161, 164
invited spaces, 64–65, 142, 155–56
Isom, William, 98, 102

Jackson, Mississippi, 107
Jackson Amendment, 135
Jellico, Tennessee, 26, 31–32, 45, 106; Black community of, 44, 49, 51; services in, 22, 29
Jewell, Sally, 118
JM Huber Corporation, 107
jobs, 5–7, 30, 32, 35; joblessness, 2, 25–27, 89–90, 159; low-wage, 25–26, 44–45, 51–52; manufacturing, 45, 51; TNC and, 114–15, 121; training programs, 7, 37, 77, 127, 145, 155; women's labor, 44–45, 51–52. *See also* coal employment decrease
Johnson, Lyndon B., 16, 19, 94, 215n10
Jones, Mary Harris "Mother," 48
JP Morgan Chase, 109
Judy, Carol, 128–29
Just Associates, 61
justice: climate, energy, and environmental, 6–7; distributional, 8, 146, 152, 168–69; ecological, 8; economic, 5–8, 132–33; energy, 8, 150–51, 155; procedural, 8, 146, 169; racial, 101; recognitional, 8, 146, 152, 169; restorative, 8, 146–47, 166, 169–70
justice, environmental, 5–8, 132–33, 135, 137, 153–55; ARISE program, 37; DOE and, 150–51; early movements, 48; inequalities and, 32–34; youth activists, 70, 81–82, 136, 167
Justice, Jim, 42, 74
Justice40 Initiative, 16, 148, 153–55
just transition, 5–9, 38, 157; from below, 142–44; contested narratives, 144–48; cultural hegemony and, 58–59; Declaration on Just Transition, 5; place-based study of, 10–12, 157–59; roots of, 5–8; types and pathways, 8–9, 168–70; unions and, 6–7, 77
Just Transition Alliance, 6
Just Transition Fund, 144

Kay, Kelly, 121
Kennedy, John F., 16, 19, 88, 93–94
Kentuckians for Fair Taxation. *See* Kentuckians for the Commonwealth (KFTC)
Kentuckians for the Commonwealth (KFTC), 48, 101, 131–33, 138, 142; Appalachia's Bright Future, 143
Kentucky, 1, 27, 32; action against strip mining in, 136–37; Bell County, 22, 24–26, 28–30, 182n6; Benham, 44; Black coal towns in, 44; CCDs, 182n6; CF Ataya, 109–11; Corbin, 97–98; decline of coal in, 73; East Kentucky Social Club, 44; Fonde, 21, 23; Friends of Coal in, 79, 82; Harlan County, 44, 46–47, 102, 143; land ownership in, 42; Lynch, 44; Middlesboro, 22, 26, 29, 41, 44, 76, 106; Mountain Association, 114, 142; Pike County, 95; politics in, 95, 101, 145; power of coal companies in, 69, 72–75, 82; Pruden, 21, 23, 182n6; SOAR, 143, 145; union decline in, 75–76; Whitley County, 22, 24–25, 29–30, 44, 182n6; Williamsburg, 32; Yellow Creek, 41
Kerry, John, 91
Kimble Companies, 108
Kirby, Rich, 83; "Wars and Rumors of Wars," 82
Klein, Naomi, 117
knowledge: local, 119, 128–30, 133–34, 144, 165, 167, 169; power and, 54–55, 162, 165; recognition of, 8–9, 170, 175; TNC and, 118–19, 164–65
Knoxville, Tennessee, 115, 136–37; Teamsters Union, 151, 154
Kopper Glo, 32–33, 108
Kreps, Brad, 108
Kretzmann, John, 126
Krippner, Greta, 105
Krug-Lewis Agreement of 1946, 46–47
Ku Klux Klan, 44
Kyoto Agreement (1997), 15, 71

Labor at the Table (LATT), 150, 154
labor unions. *See* unions
LaFollette, Tennessee, 22, 29, 32, 44–45

landfills, 134–35
land ownership, 62; absentee, 40–43, 105–9, 116; of the American Association, 40–42; Appalachian Land Ownership Task Force (1979), 42; challenges, 40–41; changing in Appalachia, 105–8; effect on organizing, 133; impacts of TNC, 112–15; power relations and, 116–20
landscapes, 57–58, 63–64, 170
landslides, 32
Latinx communities, 21, 49, 97
Leach, Melissa, 120; *Politics of Green Transformations,* 9
Lego, Brian, 50
Lewis, Anne, 51–52
Lewis, John L., 46, 88
LGBTQA youth, 144
Li, Tania, 198n31
libraries, 28, 37
Lincoln School (Middlesboro), 44
listening projects, 129, 137, 148; Alliance for Appalachia, 143–44
lobbying, 56; by activists, 131, 139, 147, 167; by coal companies, 72–75, 81; by TNC, 117–18
local knowledge. *See* knowledge
local union halls, 75–76, 78
Logan County, West Virginia, 49
logging, 107, 119, 121. *See also* forestry, sustainable
Louisville Courier Journal, 85
Lowson, Denys, 105
Lukes, Steven, 14, 54, 62, 67, 199n44; *Power,* 60–61
Lynch, Kentucky, 44
Lynd, Helen, 11
Lynd, Robert, 11

Macy, Beth, 31
Make America Great Again (MAGA) movement, 14, 87, 89, 92, 98, 103
Make Coal Great Again movement, 14, 92, 173
"Make Coal King Again," 87
Manchin, Joe, 42, 72–74, 81, 153
manufacturing, 27, 45, 51
marginalized groups, 10, 132, 148; gaining power, 64, 67–68, 157, 164–65, 169
Marxism, 54, 84, 196n8
Massey Energy, 42, 47, 76
material base, 54, 70, 161, 196n8
Matheny, Ann, 44
Mayer, Adam, 85
Mazzocchi, Tony, 5–6
McCain, John, 91–92
McCarty, Christopher, 138
McConnell, Mitch, 72–74, 85, 145
McDowell County, West Virginia, 51
McKnight, John, 126
mechanization, 4, 50–51, 76
Mercury and Air Toxics Standards Rule, 50
methane gas. *See* natural gas
micro-protests, 133
Middlesboro, Kentucky, 22, 26, 29, 41, 44, 76, 106
migration from and back to Clearfork Valley, 20, 24–27
military power, 55–56
mineral rights, 42, 107–8, 120, 132–33, 163
mineral wealth, 107–8, 131, 174
Miners for Democracy, 47
Mine Wars Museum, 83
Mingo County, West Virginia, 42
mobilization, 47–49; around RECLAIM, 147; from below, 148–55, 158–61, 165–68; of bias, 61–63, 98, 118–19, 153, 160; of companies, 55; ecology of, 56–57; power and, 65, 67, 139–42, 172; suppression of, 43, 101–2, 124, 140. *See also* campaigns, pro-coal; grassroots organizing; nonparticipation
Mockbee, Michelle, 128–29
Model Valley, 23, 107, 126–28, 215n10
Molpus Woodlands Group, 107
Monckton, Christopher, 82
Monnat, Shannon, 89–90, 99
Morris, Jennifer, 119
Morristown, Tennessee, 34
Mountain Association (Kentucky), 114, 142
Mountain Justice, 15, 135–38

mountaintop removal (MTR), 32–33, 71–74, 78; protests against, 79, 83, 135–38
Movement Generation, 8
Multi-actor Perspective (MaP), 57
Multilevel Perspective (MLP), 13–14, 53, 57, 66

National Coal Corporation, 136–37
National Congress of Neighborhood Women, 128
National Environmental Policy Act (1970), 15
National Fish and Wildlife Foundation, 112
National Geographic (magazine), 112–13
National Labor Relations Act of 1935, 46, 63
National Labor Relations Board (NLRB), 47, 76
National Mining Association (NMA), 81
National Pollution Discharge Elimination System, 135
National Public Radio (NPR), 101
National Rifle Association, 81
Native American communities. *See* indigenous communities
natural gas, 50, 108
Natural Resource Partners (NRP), 107–8
nature-based solutions, 9, 14–15, 118
The Nature Conservancy (TNC), 14–15, 55, 150–51; Advisory Business Council, 117; community dialogue, 116–17, 119–20, 164–65; conservation easements, 111–12; corporate structure, 110; critiques of, 113, 119–20; Cumberland Forest Community Fund, 114–15; fossil fuel industry and, 117–18; impacts of land ownership, 112–15; influence of, 116–20; investments of, 104–5; investors and, 2, 104–5, 107–13, 115–16, 118–21; lobbying by, 117–18; NatureVest, 2, 104–5, 109, 121; power and, 1, 164–65; transparency of, 164. *See also* Cumberland Forest Limited Partnership
NatureVest, 2, 104–5, 109, 121
Navajo Nation, 4, 11
Nelson, Scott, 43
Nelson, Timothy J., 21, 182n6
neoliberalism, 8, 37, 83, 99, 114, 145; Biden administration and, 16, 172–73; TNC and, 117; union decline and, 76
New Deal, 94, 171
Newell, Peter, 55–57; *Politics of Green Transformations,* 9; *Power Shift,* 54
New Yorker (magazine), 89
niches, 57–58, 64, 170, 197n24
"No Hate in My Holler," 97
non-elites, 56, 67–68
non-governmental organizations (NGOs), 2, 7, 55–57, 117–18. *See also* The Nature Conservancy (TNC)
nonparticipation, 90, 124–26
nonviolence, 76–77
North Carolina, 89, 107
Nye, Joseph, 117

Oak Ridge National Laboratory, 150
Obama, Barack, 70, 72–74, 91–92, 96–97
Obama administration, 118, 123, 138, 145, 160–61, 167–68; Clean Power Plan, 87; Climate Action Plan, 15; POWER Initiative, 37, 145, 152; "War on Coal," 14, 81, 85
off-highway vehicles (OHVs), 26, 111–12, 114
Office of Clean Energy Demonstration (OCED), 150–51
Office of Economic Opportunity (OEO), 36
Office of Surface Mining Reclamation and Enforcement (OSMRE), 134
Ohio, 20, 91, 94, 138, 149–50
Oil Chemical and Atomic Workers Union, 5
Open Secrets, 74
opioid crisis. *See* addiction
Organization for Economic Cooperation and Development (OECD), 3

organizing. *See* bottom-up organizing; grassroots organizing
The Other America (Harrington), 19
Oxford University, 60

Paint Creek, West Virginia, 46
Paris Agreement (2015), 3, 5, 15, 74, 87, 177n5
participation, 61, 63, 124; nonparticipation, 90, 124–26; spaces of, 64–65
participatory action research, 12, 128–29
Partnerships for Opportunity and Workforce and Economic Revitalization (POWER) Initiative, 37, 145, 152
Peck, Jamie, 37
Peck, Janice, 170–71
Perdue, Robert Todd, 138
Pied, Claudine, 93
Pike County, Kentucky, 95
Pine Mountain Settlement School, 102
pipeline protests, 137
Pittston Coal, 47, 109
Pittston strike, 15, 76–77
place, importance of, 159–60
pluralism, 60–61
pneumoconiosis, 24
polarization, political, 2, 81–82, 85, 88, 96, 100–102, 160
policymaking, 56, 61–62, 84–85
political action committee (PAC), 72
political economies, 6–11, 158–61
political lobbying. *See* lobbying
Politico (magazine), 4, 69
Politics of Green Transformations (Scoones, Leach, and Newell), 9
Politics of Resentment (Cramer), 95
pollution, 51, 103; Biden administration policies about, 148–49; in California, 111, 113, 121; dust, 32, 133–34; health effects from, 32–33; legacy, 34, 144–45; from MTR, 135; National Pollution Discharge Elimination System, 135; water, 32–33, 72, 128, 131, 134–35, 147–48, 169
poverty, 28–30, 159; twentieth century challenges to, 47–48; in Clearfork Valley, 2, 19–20, 29; persistent, 34; place-based, 21. *See also* War on Poverty
Poverty, by America (Desmond), 29
Powder River Basin, 50
power, 1, 8–9, 13; collective, 70, 75–77, 123–40, 166–68; community studies, 11, 60–61; cracks in, 45, 58–63, 67, 71, 133, 162, 170; in "cramped" spaces, 152–55, 161; debates about, 60–62; discursive, 54; as domination, 63; entrenched, 161–63; for, 66, 142–44, 155–56, 166; global, 64–65; hard, 117; hidden, 61–65, 160, 164; household, 64–65; incumbent, 55–56, 59, 63–64, 67, 69, 158–59; inequalities and, 41–42; institutional, 54; instrumental, 54; invisible, 61–65, 161, 164; local, 64–65; material basis of, 54, 196n8; national, 64–65; oppositional, 68; over, 71, 124, 126, 139–40, 166; participation and, 61; place-based study of, 10–12, 17–18; in the political arena, 71–75; propositional, 68; soft, 117; spaces of, 64–65; structural, 54; systemic, 61; three dimensions of, 14, 60–64, 139, 152–54, 160–67; through organizing, 130–35; TNC and, 116–21; to, 66, 126, 142, 166; transition theory and, 53–54, 157–58; visible, 61–65, 160; within, 66, 139, 166; with, 130, 139
Power (Lukes), 60–61
Power and Powerlessness (Gaventa), 1–2, 10, 17; inaction in, 123–124; politics during, 88; poverty in, 19–20; three dimensions of power in, 60–64; voting in, 90
powercube, 54, 64–66, 167
powerlessness, 62–64, 139; legacy of, 124, 158, 165–66; overcoming, 66–68
power levels, 65–66
power plants, 50, 74–75, 87
Power Shift, 136
Power Shift (Newell), 54

presidential elections, 90–93; of 2016, 14, 87–100, 103, 148, 173; of 2020, 2, 16, 87, 103, 148, 168; of 2024, 2, 16, 85–88, 91–93, 103, 172–73. *See also* Clinton, Hillary; Trump, Donald
private equity funds, 113
procedural justice, 8, 146, 169
production of difference, 45
propaganda, pro-coal, 78–85
propositional politics, 166–67
protests, 65, 97, 166; twentieth century, 45–49, 171; ecology of mobilizations, 56–57; of KFTC, 143; micro, 133, 139; against MTR, 79, 83, 135–38; against pain clinics, 31; pipeline, 137; against strip mining, 20, 48, 133–34; suppression of, 44, 78, 124–25, 140; violence and, 124; youth activist, 81–82. *See also* civil disobedience; direct action
Pruden, Kentucky, 21, 23, 182n6
Pudup, Mary Beth, 40
Purdue Pharma, 31

queer youth, 144, 167
quiescence, 2, 64, 123–24, 140

race, politics and, 93–100
racialized labor, 43–44, 50–51
racial justice, 101
racial solidarity, 44, 49
racism, environmental, 5–6, 48, 51
railroad companies, 40–41, 43, 50
Rand Corporation, 29–30
Reagan, Ronald, 36, 47, 76
RECLAIM (Revitalizing the Economy of Coal Communities by Leveraging Local Activities and Investing More) Act, 146–47, 169
reclamation bonds, 33, 74, 146–48
recognitional justice, 8, 146, 152, 169
recreation, 111–12, 121
Recreational Economies for Rural Communities, 151–52, 154
Redwood Summer, 136
regimes, 57–58, 63–64, 170
Reimagine Appalachia, 149–50
renewable energy, 9, 50, 55–56, 77, 94, 171; pushback against, 72–74; solar energy, 26, 150, 155
rentierism, 105, 120–21, 160, 163
reparative economies, 169–70
Republicanism, 2, 14–15, 17, 71–73, 84–92, 100–103
research methods, 11–12
resentment, 70, 82, 88, 93, 95–100, 102, 160
resistance. *See* protests
restorative justice, 8, 146–47, 166, 169–70
revisit studies, 11–12
Riley, William, 49
RMK Timberland Group, 107
roads, 21, 23, 27, 36–37, 133–34
Roberts, Cecil, 7
Rogers, Hal, 25–26, 146
Rogers, Katrina S., 117–18
Romney, Mitt, 72
Roosevelt, Franklin D., 88, 93–94
Roses Creek, 21, 23
Route 90, 21, 23
Rubik's cube, 64–66
Rust Belt, 90
Ryerson, Sylvia, 78, 80, 84

sacrifice zones, 27
sandwich model, 149
Save Our Cumberland Mountains (SOCM). *See* Statewide Organizing for Community eMpowerment (SOCM)
Scaling Up Renewable Energy Program (SREP) (World Bank), 55
scholar activism, 12
schools, 25, 27, 37, 44
Schwartzman, Gabe, 1–2, 12, 86
scientific knowledge, 118–19, 128, 213n74
Scoones, Ian, 93, 120; *Politics of Green Transformations,* 9
Scott, Rebecca, 80
Selections from the Prison Notebooks (Gramsci), 157
severance taxes, 27, 131, 134
Sexy SexEd, 101
Shaefer, Luke, 21, 182n6

shame, 95–96
Shaping Our Appalachian Region (SOAR), 143, 145
Shifflett, Crandall, 43
Sierra Club, 33, 134, 137–38, 148, 154
sludge, 32
Smith, Al, 36
Smith, Barbara Ellen, 47, 76
social capital, 28, 125, 129
social media, 79–80
social reproductive labor, 45
Social Security Disability Insurance program, 20
social welfare programs, 37
solar energy, 26, 150, 155
solar site (proposed) of TNC, 23, 26, 112
SolveIt Prize, 152
Southern Appalachian Mountain Stewards, 122
Southern Connected Communities Project, 127, 147
South Texas border communities, 21, 29
Sovacool, Benjamin, 56
spaces, 64–65, 142, 155–56
Spearhead Trails, 112
springs, 32–33, 134
state-facilitated market rule, 37
state-led pathways, 9
Statewide Organizing for Community eMpowerment (SOCM), 48, 83–84, 101, 125, 130–36, 138, 147; Teamsters Union and, 151, 154
Staying Together Appalachian Youth (STAY) Project, 144
Stevis, Dimitris, 8
Stolen Pride (Hochschild), 95
Strangers in Their Own Land (Hochschild), 95
Strategic Lawsuit Against Public Participation (SLAPP), 137
streams, 147, 159
strikes, 46–48, 76–77
strip mining, 13, 32–33, 146, 148; growth of, 49–50, 76–78, 135, 160; by JM Huber, 107; legislation, 83, 131–32, 167; protests against, 20, 48, 131–39. *See also* Statewide Organizing for Community eMpowerment (SOCM); Surface Mining Control and Reclamation Act (SMCRA) of 1977
structural theories, 14
subsurface rights, 107–8
sulfur dioxide emissions, 50
Sunbelt, 35
SunTribe, 112
Sunup Initiative, 97–98
Superfund for Workers (Mazzocchi), 5–6
Superfund sites, 5, 26
surface coal mining. *See* strip mining
Surface Mining Control and Reclamation Act (SMCRA) of 1977, 15, 33, 131, 133–34, 136, 146–48, 167
sustainability studies, 13–14
sustainable forestry, 104–5, 111, 114, 119, 121
Swinford, Bonnie, 137–38

Tackett Creek, Tennessee, 21, 23; Tackett Creek Wildlife Management Area, 26, 112
Tackett Flats, 112
Tarus, Lyndsay, 144
taxation, 27, 29–30, 131, 134
Taylor, Betsy, 144
Tazewell, Tennessee, 22
Teamsters Union, 7, 151, 154
Tea Party movement, 93
technology-based pathway, 9
Tennessee, 42, 74, 102, 108, 150; Bean Station, 97; Buffalo, 23; Campbell County, 23–31, 44, 86, 107, 115, 136, 182n6; Census Tracts, 182n6; CF Ataya, 109–112; Claiborne County, 21–30, 44, 154, 182n6; Clairfield, 21, 23–25, 29, 91, 127, 182n6; Clinch-Powell Resource Conservation and Development organization, 114; Coal Creek War, 46; Department of Environment and Conservation (TDEC), 151; Duff, 21, 23; Eagan, 1, 21, 23, 127; Elk Valley, 137; Fork Ridge, 44; Friends of Coal

in, 79–80; Habersham, 91, 182n6; Highlander Center, 144–45; Jellico, 22, 26, 31–32, 44–45, 49, 51, 106; Knoxville, 115, 136–37, 151, 154; LaFollette, 22, 29, 32, 44–45; Morristown, 34; SOCM, 101; Tackett Creek, 21, 23, 26, 112; Tazewell, 22; unions in, 48, 75; University of, 155; Valley Creek, 23, 44, 51, 97; voting in, 90–91; Westbourne, 26, 112; Wetlands Acquisition Fund, 112; White Oak, 21, 23, 91, 134; Wildlife Resources Agency (TWRA), 112–14. *See also* Central Appalachian region; Statewide Organizing for Community eMpowerment (SOCM)

Tennessee Appalachian Community Economics (TNACE), 130, 138, 141, 147–48, 150–55

Terra Strata LLC, 115

Thaler, Gregory, 117

Thatcher, Margaret, 59, 82

Theodore, Nick, 37

This Changes Everything (Klein), 117

three dimensions of power, 14, 60–64, 139, 152–54, 160–67

Three Rivers Earth First!, 136

timber companies, 40, 111

timber investment management organizations (TIMOs), 107, 121

timeline of key trends, 15

top-down policies, 141–42; bottom-up organizing and, 148–50. *See also* bottom-up organizing

To Save the Land and the People movement, 48

tourism, 26

training programs, 7, 37, 77, 127, 145, 155

transformation, 7–8, 172; ecology of mobilizations, 56–57

transformative theory of change, 64–66

transition studies, 13–14

trasformismo, 59

"tree huggers," 70, 80–83, 137, 162

Trump, Donald, 15, 78, 112, 140; 2016 election, 14, 91, 148; 2024 election, 16, 91, 172–73; climate legislation rollbacks of, 73–74, 85, 87, 147, 156, 168, 173; support for, 2, 87–103, 162. *See also* Make America Great Again (MAGA) movement; Make Coal Great Again movement; presidential elections; Republicanism

Trumpka, Rich, 7

trust, 125, 129–30

unemployment. *See* coal employment decrease; jobs

unions, 24, 150, 156, 172; AFL-CIO, 7; apprenticeship programs, 155; coal company towns and, 43–44; decline of, 51–52, 75–78, 84, 144, 159; economic development and, 37; Just Transition Alliance and, 6–7; local union halls, 75–76, 78; Oil Chemical and Atomic Workers Union, 5; power relations and, 57, 66; race and, 49–50; reform movements, 45, 47; repression of, 46–48; Teamsters Union, 7, 151, 154. *See also* United Mine Workers of America (UMWA)

United Kingdom, 70

United Mine Workers Journal, 78

United Mine Workers of America (UMWA), 2, 7, 15, 47; Lewis, 46, 88; racial equality and, 49, 97; support for Gore, 90–91; weakening of, 70, 75–78, 84, 159

United Mountain Defense, 136

United Nations Framework Convention on Climate Change (UNFCCC), 3, 87, 177n5

United States Department of Agriculture (USDA) Rural Development, 150

United Steelworkers, 77

University of Tennessee, 155

University of Virginia, 114

the Valley. *See* Clearfork Valley

Valley Creek, Tennessee, 23, 44, 51, 97

Vance, JD, 87, 89, 203n2

Vanity Fair (magazine), 89

Van Zee, Art, 30–31
violence, 40, 44, 124–25, 131
Virginia, 26, 30–31, 42, 95, 108, 115; Appalachia, 135; Appalachian Sustainable Development, 142; CF Highlands, 109–10, 112; Clean Water Revolving Loan Fund, 109; Clinch Coalition, 122; Dickenson County, 115; Inman, 135; Pittston Strike, 76–77; University of, 114; Wise County, 42, 106, 114–15
visible power, 61–65, 160
voluneering, 127–28
voting. *See* Democratic voting; Republicanism
vulture capitalism, 76

Wagner Act, 46
Wallace, George, 36
Waller, Altina, 40
"War on Coal," 14–15, 81–85, 92, 94–95, 137
War on Poverty, 2, 13, 16, 29, 94, 141, 215n10; early years, 47–48; effects of, 19, 155; OEO, 35–37; participation and, 63, 153, 156, 171–72
Warren County, North Carolina, 48
"Wars and Rumors of Wars" (Kirby), 82
Washington, DC, 36, 101, 136–37, 147
Washington Post, 89, 108, 117–18
water, drinking, 32–33, 127–28, 134
water pollution, 32–33, 72, 128, 131, 134–35, 147–48, 169
Waymakers Collective, 101–2
Westbourne, Tennessee, 26, 112
West Virginia, 28, 41–43, 69–76, 138, 145; Blair, 83; Blair Mountain, 46; Cabin Creek, 46; Citizens for Coal, 83; Coal Association, 79–80, 91; Coalfield Development, 150; Logan County, 49; McDowell County, 51; Mine Wars, 46; Mingo County, 42; Paint Creek, 46
Wetlands Acquisition Fund (Tennessee), 112
What Happened (Clinton), 94–95
White, Connie, 132
whiteness, 98–100
White Oak, Tennessee, 21, 23, 91, 134
white supremacist movements, 93, 98, 100
Whitley County, Kentucky, 22, 24–25, 29–30, 44, 182n6
wildlife migration corridors, 109
Wilkerson, Isabel, 99
Williams, Hank, Jr., 82
Williamsburg, Kentucky, 32
Winkler, Harald, 58–59
Wise County, Virginia, 42, 106, 114–15
Wittmayer, Julia M., 57
WMMT radio, 82–83
women, labor of, 44–45, 51–52
women-led organizing, 48, 128, 167
Woodland Community Land Trust, 31, 115, 126–28, 150, 152, 155; map, 23
Woods, Clyde, 171
World Bank, 4, 55, 55, 118
World Wildlife Fund, 55
Wright, Chris, 173

Yellow Creek, Kentucky, 41
York, Richard, 79–80, 84
youth activists, 70, 81–82, 136, 167

Zeb Mountain Removal Coal Mining Operation, 136–37

JOHN GAVENTA is a professor and research fellow at the Institute of Development Studies at the University of Sussex. He is the author of *Power and Powerlessness: Quiescence and Rebellion in an Appalachian Valley*.

GABE SCHWARTZMAN is an assistant professor of geography and sustainability at the University of Tennessee and has been deeply engaged in community mobilization efforts in the Clearfork Valley.

The University of Illinois Press
is a founding member of the
Association of University Presses.

Composed in 10.5/13 Mercury Text
with Trade Gothic display
by Jim Proefrock
at the University of Illinois Press
Manufactured by Sheridan Books, Inc.

University of Illinois Press
1325 South Oak Street
Champaign, IL 61820-6903
www.press.uillinois.edu

"When it comes to motivating writers, self-selected goals are much more powerful than school-selected goals, and this book offers practical steps that not only help students to make and revise goals, it also offers reflective practices that foster continual improvement. I like how *Goal Setting in the Writing Classroom* positions the students to do the thinking."

—Kelly Gallagher, author of *Write Like This* and *Teaching Adolescent Writers*

"Valerie skillfully blends her experience as a children's author and middle school writing teacher to offer practical strategies that help students set and achieve personal writing goals. This book is a valuable tool for educators."

—Dr. Towanda Harris, author of *The Right Tools: A Guide to Selecting, Evaluating, and Implementing Classroom Resources and Practices*

"In *Goal Setting in the Writing Classroom*, Valerie Bolling shares her knowledge and experience as an educator, author, and human that gives new meaning to the term mentor author. Students will love learning about her process, can reflect on her work and find easy to implement steps to improve their own writing. She shares her secrets to meaningful goal setting 'that leads to confidence, perseverance, and self-reflection.' Read, write, reflect, and repeat."

—JoEllen McCarthy, educator, literacy advisor, and author of *Layers of Learning: Using Read Alouds to Connect Literacy and Caring Conversations*